the ULTIMATE
SOUP
COOKBOOK

the ULTIMATE SOUP COOKBOOK

VICE PRESIDENT, EDITOR-IN-CHIEF:	Catherine Cassidy
VICE PRESIDENT, EXECUTIVE EDITOR/BOOKS:	Heidi Reuter Lloyd
CREATIVE DIRECTOR:	Howard Greenberg
FOOD DIRECTOR:	Diane Werner, RD
SENIOR EDITOR/BOOKS:	Mark Hagen
EDITOR:	Amy Glander
ASSOCIATE CREATIVE DIRECTOR:	Edwin Robles Jr.
ART DIRECTOR:	Jessie Sharon
CONTENT PRODUCTION MANAGER:	Julie Wagner
LAYOUT DESIGNER:	Emma Acevedo
COPY CHIEF:	Deb Warlaumont Mulvey
COPY EDITORS:	Alysse Gear, Dulcie Shoener
RECIPE ASSET SYSTEM MANAGER:	Coleen Martin
RECIPE TESTING AND EDITING:	Taste of Home Test Kitchen
FOOD PHOTOGRAPHY:	Taste of Home Photo Studio
COVER PHOTOGRAPHER:	Dan Roberts
COVER FOOD STYLIST:	Shannon Roum
COVER SET STYLIST:	Dee Dee Jacq
ADMINISTRATIVE ASSISTANT:	Barb Czysz
NORTH AMERICAN CHIEF MARKETING OFFICER:	Lisa Karpinski
VICE PRESIDENT/BOOK MARKETING:	Dan Fink
CREATIVE DIRECTOR/CREATIVE MARKETING:	Jim Palmen

The Reader's Digest Association, Inc.

PRESIDENT AND CHIEF EXECUTIVE OFFICER:	Tom Williams
EXECUTIVE VICE PRESIDENT, RDA, AND PRESIDENT, NORTH AMERICA:	Dan Lagani

Front Cover, counter-clockwise from top: Pasta Sausage Soup (p. 113), Versatile Ham & Corn Chowder (p. 110), Onion Soup with Sausage (p. 116), Pretty Autumn Soup (p. 165), Chicken & Dumpling Soup (p. 100)

Back Cover, top to bottom: Italian Sausage Tortellini Soup (p. 108), Classic Broccoli Cheese Soup (p. 180), Anytime Turkey Chili (p. 261), Hearty Chipotle Chicken Soup (p. 72)

International Standard Book Number (10): 0-89821-906-X
International Standard Book Number (13): 978-0-89821-906-7
Library of Congress Control Number: 2011932530

Printed in U.S.A.
Second Printing
For other Taste of Home books and products, visit ShopTasteofHome.com

© 2011 Reiman Media Group, LLC
5400 S. 60th St., Greendale WI 53129
All rights reserved.
Taste of Home is a registered trademark of The Reader's Digest Association, Inc.

74   115   118

table of contents

the **ULTIMATE SOUP** cookbook

serve ladles of
HOME-COOKED COMFORT!

soups for all seasons

Featuring everything from basic broths and classic weeknight favorites to impressive first-course starters and cool and refreshing dessert soups, *The Ultimate Soup Cookbook* offers an endless variety of succulent dishes that are ideal for any season or occasion.

When the temperatures take a tumble, warm up with steamy spoonfuls of Lemon-Chicken Velvet Soup (p. 101) and fiery Spicy Pork Chili (p. 255). Say hello to spring with Asparagus Cheese Soup (p. 185) and Carrot Broccoli Soup (p. 136) for a meal brimming with garden-fresh veggies.

On a hot summer's day, you can even enjoy a sweet sip of Smooth Strawberry Soup (p. 236) for a dessert that's a breeze.

Choose from meaty beef, pork or poultry, or satisfying meatless, bean or tomato soups. Chunky chowders, smooth bisques, creamy soups and, of course, zesty chilis are also perfect choices. And don't pass by our selection of fresh-baked breads to turn a steamy bowl into a complete meal.

one-dish wonders

It's not just the amazing flavors and textures that make these soups so delicious. They're also versatile and easy on the wallet! Some even rely on the convenience of a slow cooker to keep preparation simple.

The recipes come from the personal files of real home cooks just like you, and each soup has been tested by our staff of Test Kitchen experts. You can trust that every recipe is easy to prepare and calls for fresh, wholesome ingredients as well as affordable, everyday staples you likely already have stocked in the pantry.

You'll also find recipes sized perfectly for small-scale cooking and more than 100 handy kitchen tips to make whipping up any of these heartwarming soups a snap.

soup's on!

Soup was Mom's go-to food, and now it can be yours, too! With *The Ultimate Soup Cookbook*, it's easy to simmer up timeless home-style fare any night of the week. From nostalgic favorites to flavorful new sensations, this huge collection is brimming with delicious soups, chilis, breads and more that are guaranteed to warm spirits and satisfy even the heartiest of appetites!

beans
& lentils

This chapter is chock-full of all the beans your heart desires.
You can choose from split or black-eyed peas, lentils and
great northern, pinto, black, lima, kidney, navy or cannellini
beans to pack a nutritional punch in your next soup recipe.
And since beans are inexpensive, you'll have a full wallet to
go with your family's empty soup bowls!

22

23

31

sandra bonde

BRAINERD, MINNESOTA

Turkey kielbasa brings great flavor to simple split pea soup. It's always a hit with my entire family.

split pea primer

Unlike other dried beans, split peas should not be soaked before cooking—but they should be sorted to remove any damaged peas, pebbles or grit. After sorting, rinse split peas with cold water in a colander, and cook according to the recipe instructions.

kielbasa split pea soup

2 celery ribs, thinly sliced

1 medium onion, chopped

1 package (16 ounces) dried green split peas

9 cups water, *divided*

1 package (14 ounces) smoked turkey kielbasa, halved and sliced

4 medium carrots, halved and thinly sliced

2 medium potatoes, peeled and cubed

1 tablespoon minced fresh parsley

1 teaspoon dried basil

1-1/2 teaspoons salt

1/2 teaspoon pepper

In a Dutch oven coated with cooking spray, cook celery and onion until tender. Stir in split peas and 6 cups water. Bring to a boil. Reduce heat; cover and simmer for 25 minutes.

Stir in the kielbasa, carrots, potatoes, parsley, basil, salt, pepper and remaining water. Return to a boil. Reduce heat; cover and simmer for 20-25 minutes or until peas and vegetables are tender.

YIELD: 12 servings.

sandi lee

HOUSTON, TEXAS

You'll get a kick out of this hearty Southwestern soup. Feel free to dunk your tortilla chips right into it!

flavorful taco soup

1/2 pound lean ground beef (90% lean)

1 can (15 ounces) pinto beans, rinsed and drained

1 can (10 ounces) diced tomatoes with mild green chilies, undrained

1 can (8-3/4 ounces) whole kernel corn, drained

1-1/2 cups water

2 tablespoons taco seasoning

4-1/2 teaspoons ranch salad dressing mix

TOPPINGS:

1/2 medium ripe avocado, peeled and cubed

2 tablespoons shredded cheddar cheese

2 teaspoons minced fresh cilantro

Tortilla chips

In a large saucepan, cook beef over medium heat until it is no longer pink; drain. Stir in the beans, tomatoes, corn, water, taco seasoning and salad dressing mix. Bring to a boil. Reduce heat; cover and simmer for 30-35 minutes or until heated through.

Spoon into bowls; top with avocado, cheese and cilantro. Serve with tortilla chips.

YIELD: 4 servings.

bart's black bean soup

1 can (15 ounces) black beans, rinsed and drained

1-1/2 cups chicken broth

3/4 cup chunky salsa

1/2 cup canned whole kernel corn, drained

Dash hot pepper sauce

2 teaspoons lime juice

1 cup (4 ounces) shredded cheddar cheese

2 tablespoons chopped green onions

In a microwave-safe bowl, combine the first five ingredients. Cover and microwave on high for 2 minutes or until heated through. Pour into four serving bowls; drizzle each with lime juice. Sprinkle with cheese and green onions.

YIELD: 4 servings.

EDITOR'S NOTE: This recipe was tested in a 1,100-watt microwave.

sharon ullyot
LONDON, ONTARIO

You can whip up my friend Bart's famous soup in mere minutes. We enjoy it with rolls and a salad for a complete meal that's both tasty and easy.

nelda cameron
CLEVELAND, TEXAS

Looking for a crowd-pleaser that will fill hungry tummies? My easy recipe is guaranteed to be a winner. Serve with fresh corn bread for a complete meal-in-one.

hearty bean soup

1 large onion, chopped

1/2 cup chopped green pepper

2 tablespoons butter

2 garlic cloves, minced

2 cans (15-1/2 ounces *each*) great northern beans, rinsed and drained

2 cans (15 ounces *each*) pinto beans, rinsed and drained

2 cans (11-1/2 ounces *each*) condensed bean with bacon soup, undiluted

2 cups diced fully cooked ham

2 cups water

2 tablespoons canned diced jalapeno peppers

In a small skillet, saute onion and green pepper in butter for 3 minutes. Add the garlic; cook 1 minute longer. Transfer to a Dutch oven or soup kettle. Stir in the remaining ingredients. Cover and cook over medium-low heat for 20 minutes or until heated through, stirring occasionally.

YIELD: 10 servings.

EDITOR'S NOTE: We recommend wearing disposable gloves when cutting hot peppers. Avoid touching your face.

bean, chicken and sausage soup

1-1/2 pounds bulk Italian sausage
2 cups chopped onion
6 bacon strips, diced
2 quarts water
2 cans (14-1/2 ounces *each*) diced tomatoes, undrained
2 bay leaves
2 teaspoons garlic powder
1 teaspoon *each* dried thyme, savory and salt
1/2 teaspoon *each* dried basil, oregano and pepper
4 cups cubed cooked chicken
2 cans (15 to 16 ounces *each*) great northern beans, rinsed and drained

In a heavy 8-qt. Dutch oven, cook the sausage, onion and bacon over medium-high heat until sausage is no longer pink; drain. Add the water, tomatoes and seasonings. Cover and simmer for 30 minutes.

Add chicken and beans. Simmer, uncovered, for 30-45 minutes. Discard bay leaves.

YIELD: 18 servings.

linda johnson
SEVIERVILLE, TENNESSEE

I found this recipe in a magazine and have had fun experimenting with different ingredients throughout the years. My husband thinks this version is the best.

mexican bean barley soup

2 medium onions, chopped
3 garlic cloves, minced
2 tablespoons canola oil
1 medium turnip, peeled and diced
1 medium carrot, diced
2 tablespoons finely chopped jalapeno pepper
1-1/2 teaspoons ground cumin
1/2 teaspoon ground coriander
3 cans (14-1/2 ounces *each*) vegetable broth
2 cups cooked barley
1 can (15 ounces) pinto beans, rinsed and drained
2 teaspoons lemon juice

In a large saucepan, saute the onions and garlic in oil until tender. Add the turnip, carrot and jalapeno; cook and stir until all are tender. Add cumin and coriander; cook and stir for 2 minutes. Add the broth. Bring to a boil. Reduce the heat; cover and simmer for 20 minutes.

Add the barley, beans and lemon juice. Simmer, uncovered, 10-15 minutes longer or until the soup thickens slightly.

YIELD: 7 servings.

EDITOR'S NOTE: We recommend wearing disposable gloves when cutting hot peppers. Avoid touching your face.

elizabeth cole
MUCKPORT, INDIANA

I include this soup on the menu for the retreats we host on our woodland farm. Everyone enjoys spooning up its yummy vegetable broth and hearty mix of beans and barley. Homemade onion-herb bread makes a great accompaniment.

potato soup with beans

2 medium carrots, shredded
1 tablespoon butter
4 cups chicken *or* vegetable broth
3 medium potatoes, peeled and cubed
1 garlic clove, minced
1-1/2 teaspoons dill weed
1 can (15-1/2 ounces) great northern beans, rinsed and drained
4-1/2 teaspoons all-purpose flour
3/4 cup sour cream
Pepper to taste

In a large saucepan, cook the carrots in butter for 4 minutes or until tender. Stir in broth, potatoes, garlic and dill. Bring to a boil. Reduce heat; cover and simmer for 25 minutes or until potatoes are tender.

With a slotted spoon, remove half of the potatoes to a bowl; mash with a fork. Return to the pan. Stir in the beans. In a small bowl, combine the flour, sour cream and pepper; add to soup. Cook over low heat for 5 minutes or until heated through (do not boil).

YIELD: 6 servings.

christine ecker
LINWOOD, NEW JERSEY

Winter winds can blow strong here on the Jersey shore. But my rich soup featuring potatoes, beans and sour cream is sure to warm both body and soul.

lois dean
WILLIAMSON, WEST VIRGINIA

I wanted to make a meatless soup for a Lenten lunch. I came up with this colorful vegetable dish and got rave reviews.

veggie bean soup

1/2 cup chopped onion
1/2 cup sliced celery
1/2 cup sliced fresh carrots
1 tablespoon olive oil
1/2 teaspoon minced garlic
2 cups water
1 can (15-1/2 ounces) great northern beans, rinsed and drained
3/4 cup chicken broth
3/4 cup Italian stewed tomatoes
1/2 cup cubed peeled potato
1/2 cup frozen cut green beans
1 bay leaf
1/2 teaspoon salt, optional
1/4 teaspoon pepper

In a large saucepan, saute the onion, celery and carrots in oil until tender. Add garlic; cook 1 minute longer. Stir in the remaining ingredients. Bring to a boil. Reduce heat; simmer, uncovered, for 15 minutes or until heated through. Discard bay leaf.

YIELD: 4 servings.

shannon kohn
SIMPSONVILLE,
SOUTH CAROLINA

You'll enjoy my quick and easy version of a tasty bean soup I tried at a Mexican restaurant. I added dumplings to make it more filling.

bean soup with cheddar cornmeal dumplings

1/4 cup chopped onion
1/4 cup fresh baby carrots, cut into 1/4-inch slices
1 can (15 ounces) pinto beans, rinsed and drained

1 cup chicken broth
1 cup chunky salsa
1/3 cup self-rising flour
2 tablespoons cornmeal
1/8 teaspoon salt
1/4 cup 2% milk
2 tablespoons shredded cheddar cheese

In a large saucepan coated with cooking spray, saute the onion and carrots until tender. Stir in the beans, broth and salsa. Bring to a boil. Reduce the heat; simmer, uncovered, for 3-5 minutes or until reduced slightly.

For dumplings, in a small bowl, combine the flour, cornmeal and salt. Stir in the milk and cheese just until moistened. Drop by tablespoonfuls onto simmering soup.

Cover and simmer for 15 minutes or until a toothpick inserted near center of a dumpling comes out clean (do not lift cover while simmering).

YIELD: 2 servings.

EDITOR'S NOTE: As a substitute for 1/3 cup of self-rising flour, place 1/2 teaspoon baking powder and 1/8 teaspoon salt in a measuring cup. Add all-purpose flour to measure 1/3 cup.

bean and pasta soup

- 1 cup uncooked small pasta
- 2 celery ribs, thinly sliced
- 2 medium carrots, thinly sliced
- 1 medium onion, chopped
- 1 garlic clove, minced
- 1 tablespoon olive oil
- 2 cups water
- 1 can (14-1/2 ounces) diced tomatoes, undrained
- 1-1/4 cups reduced-sodium chicken broth or vegetable broth
- 1 teaspoon dried basil
- 1/2 teaspoon dried rosemary, crushed
- 1/4 teaspoon salt
- 1/8 teaspoon pepper
- 1 can (15 ounces) white kidney or cannellini beans, rinsed and drained
- 2 cups shredded fresh spinach
- 1/4 cup shredded Parmesan cheese, optional

Cook pasta according to the package directions. Meanwhile, in a large nonstick saucepan, saute the celery, carrots, onion and garlic in oil for 5 minutes. Stir in the water, tomatoes, broth, basil, rosemary, salt and pepper. Bring to a boil. Reduce the heat; cover and simmer for 10 minutes or until the carrots are tender.

Drain pasta; stir into vegetable mixture. Add the beans; heat through. Stir in the spinach; cook until spinach is wilted, about 2 minutes. Sprinkle with Parmesan cheese if desired.

YIELD: 5 servings.

maria gooding
ST. THOMAS, ONTARIO

We're always on the lookout for great low-fat recipes, and this soup fits the bill. Loaded with veggies and pasta, it's fast, filling and delicious.

cannellini beans

Cannellini beans are large white kidney beans and are generally available dry and canned. Some canned products will list both cannellini beans and large white kidney beans on the label. If you can't find them in your area, feel free to substitute navy beans or great northern beans.

yvonne andrus
HIGHLAND, UTAH

My recipe for minestrone is so convenient. Just toss the ingredients in the slow cooker in the morning and forget about it for the rest of the day. A few hours later, a hot, steamy bowl of hearty soup awaits you.

easy minestrone

4 medium tomatoes, chopped

2 medium carrots, chopped

2 celery ribs, chopped

1 medium zucchini, halved and sliced

1-1/2 cups shredded cabbage

1 can (16 ounces) kidney beans, rinsed and drained

1 can (15 ounces) garbanzo beans *or* chickpeas, rinsed and drained

6 cups reduced-sodium chicken broth *or* vegetable broth

1-1/4 teaspoons Italian seasoning

1 teaspoon salt

1/4 teaspoon pepper

2 cups cooked elbow macaroni

5 tablespoons shredded Parmesan cheese

In a 5-qt. slow cooker, combine the first 11 ingredients. Cover and cook on low for 6-8 hours or until the vegetables are tender.

Just before serving, stir in macaroni and heat through. Serve with cheese.

YIELD: 10 servings.

too-easy tortellini soup

4 cups chicken broth
1 package (9 ounces) refrigerated cheese tortellini
1 can (15 ounces) white kidney *or* cannellini beans, rinsed and drained
1 can (14-1/2 ounces) Italian diced tomatoes, undrained
1-1/2 teaspoons dried basil
1 tablespoon red wine vinegar
Shredded Parmesan cheese and coarsely ground pepper, optional

In a large saucepan, bring broth to a boil. Stir in tortellini. Reduce heat; simmer, uncovered, for 4 minutes, stirring occasionally. Stir in the beans, tomatoes and basil. Simmer for 4-6 minutes or until pasta is tender. Stir in the vinegar. Sprinkle with cheese and pepper if desired.

YIELD: 6 servings.

beth daley
CHESTERFIELD, MISSOURI

One day I was craving a quick, hearty soup, so I combine packaged tortellini and canned goods for a minute-made dinner. Dried basil and Parmesan cheese round out the flavor.

black-eyed pea soup

4 bacon strips, diced
1 medium green pepper, chopped
1 small onion, chopped
2 garlic cloves, minced
2 cans (15-1/2 ounces *each*) black-eyed peas, undrained
2 cans (14-1/2 ounces *each*) diced tomatoes, undrained
1 cup water
1-1/2 teaspoons salt
1 to 1-1/4 teaspoons ground cumin
1 to 1-1/4 teaspoons ground mustard
1 teaspoon chili powder
1/2 teaspoon curry powder
1/2 teaspoon pepper
1/4 to 1/2 teaspoon sugar, optional
Shredded Colby-Monterey Jack cheese and minced fresh parsley

In a large saucepan, cook bacon over medium heat until crisp; remove to paper towels. Drain, reserving 1 tablespoon drippings. In the drippings, saute the green pepper, onion and garlic until tender.

Add the peas, tomatoes, water and seasonings. Bring to a boil. Reduce the heat; cover and simmer for 15-20 minutes. Sprinkle with the cheese, parsley and bacon.

YIELD: 8 servings.

donna ambrose
MT. WOLF, PENNSYLVANIA

Even people who don't care for black-eyed peas will enjoy this soup. With a crusty loaf of bread, it's a heartwarming meal for cold winter days.

zuppa di fagioli

2 tablespoons dry bread crumbs
1 tablespoon grated Parmesan cheese
1/4 pound bulk Italian sausage
1 cup sliced leeks (white portion only)
1 medium carrot, chopped
1 celery rib, chopped
1 tablespoon canola oil
1 garlic clove, minced
2 cans (15-1/2 ounces *each*) great northern beans, rinsed and drained
2 cans (14-1/2 ounces *each*) reduced-sodium chicken broth
1 can (14-1/2 ounces) reduced-sodium beef broth
1 can (14-1/2 ounces) diced tomatoes in sauce
1 package (6 ounces) fresh baby spinach
3 tablespoons minced fresh basil
2 tablespoons minced fresh parsley
1/2 teaspoon salt
1/4 teaspoon pepper

In a large bowl, combine bread crumbs and cheese. Crumble sausage over mixture and mix well. Shape into 1/2-in. balls.

Place in a greased 15-in. x 10-in. x 1-in. baking pan. Bake at 350° for 8-10 minutes or until juices run clear; drain and set aside.

In a Dutch oven, saute the leeks, carrot and celery in oil until tender. Add garlic; cook 1 minute longer. Stir in the beans, broths, tomatoes, spinach, basil, parsley, salt, pepper and reserved meatballs. Cover and cook until spinach is tender and meatballs are heated through.

YIELD: 10 servings.

mary caron
EDENTON, NORTH CAROLINA

I like to welcome my family home with steaming bowls of classic white bean soup. It features plenty of fresh veggies as well as tender Italian meatballs.

beverly ballaro
LYNNFIELD, MASSACHUSETTS

We savor this thick, filling soup during our chilly New England winters. You can use small shell pasta or elbow macaroni.

pasta bean soup

1 large onion, chopped
1 large carrot, chopped
1 celery rib, chopped
2 tablespoons olive oil
3 garlic cloves, minced
4 cups vegetable *or* chicken broth
3/4 cup uncooked small pasta shells
2 teaspoons sugar
1-1/2 teaspoons Italian seasoning
1/4 teaspoon crushed red pepper flakes
2 cans (15 ounces *each*) white kidney *or* cannellini beans, rinsed and drained
1 can (28 ounces) crushed tomatoes
3 tablespoons grated Parmesan cheese

In a Dutch oven, saute the onion, carrot and celery in oil until crisp-tender. Add garlic; saute 1 minute longer. Add the broth, pasta, sugar, Italian seasoning and pepper flakes.

Bring to a boil. Reduce heat; simmer, uncovered, for 15 minutes or until pasta is tender. Add the beans and tomatoes; simmer, uncovered, for 5 minutes. Garnish with Parmesan cheese.

YIELD: 6 servings.

onions

Onions are low in calories but high in taste—they're an excellent way to boost flavor in light and savory dishes. They add nutrition, too. Onions contain only a trace amount of calcium and iron, but just one half cup of chopped onions yields about 240 mg of potassium.

andi haug
HENDRUM, MINNESOTA

Here, I combined two family favorite recipes. I often serve the recipe for Sunday dinner, making enough to leave leftovers for my husband's Monday lunch thermos. He's a bricklayer and works outdoors during the cold weather months.

ham and lentil soup

1 meaty ham bone
6 cups water
1-1/4 cups dried lentils, rinsed
1 can (28 ounces) diced tomatoes, undrained

2 to 3 carrots, sliced
2 celery ribs, sliced
1/4 cup chopped green onions
1/2 teaspoon salt
1/2 teaspoon garlic powder
1/2 teaspoon dried oregano
1/8 teaspoon pepper
12 ounces bulk pork sausage, cooked and drained
2 tablespoons chopped fresh parsley

In a Dutch oven, bring ham bone and water to a boil. Reduce heat; cover and simmer for 1-1/2 hours.

Remove the ham bone. To broth, add the lentils, tomatoes, carrots, celery, onions and seasonings; bring to a boil. Reduce the heat; cover and simmer for 30-40 minutes or until the lentils and vegetables are tender.

Meanwhile, remove the ham from bone; coarsely chop. Add the ham, sausage and parsley to soup; heat through.

YIELD: 10-12 servings.

zesty italian soup

- 1 pound bulk Italian sausage
- 3 cans (14-1/2 ounces *each*) reduced-sodium chicken broth
- 1 can (15 ounces) black beans, rinsed and drained
- 1 can (15 ounces) pinto beans, rinsed and drained
- 1 can (14-1/2 ounces) diced tomatoes and green chilies, undrained
- 1 can (14-1/2 ounces) Italian diced tomatoes
- 1 large carrot, chopped
- 1 jalapeno pepper, seeded and chopped
- 1-1/2 teaspoons Italian seasoning
- 1 teaspoon dried minced garlic
- 1-1/2 cups cooked elbow macaroni

In a large skillet, cook sausage over medium heat until no longer pink; drain.

Transfer to a 5-qt. slow cooker. Stir in the broth, beans, tomatoes, carrot, jalapeno, Italian seasoning and garlic. Cover and cook on low for 7-8 hours or until heated through. Just before serving, stir in the macaroni.

YIELD: 10 servings.

EDITOR'S NOTE: We recommend wearing disposable gloves when cutting hot peppers. Avoid touching your face.

myrna sippel
THOMPSON, ILLINOIS

I tried a delicious Italian soup at a local restaurant while visiting my sister-in-law. I decided to create my own version at home and came up with this recipe. You can vary the seasonings and the types of tomatoes to suit your family's tastes.

stacy's black bean soup

stacy marti
JENKS, OKLAHOMA

My clan loves my low-fat black bean soup, and you will, too! It's packed with good-for-you veggies and beans. If you prefer a vegetarian version, simply substitute vegetable broth for the chicken broth.

1-1/2 cups dried black beans
  3 celery ribs, chopped
  3 medium carrots, chopped
  1 large onion, chopped
  2 teaspoons olive oil
  2 garlic cloves, minced
6-1/2 cups reduced-sodium chicken broth
  1 teaspoon dried oregano
1/2 teaspoon dried thyme
1/2 teaspoon salt
1/4 teaspoon cayenne pepper
  1 bay leaf
  3 tablespoons lime juice
1/2 cup reduced-fat sour cream
1/4 cup minced fresh cilantro

Place beans in a large saucepan; add water to cover by 2 in. Bring to a boil; boil for 2 minutes. Remove from the heat; cover and let stand for 1 to 4 hours or until beans are softened. Drain and rinse beans, discarding liquid.

In a Dutch oven coated with cooking spray, saute the celery, carrots and onion in oil until the vegetables are tender. Add garlic; cook 1 minute longer. Add the beans, broth, oregano, thyme, salt, cayenne and bay leaf. Bring to a boil. Reduce heat; cover and simmer for 1 to 1-1/4 hours or until beans are tender. Discard bay leaf. Cool slightly.

In a blender, cover and process soup in batches until smooth. Return to pan; heat though. Stir in lime juice. Garnish each serving with sour cream and cilantro.

YIELD: 8 servings.

split pea vegetable soup

1-1/2 cups dried green split peas, rinsed

2-1/2 quarts water

7 to 8 whole allspice, tied in a cheesecloth bag

2 teaspoons salt

1/2 teaspoon pepper

6 large potatoes, peeled and cut into 1/2-inch cubes

6 medium carrots, chopped

2 medium onions, chopped

2 cups cubed cooked ham

1/2 medium head cabbage, shredded

In a Dutch oven, combine the peas, water, allspice, salt and pepper; bring to a boil. Reduce heat; cover and simmer for 1 hour.

Stir in the potatoes, carrots, onions, ham and cabbage; return to a boil. Reduce heat; cover and simmer for about 30 minutes or until vegetables are tender, stirring occasionally. Discard allspice.

YIELD: 16-20 servings.

maureen ylitalo
WAHNAPITAE, ONTARIO

This recipe originated with the master chef of our family: my father-in-law. It freezes so well that I frequently make an extra batch to enjoy later.

veggie soup shortcut

Purchase a package of coleslaw mix instead of a whole head of cabbage. This is a time-saver, since the cabbage and carrots are already washed and chopped. Simply add it to your simmering soup for 4-5 minutes before serving.

black bean & salsa soup

3/4 cup chopped celery

1 medium onion, chopped

1 tablespoon canola oil

3 garlic cloves, minced

3 cans (14-1/2 ounces each) chicken broth

2 cans (15 ounces each) black beans, rinsed and drained

1 jar (16 ounces) salsa

1 cup cubed cooked chicken breast

1 cup cooked long grain rice

1 tablespoon lime juice

1 teaspoon ground cumin

In a large saucepan, saute celery and onion in oil until tender. Add garlic; cook 1 minute longer. Stir in the remaining ingredients; heat through.

YIELD: 10 servings.

mary buhl
DULUTH, GEORGIA

Salsa and cumin add just the right amount of zip to my chunky black bean soup. Serve it with warm corn bread for a delicious Southwestern meal.

**taste of home
test kitchen**
GREENDALE, WISCONSIN

We simmered up a garden-fresh meatless soup with two kinds of beans, making for a satisfying entree.

zucchini

Zucchini contains a lot of water, and freezing pulls the moisture to the surface, leaving a puddle upon thawing. It's fine to add frozen zucchini directly to soup without thawing, but if you're baking, you should thaw it and blot it dry.

vegetarian white bean soup

2 small zucchini, quartered lengthwise and sliced

1 cup *each* chopped onion, celery and carrot

2 tablespoons canola oil

3 cans (14-1/2 ounces *each*) vegetable broth

1 can (15-1/2 ounces) great northern beans, rinsed and drained

1 can (15 ounces) white kidney *or* cannellini beans, rinsed and drained

1 can (14-1/2 ounces) diced tomatoes, undrained

1/2 teaspoon dried thyme

1/2 teaspoon dried oregano

1/4 teaspoon pepper

In a large saucepan, saute the zucchini, onion, celery and carrot in oil for 5-7 minutes or until crisp-tender. Add the remaining ingredients. Bring to a boil.

Reduce heat; cover and simmer for 15 minutes or until vegetables are tender.

YIELD: 7 servings.

carolyn burbidge
BOUNTIFUL, UTAH

Looking for a quick and satisfying soup? Give my recipe a try...but be warned that it may not last long! Any leftovers taste even more delicious the next day.

beefy bean soup

1 can (29 ounces) tomato puree

1 can (14-1/2 ounces) diced tomatoes, undrained

1 cup water

1 cup beef broth

4-1/2 teaspoons chicken bouillon granules

3/4 teaspoon salt

3/4 teaspoon dried basil

3/4 teaspoon dried oregano

3/4 cup uncooked elbow macaroni

1/2 pound lean ground beef (90% lean)

1 cup chopped celery

1/2 cup chopped onion

1/2 teaspoon dried minced garlic

1 can (16 ounces) kidney beans, rinsed and drained

1 can (15-1/2 ounces) great northern beans, rinsed and drained

In a Dutch oven, combine the first eight ingredients. Bring to a boil. Stir in the macaroni. Reduce heat; simmer, uncovered, for 10-15 minutes or until the macaroni is tender.

Meanwhile, in a large skillet, cook the beef, celery, onion over medium heat until meat is no longer pink. Add the garlic; cook 1 minute longer. Drain. Add to the tomato mixture. Stir in the beans; heat through.

YIELD: 8 servings.

three-bean soup

1 medium onion, chopped
1 tablespoon canola oil
3 small potatoes, peeled and cubed
2 medium carrots, sliced
3 cans (14-1/2 ounces *each*) chicken *or* vegetable broth
3 cups water
2 tablespoons dried parsley flakes
2 teaspoons dried basil
1 teaspoon dried oregano
1 garlic clove, minced
1/2 teaspoon pepper

1 can (15-1/2 ounces) great northern beans, rinsed and drained
1 can (15 ounces) pinto beans, rinsed and drained
1 can (15 ounces) garbanzo beans *or* chickpeas, rinsed and drained
3 cups chopped fresh spinach

In a Dutch oven, saute onion in oil. Add the next nine ingredients. Simmer, uncovered, until vegetables are tender. Add beans and spinach; heat through.

YIELD: 12 servings.

valerie lee
SNELLVILLE, GEORGIA

When I was growing up, my mother prepared many different soups, each seasoned just right. She often made this colorful combination that's chock-full of harvest-fresh goodness. It showcases an appealing assortment of beans, potatoes, carrots and spinach.

rebecca phipps
RURAL HALL, NORTH CAROLINA

My husband and I are both diabetic, so I always get excited when I find delicious recipes that are in line with our dietary requirements. I serve this soup with baked wheat tortilla triangles, fresh fruit and a variety of cubed cheeses for a complete meal.

meatball soup

1 pound lean ground turkey

2-1/2 teaspoons Italian seasoning, *divided*

1/4 teaspoon paprika

1/4 teaspoon salt, *divided*

1/4 teaspoon coarsely ground pepper, *divided*

4 teaspoons olive oil, *divided*

2 celery ribs, chopped

15 fresh baby carrots, chopped

1 small onion, chopped

1 can (15 ounces) white kidney *or* cannellini beans, rinsed and drained

1 can (14-1/2 ounces) Italian diced tomatoes, undrained

1 can (14-1/2 ounces) reduced-sodium chicken broth

3/4 cup chopped cabbage

3/4 cup cut fresh green beans

3 tablespoons shredded part-skim mozzarella cheese

In a large bowl, combine the turkey, 1-1/2 teaspoons Italian seasoning, paprika, 1/8 teaspoon salt and 1/8 teaspoon pepper. Shape into 36 meatballs.

In a large nonstick skillet coated with cooking spray, brown meatballs in batches in 2 teaspoons oil until no longer pink. Remove and keep warm.

In a large saucepan coated with cooking spray, saute the celery, carrots and onion in remaining oil until tender. Stir in the white kidney beans, tomatoes, broth, cabbage, green beans and remaining Italian seasoning, salt and pepper.

Bring to a boil. Reduce heat; stir in meatballs. Simmer, uncovered, for 15-20 minutes or until green beans are tender. Sprinkle with cheese.

YIELD: 6 servings.

hearty minestrone soup

2 cans (one 28 ounces, one 14-1/2 ounces) diced tomatoes, undrained
2 cups water
2 medium carrots, sliced
1 medium onion, chopped
1 medium zucchini, chopped

1 package (3-1/2 ounces) sliced pepperoni
2 teaspoons minced garlic
2 teaspoons chicken bouillon granules
1/2 teaspoon dried basil
1/2 teaspoon dried oregano
2 cans (16 ounces each) kidney beans, rinsed and drained
1 package (10 ounces) frozen chopped spinach, thawed and squeezed dry
1-1/4 cups cooked elbow macaroni
Shredded Parmesan cheese

In a 5-qt. slow cooker, combine the first 10 ingredients. Cover and cook on low for 6-8 hours or until the vegetables are tender.

Stir in the beans, spinach and macaroni. Cover and cook 15 minutes longer or until heated through. Sprinkle with cheese.

YIELD: 7 servings.

bonnie hosman
YOUNG, ARIZONA

I picked up this recipe in California in the '80s and have been making it ever since. I love it partly because it's simple to put together and partly because the flavor is just so wonderful!

classic ham and bean soup

1 pound dried navy beans
2 medium onions, chopped
2 teaspoons canola oil
2 celery ribs, chopped
10 cups water
4 cups cubed fully cooked ham
1 cup mashed potatoes (without added milk and butter)
1/2 cup shredded carrot
2 tablespoons Worcestershire sauce
1 teaspoon salt
1/2 teaspoon dried thyme
1/2 teaspoon pepper
2 bay leaves
1 meaty ham bone *or* 2 smoked ham hocks
1/4 cup minced fresh parsley

Place beans in a Dutch oven; add water to cover by 2 in. Bring to a boil; boil for 2 minutes. Remove from heat; cover and let stand for 1 to 4 hours or until the beans are softened. Drain and rinse the beans, discarding liquid.

In the same pan, saute onions in oil for 2 minutes. Add the celery; cook until tender. Stir in the beans, water, ham, potatoes, carrot, Worcestershire sauce, salt, thyme, pepper and bay leaves. Add ham bone.

Bring to a boil. Reduce heat; cover and simmer for 1-1/4 to 1-1/2 hours or until beans are tender.

Discard the bay leaves. Remove ham bone; when cool enough to handle, remove meat from bone. Discard bone and cut meat into cubes; return to the soup. Heat through. Garnish soup with parsley.

YIELD: 15 servings.

amanda reed
MILFORD, DELAWARE

I first learned to make ham and bean soup when we lived in Pennsylvania near several Amish families. It's a great way to use up leftover ham and mashed potatoes. It freezes well, too.

pre-cut ham

Instead of using ham hocks in soups, buy a fully cooked ham and ask the butcher to cut it into large chunks. Freeze the ham until needed. The large chunks require less trimming and provide more meat than ham hocks.

gail wilkerson
HOUSE SPRINGS, MISSOURI

This soup is simple to assemble with ingredients that are a breeze to keep on hand, and it's delicious to boot.

sausage bean soup

4 cups water
1 medium potato, peeled and chopped
6 brown-and-serve turkey sausage links (1 ounce *each*)
2 cans (16 ounces *each*) kidney beans, rinsed and drained
1 can (28 ounces) diced tomatoes, undrained
1 cup chopped onion
1 medium green pepper, chopped
1 bay leaf
1/2 teaspoon garlic salt
1/2 teaspoon seasoned salt
1/2 teaspoon pepper
1/2 teaspoon dried thyme

In a large saucepan, bring water and potato to a boil. Cover and cook for 10-15 minutes or until tender (do not drain). Meanwhile, crumble sausage into a skillet; cook over medium heat until browned. Drain if necessary. Add to saucepan.

Stir in the remaining ingredients. Bring to a boil. Reduce heat; simmer, uncovered, for 8-10 minutes or until heated through, stirring occasionally. Discard bay leaf.

YIELD: 10 servings.

angee owens
LUFKIN, TEXAS

My zesty meatless soup will fill your tummy without expanding your waistline. If you prefer meat, add lean beef or chicken to pack in a little extra protein.

black bean soup

3 cans (15 ounces *each*) black beans, rinsed and drained, *divided*
3 celery ribs with leaves, chopped
1 large onion, chopped
1 medium sweet red pepper, chopped
1 jalapeno pepper, seeded and chopped
2 tablespoons olive oil
4 garlic cloves, minced
2 cans (14-1/2 ounces *each*) reduced-sodium chicken broth *or* vegetable broth
1 can (14-1/2 ounces) diced tomatoes with green peppers and onions, undrained
3 teaspoons ground cumin
1-1/2 teaspoons ground coriander
1 teaspoon Louisiana-style hot sauce
1/4 teaspoon pepper
1 bay leaf
1 teaspoon lime juice
1/2 cup reduced-fat sour cream
1/4 cup chopped green onions

In a small bowl, mash one can black beans; set aside. In a large saucepan, saute the celery, onion, red pepper and jalapeno in oil until tender. Add garlic; cook 1 minute longer.

Stir in the broth, tomatoes, cumin, coriander, hot sauce, pepper, bay leaf, remaining beans and reserved mashed beans. Bring to a boil. Reduce heat; cover and simmer for 15 minutes.

Discard bay leaf. Stir in lime juice. Garnish each serving with 1 tablespoon sour cream and 1-1/2 teaspoons green onion.

YIELD: 8 servings.

EDITOR'S NOTE: We recommend wearing disposable gloves when cutting hot peppers. Avoid touching your face.

sportsman's bean soup

2 pounds dried navy beans
3 large onions, chopped
2 tablespoons butter
4 medium carrots, chopped
2 smoked ham hocks
1 tablespoon marinade for chicken
12 orange peel strips (1 to 3 inches)
1 teaspoon salt
1/2 teaspoon dried thyme
2 bay leaves
3 cups cubed fully cooked ham
1 can (28 ounces) diced tomatoes, undrained
1/4 cup cider vinegar

Sort beans and rinse with cold water. Place in a stock pot; add water to cover by 2 in. Bring to a boil; boil for 2 minutes. Remove from the heat; cover and let stand for 1-4 hours or until beans are softened.

Drain and rinse beans; discard liquid and set beans aside. In the same pan, saute the onions in butter until tender. Add the carrots; saute 4-5 minutes longer.

Add the ham hocks, marinade for chicken, orange peel, salt, thyme, bay leaves, beans and enough water to cover by 2 in. Bring to a boil. Reduce heat; cover and simmer for 2 hours or until beans are tender.

Remove the ham hocks; when cool enough to handle, remove meat from bones. Discard bones and cut meat into cubes; return to the soup. Add the additional ham, tomatoes and vinegar; heat through. Discard the bay leaves and orange peel before serving.

YIELD: 27 servings.

EDITOR'S NOTE: This recipe was tested with Lea & Perrins Marinade for Chicken.

howell vincent
GEORGETOWN, KENTUCKY

I've been cooking soups and stews for over 45 years. My wife ranks this wholesome creation as one of her all-time favorites. In fact, I'm proud to say it was one of the dishes that won me my lady's heart.

swiss chard bean soup

taste of home test kitchen

GREENDALE, WISCONSIN

This good-for-you soup combines nutritious Swiss chard with other fresh garden favorites. Its light broth is surprisingly rich in flavor and the grated Parmesan cheese packs a tasty punch.

1 medium carrot, coarsely chopped
1 small zucchini, coarsely chopped
1 small yellow summer squash, coarsely chopped
1 small red onion, chopped
2 tablespoons olive oil
2 garlic cloves, minced
3 cans (14-1/2 ounces *each*) reduced-sodium chicken broth
4 cups chopped Swiss chard
1 can (15-1/2 ounces) great northern beans, rinsed and drained
1 can (14-1/2 ounces) diced tomatoes, undrained
1 teaspoon dried thyme

1/2 teaspoon salt
1/2 teaspoon dried oregano
1/4 teaspoon pepper
1/4 cup grated Parmesan cheese

In a Dutch oven, saute the carrot, zucchini, yellow squash and onion in oil until tender. Add garlic; saute 1 minute longer. Add the broth, Swiss chard, beans, tomatoes, thyme, salt, oregano and pepper.

Bring to a boil. Reduce heat; simmer, uncovered, for 15 minutes or until chard is tender. Just before serving, sprinkle with cheese.

YIELD: 10 servings.

shrimp and black bean soup

1 large onion, chopped
1 tablespoon olive oil
2 cans (14-1/2 ounces *each*) reduced-sodium chicken broth
2 cans (10 ounces *each*) diced tomatoes and green chilies, undrained
2 cups frozen corn
1 can (15 ounces) black beans, rinsed and drained
1 can (14-1/2 ounces) diced tomatoes, undrained
4-1/2 teaspoons chili powder
1 teaspoon sugar
1/2 teaspoon salt
1 pound uncooked medium shrimp, peeled and deveined
1/4 cup minced fresh parsley

In a Dutch oven, saute onion in oil for 3-4 minutes or until tender. Add the broth, tomatoes and green chilies, corn, black beans, tomatoes, chili powder, sugar and salt. Bring to a boil, stirring occasionally. Reduce heat; cover and simmer for 20 minutes.

Stir in shrimp; cook 5-6 minutes longer or until shrimp turn pink. Stir in parsley.

YIELD: 8 servings.

elizabeth lewis
HAYDEN, ALABAMA

My hungry clan can't get enough of this bold and spicy soup packed with tomatoes, beans, corn and shrimp. It's a flavorful Creole dish that can be enjoyed any time of year.

chicken lima bean soup

1 pound dried large lima beans
1 broiler/fryer chicken (3 to 3-1/2 pounds)
3 quarts water
2 celery ribs with leaves, sliced
4 chicken bouillon cubes
2-1/2 teaspoons salt
1/2 teaspoon pepper
3 medium carrots, chopped
4 cups chopped fresh spinach
2 tablespoons minced fresh parsley

In a Dutch oven, combine the beans, chicken, water, celery, bouillon, salt and pepper; bring to a boil. Reduce heat; cover and simmer for 2 hours or until beans are tender.

Remove chicken. When cool enough to handle, remove meat from bones; discard bones. Cut meat into bite-size pieces; return to pan. Add carrots; simmer for 30 minutes or until tender. Stir in the spinach and parsley; heat through.

YIELD: 12-14 servings.

carol ann kaiser
PENDLETON, OREGON

When I was a little girl, my father could be found standing over the stove perfecting his chicken lima bean soup. It's one of his most memorable dishes... and one of my most treasured recipes.

macaroni bean soup

4 cups chicken broth
2 cups tomato juice
1 cup uncooked elbow macaroni
1 cup sliced fresh carrots
1 teaspoon minced garlic
2 medium yellow summer squash, sliced
1 can (16 ounces) kidney beans, rinsed and drained
1 teaspoon seasoned salt
1/8 teaspoon pepper
1/4 cup grated Parmesan cheese
1 tablespoon lemon juice

In a large saucepan, bring the broth, tomato juice, macaroni, carrots and garlic to a boil. Reduce heat; cover and simmer for 5 minutes or until the carrots are tender.

Stir in the squash, beans, seasoned salt and pepper; simmer for 10 minutes or until macaroni and vegetables are tender. Remove from the heat; stir in cheese and lemon juice.

YIELD: 9 servings.

sundra hauck
BOGALUSA, LOUISIANA

Ready in just 25 minutes, my chunky soup makes a great meatless main dish.

alice mceachern
SURREY, BRITISH COLUMBIA

This stew became a favorite after my children requested more meatless dishes. Red wine vinegar perks up the flavor and carrots add color. We like to ladle helpings over cooked rice.

spinach lentil stew

1/2 cup chopped onion
2 garlic cloves, minced
1 tablespoon canola oil
5 cups water
1 cup lentils, rinsed
4 teaspoons vegetable *or* chicken bouillon granules
3 teaspoons Worcestershire sauce
1/2 teaspoon salt
1/2 teaspoon dried thyme
1/4 teaspoon pepper
1 bay leaf
1 cup chopped carrots
1 can (14-1/2 ounces) diced tomatoes, undrained
1 package (10 ounces) frozen chopped spinach, thawed and squeezed dry
1 tablespoon red wine vinegar

In a large saucepan, saute the onion and garlic in oil until tender. Add the water, lentils, bouillon, Worcestershire sauce, salt, thyme, pepper and bay leaf; bring to a boil. Reduce heat; cover and simmer for 20 minutes.

Add the carrots, tomatoes and spinach; return to a boil. Reduce heat; cover and simmer 15-20 minutes longer or until lentils are tender. Stir in vinegar. Discard bay leaf.

YIELD: 6 servings.

lucille schreiber
GLEASON, WISCONSIN

There's not a winter that goes by that I don't fix at least one batch of split pea soup. It's a hot and hearty meal that warms us up on chilly nights.

split pea and ham soup

1 pound dried green split peas (2 cups)
7 cups water
1 teaspoon canola oil
2 cups cubed fully cooked ham
2 cups chopped carrots
1 cup chopped celery

1 cup chopped onion
1 cup diced peeled potato
1 teaspoon salt, optional
1/2 teaspoon garlic powder
1/2 teaspoon pepper
1/4 cup minced fresh parsley

In a Dutch oven or soup kettle, bring the peas, water and oil to a boil. Reduce heat; cover and simmer for 2 hours, stirring occasionally. Add the next eight ingredients; cover and simmer for 30 minutes or until vegetables are tender. Stir in parsley.

YIELD: 10 servings.

vegetable bean soup

3 medium carrots, sliced
1-1/2 cups chopped onions
1 cup sliced celery
1 tablespoon canola oil
2 to 3 garlic cloves, minced
2 cans (14-1/2 ounces *each*) chicken broth
2 cans (15 ounces *each*) navy *or* great northern beans, rinsed and drained, *divided*
2 cups fresh broccoli florets
1/2 teaspoon salt
1/2 teaspoon dried rosemary, crushed
1/4 teaspoon dried thyme
1/4 teaspoon pepper
1 cup fresh baby spinach, optional

In a Dutch oven, saute the carrots, onions and celery in oil until tender. Add garlic; cook 1 minute longer. Stir in broth, one can of beans, broccoli and seasonings; bring to a boil. Reduce heat; simmer, uncovered, for 5-7 minutes.

Place remaining beans in a blender; cover and process until smooth. Add beans to the soup with spinach if desired; simmer for 2 minutes or until heated through.

YIELD: 8 servings.

bean education and awareness network
SCOTTSBLUFF, NEBRASKA

Navy beans add extra texture and flavor to this veggie-packed soup. It will definitely fill you up.

chopped carrots

To easily chop carrots coarsely for your soups, simply peel the carrots, remove the ends and slice into quarters. Then toss the slices in the food processor and let it do the chopping!

pasta fagioli soup

brenda thomas
SPRINGFIELD, MISSOURI

My hubby enjoys my classic Italian soup far more than any restaurant version. Loaded with fresh spinach, macaroni and seasoned sausage, it's a meal all by itself.

1/2 pound Italian turkey sausage links, casings removed, crumbled

1 small onion, chopped

1-1/2 teaspoons canola oil

1 garlic clove, minced

2 cups water

1 can (15-1/2 ounces) great northern beans, rinsed and drained

1 can (14-1/2 ounces) diced tomatoes, undrained

1 can (14-1/2 ounces) reduced-sodium chicken broth

3/4 cup uncooked elbow macaroni

1/4 teaspoon pepper

1 cup fresh spinach leaves, cut into strips

5 teaspoons shredded Parmesan cheese

In a large saucepan, cook sausage over medium heat until no longer pink; drain and set aside. In the same pan, saute onion in oil until tender. Add garlic; saute 1 minute longer.

Add the water, beans, tomatoes, broth, macaroni and pepper; bring to a boil. Cook, uncovered, for 8-10 minutes or until macaroni is tender.

Reduce heat to low; stir in sausage and spinach. Cook for 2-3 minutes or until the spinach is wilted. Garnish with cheese.

YIELD: 5 servings.

peasant bean soup

1 pound dried great northern beans, washed and sorted
2-1/2 quarts cold water, *divided*
3 medium carrots, sliced
3 celery ribs, sliced
2 medium onions, chopped
1 garlic clove, minced
1 can (16 ounces) stewed tomatoes, cut up
1 to 2 bay leaves
2 tablespoons olive oil
Salt and pepper to taste

Soak beans overnight in 2 qts. water.

Add remaining water to softened beans and bring to a boil; reduce heat and simmer 30 minutes.

Stir in the remaining ingredients; simmer 1 hour or until beans are tender. Discard bay leaves.

YIELD: 8 servings.

bertha mcclung
SUMMERSVILLE, WEST VIRGINIA

Give this soup a try the next time you're looking for something hearty to serve a crowd. I often double or triple the recipe for parties or potlucks.

creamy split pea soup

1/2 pound sliced bacon, diced
1 large onion, chopped
2 ribs celery, sliced
1 pound dried green split peas
2 quarts water
2 medium potatoes, peeled and diced
2 cups diced fully cooked ham
2 teaspoons salt
1 bay leaf
1/4 teaspoon pepper
1 cup heavy whipping cream

In a Dutch oven or soup kettle, cook bacon over medium heat until crisp. Using a slotted spoon, remove bacon to paper towels; drain, reserving drippings. Add onion and celery to drippings. Saute until vegetables are tender; drain. Add the peas, water, potatoes, ham, salt, bay leaf and pepper. Bring to a boil. Reduce heat; cover and simmer for 45 minutes or until peas are very tender, stirring occasionally. Discard bay leaf.

Cool slightly. Process in small batches in a blender until smooth. Return to Dutch oven; stir in cream. Heat through (do not boil). Garnish with reserved bacon.

YIELD: 12 servings.

sherry smith
SALEM, MISSOURI

A friend shared this with me over 25 years ago. At the time, she was in her 60s and working as a cook on a riverboat barge. A recipe from someone with that much moxie was definitely worth keeping!

yankee bean soup

1-1/2 cups dried navy beans
1/2 pound sliced bacon, diced
3/4 cup chopped onion
1/2 cup chopped carrot
1/3 cup chopped celery leaves
4 cups water
2 cups milk
2 teaspoons molasses
1-1/2 teaspoons salt

Place the beans in a Dutch oven; add water to cover by 2 in. Bring to a boil; boil for 2 minutes. Remove from the heat; cover and let stand for 1 hour.

Drain and rinse beans, discarding liquid. Set beans aside. In the same pan, cook the bacon over medium heat until crisp. Using a slotted spoon, remove bacon to paper towels; drain, reserving 2 tablespoons drippings.

In the drippings, saute the onion until tender. Stir in carrot and celery leaves. Return beans to the pan. Add water. Bring to a boil. Reduce heat; cover and simmer for 1-3/4 to 2 hours or until the beans are tender.

Stir in the milk, molasses, salt and bacon. Remove about 2-1/2 cups of soup; cool slightly. Place in a blender or food processor; cover and process until pureed. Return to the pan; heat through.

YIELD: 6 servings.

ann nace
PERKASIE, PENNSYLVANIA

Bacon, molasses and onion add great flavor to my special bean soup. It's perfect for a wintry day.

secret spice

Liven up navy bean soup by tossing in a few whole cloves while the soup is simmering and removing them just before serving. Folks will notice the special taste but won't be able to identify the source.

beef & ground beef

Beef is so versatile—and it's the perfect choice to add vigor to any soup. Whether it's ground beef, stew meat or steak, you'll find a recipe that includes it here. Partnered with vegetables, pasta, rice or even tortilla chips, you'll discover surefire family pleasers on the following pages.

34 37 44

linda fox
SOLDOTNA, ALASKA

A steaming bowl of this soup hits the spot on cold days—we have them in abundance here in Alaska. Oregano adds fast flavor to the pleasant combination of tender veggies, pasta spirals and ground beef.

mushrooms

To prepare mushrooms for soup, gently remove any dirt by rubbing with a mushroom brush or wiping with a damp paper towel. Or quickly rinse under cold water, drain and pat dry with paper towels.

pasta pizza soup

1 pound lean ground beef (90% lean)
4 ounces sliced fresh mushrooms
1 medium onion, chopped
1 celery rib, thinly sliced
1 garlic clove, minced
4 cups water
1 can (14-1/2 ounces) Italian diced tomatoes, undrained
2 medium carrots, sliced
4 teaspoons beef bouillon granules
1 bay leaf
1-1/2 teaspoons dried oregano
1-1/2 cups cooked tricolor spiral pasta

In a large saucepan over medium heat, cook the beef, mushrooms, onion, celery and garlic until meat is no longer pink; drain.

Stir in the water, tomatoes, carrots, bouillon, bay leaf and oregano. Bring to a boil. Reduce heat; cover and simmer for 20-25 minutes or until carrots are tender. Stir in pasta; heat through. Discard bay leaf.

YIELD: 8 servings.

diane mrozinski
ESSEXVILLE, MICHIGAN

You'll get a thumbs-up when you serve my hamburger soup packed with veggies. You can substitute ground turkey for the beef, if you like, and easily double or triple the recipe to serve more people.

hearty hamburger soup

1/4 pound lean ground beef (90% lean)
1/4 cup chopped onion
1-1/2 cups water
1/4 cup thinly sliced carrot
1-1/2 teaspoons beef bouillon granules
1 can (5-1/2 ounces) V8 juice
1/4 cup frozen corn
1/4 cup frozen peas
1/4 cup sliced fresh mushrooms
1/4 cup sliced zucchini
1/8 teaspoon dried basil
Dash pepper
1/2 cup cooked elbow macaroni

In a small saucepan, cook beef and onion over medium heat until meat is no longer pink; drain. Add the water, carrot and bouillon. Bring to a boil. Reduce heat; simmer, uncovered, for 5 minutes.

Add the V8 juice, corn, peas, mushrooms, zucchini, basil and pepper. Simmer 6-8 minutes longer or until vegetables are tender. Add macaroni; heat through.

YIELD: 2 servings.

beef goulash soup

2 pounds beef top sirloin steak, cut into 1/2-inch cubes

1 large onion, chopped

1 large green pepper, chopped

2 tablespoons olive oil

3 medium potatoes, peeled and cubed

3 medium carrots, chopped

4 cups beef broth

1 cup water

2 tablespoons paprika

1 tablespoon sugar

1 to 2 teaspoons salt

1/2 teaspoon pepper

1/4 teaspoon cayenne pepper

2 bay leaves

1 can (28 ounces) crushed tomatoes

1 can (6 ounces) tomato paste

2 tablespoons caraway seeds

Sour cream

In a Dutch oven over medium-high heat, cook and stir the beef, onion and green pepper in oil until meat is browned on all sides; drain. Stir in the next 10 ingredients; bring to a boil. Reduce heat; cover and simmer for 25-30 minutes or until the potatoes are tender.

Stir in the tomatoes, tomato paste and caraway seeds. Cover and simmer 25-30 minutes longer or until meat is tender. Discard bay leaves. Top each serving with a dollop of sour cream.

YIELD: 16 servings.

sharon bickett

CHESTER, SOUTH CAROLINA

Paprika, cayenne pepper and caraway spice up tender chunks of beef, potatoes and carrots in this tantalizing tomato-based soup. I like to garnish each bowl with a dollop of sour cream.

brigitte schultz

BARSTOW, CALIFORNIA

You will chase away winter's chill with a spoon when you cook up my satisfying soup. It features a rich flavor and is full of nutritious vegetables and chunks of tender steak.

easy vegetable beef soup

1 pound beef top sirloin steak, cut into 1/2-inch cubes

1/4 teaspoon pepper, *divided*

2 teaspoons olive oil

2 cans (14-1/2 ounces *each*) beef broth

2 cups cubed peeled potatoes

1-1/4 cups water

2 medium carrots, sliced

1 tablespoon onion soup mix

1 tablespoon dried basil

1/2 teaspoon dried tarragon

2 tablespoons cornstarch

1/2 cup white wine *or* additional beef broth

Sprinkle steak with 1/8 teaspoon pepper. In a Dutch oven, brown steak in batches in oil over medium heat. Add the broth, potatoes, water, carrots, onion soup mix, basil, tarragon and remaining pepper; bring to a boil. Reduce heat; cover and simmer for 20-25 minutes or until vegetables are tender.

In a small bowl, combine the cornstarch and wine until smooth; stir into soup. Bring to a boil; cook and stir for 2 minutes or until thickened.

YIELD: 7 servings.

ground beef noodle soup

1-1/2 pounds lean ground beef (90% lean)
1/2 cup *each* chopped onion, celery and carrot
7 cups water
1 envelope au jus mix
2 tablespoons beef bouillon granules
2 bay leaves
1/8 teaspoon pepper
1-1/2 cups uncooked egg noodles

In a large saucepan, cook the beef, onion, celery and carrot over medium heat until meat is no longer pink; drain.

Add the water, au jus mix, bouillon, bay leaves and pepper; bring to a boil. Stir in the noodles. Return to a boil. Cook, uncovered, for 15 minutes or until the noodles are tender, stirring occasionally. Discard bay leaves.

YIELD: 8 servings.

judy brander
TWO HARBORS, MINNESOTA

My savory specialty combines ground beef with onions, celery and carrots. Whip it up any day of the week for a quick meal that's guaranteed to please.

taco soup

2 pounds lean ground beef (90% lean)
1 small onion, chopped
3 cans (14-1/2 ounces *each*) stewed tomatoes
1-1/2 cups water
1 can (16 ounces) lima beans, rinsed and drained
1 can (16 ounces) kidney beans, rinsed and drained
1 can (15 ounces) pinto beans, rinsed and drained
1 can (14-1/2 ounces) hominy, drained
3 cans (4 ounces *each*) chopped green chilies, undrained
1 envelope taco seasoning
1 envelope ranch salad dressing mix
1 teaspoon salt
1 teaspoon pepper
Shredded cheddar cheese, optional
Tortilla chips, optional

In a large Dutch oven, cook beef and onion over medium heat until meat is no longer pink; drain.

Stir in the next 11 ingredients; bring to a boil. Reduce heat; cover and simmer for 30 minutes. Garnish soup with cheese and serve with tortilla chips if desired.

YIELD: 10 servings.

tonya jones
SUNDOWN, TEXAS

I have to admit that when a good friend gave me this recipe, I wasn't certain I'd like it. But after one taste, I changed my mind! My husband loves it, too.

spicy steak house soup

1/4 pound beef tenderloin, cut into 1/4-inch pieces
1/4 cup chopped onion
1/4 teaspoon salt
2 teaspoons olive oil
1-1/2 cups cubed peeled Yukon Gold potatoes
1 cup reduced-sodium beef broth
1/4 cup steak sauce
3/4 teaspoon chili powder
1/4 teaspoon ground cumin
1/8 teaspoon cayenne pepper
2 tablespoons minced fresh parsley

In a large nonstick saucepan, saute the beef, onion and salt in oil for 4-5 minutes or until meat is no longer pink. Stir in the potatoes, broth, steak sauce, chili powder, cumin and cayenne. Bring to a boil.

Reduce heat; cover and simmer for 30-35 minutes or until potatoes are tender. Garnish with parsley.

YIELD: 2 servings.

lisa renshaw
KANSAS CITY, MISSOURI

Think "steak dinner in a bowl" when eating this rich soup. It makes perfect game-day fare in the fall or winter. Chili powder and other seasonings give it a spicy zip that will warm you right up!

evelyn buford
BELTON, MISSOURI

I always get a great response at church suppers and potlucks whenever I bring this easy-to-fix Southwestern soup. The flavor seems to improve in the leftovers—if there are any!

chunky taco soup

1-1/2 pounds beef top sirloin *or* round steak, cut into 3/4-inch cubes
1 medium onion, chopped
1 tablespoon olive oil
2 cans (15 ounces *each*) pinto beans, rinsed and drained
2 cans (14-1/2 ounces *each*) diced tomatoes and green chilies, undrained
2 cups water
1 can (15 ounces) black beans, rinsed and drained
1 can (14-3/4 ounces) cream-style corn
1 envelope ranch salad dressing mix
1 envelope taco seasoning
1/4 cup minced fresh cilantro

In a large kettle or Dutch oven, brown beef and onion in oil. Add the pinto beans, tomatoes, water, black beans, corn, salad dressing mix and taco seasoning. Bring to a boil. Reduce heat; cover and simmer for 20-30 minutes or until the meat is tender. Sprinkle with cilantro.

YIELD: 12 servings.

carole lanthier
COURTICE, ONTARIO

This soup is really easy and takes very little time to put together. Serve it for lunch or supper with homemade bread.

easy beef barley soup

1/2 pound lean ground beef (90% lean)
2 large fresh mushrooms, sliced
1 celery rib, chopped
1 small onion, chopped
2 teaspoons all-purpose flour

3 cans (14-1/2 ounces *each*) reduced-sodium beef broth
2 medium carrots, sliced
1 large potato, peeled and cubed
1/2 teaspoon pepper
1/8 teaspoon salt
1/3 cup medium pearl barley
1 can (5 ounces) evaporated milk
2 tablespoons tomato paste

In a Dutch oven over medium heat, cook and stir the beef, mushrooms, celery and onion until meat is no longer pink; drain. Stir in flour until blended; gradually add broth. Stir in the carrots, potato, pepper and salt. Bring to a boil. Stir in barley.

Reduce heat; cover and simmer for 45-50 minutes or until barley is tender. Whisk in milk and tomato paste; heat through.

YIELD: 4 servings.

asian vegetable-beef soup

1 pound beef stew meat, cut into
   1-inch cubes

1 tablespoon canola oil

2 cups water

1 cup beef broth

1/4 cup sherry or additional beef broth

1/4 cup reduced-sodium soy sauce

6 green onions, chopped

3 tablespoons brown sugar

2 garlic cloves, minced

1 tablespoon minced fresh gingerroot

2 teaspoons sesame oil

1/4 teaspoon cayenne pepper

1-1/2 cups sliced fresh mushrooms

1-1/2 cups julienned carrots

1 cup sliced bok choy

1-1/2 cups uncooked long grain rice

Chive blossoms, optional

In a large saucepan, brown meat in oil on all sides; drain. Add the water, broth, sherry, soy sauce, onions, brown sugar, garlic, ginger, sesame oil and cayenne. Bring to a boil. Reduce heat; cover and simmer for 1 hour.

Stir in the mushrooms, carrots and bok choy; cover and simmer 20-30 minutes longer or until the vegetables are tender. Meanwhile, cook the rice according to package directions.

Divide rice among six soup bowls, 3/4 cup in each; top each with 1 cup of soup. Garnish with chive blossoms if desired.

YIELD: 6 servings.

mollie lee
ROCKWALL, TEXAS

My husband is Korean-American, and I enjoy working Asian flavors into our menu. This tasty soup was something I put together one night with a variety of ingredients I found in the refrigerator. Everyone loved it!

hearty beef barley soup

elizabeth kendall

CAROLINA BEACH,
NORTH CAROLINA

This satisfying barley soup is a favorite menu item in our house throughout the year. Everyone savors the flavor when I make it.

1 pound beef top round steak, cut into 1/2-inch cubes
1 tablespoon canola oil
3 cans (14-1/2 ounces *each*) beef broth
2 cups water
1/3 cup medium pearl barley
1 teaspoon salt
1/8 teaspoon pepper
1 cup chopped carrots
1/2 cup chopped celery
1/4 cup chopped onion

3 tablespoons minced fresh parsley
1 cup frozen peas

In a Dutch oven, brown beef in oil; drain. Stir in the broth, water, barley, salt and pepper. Bring to a boil. Reduce heat; cover and simmer for 1 hour.

Add the carrots, celery, onion and parsley; cover and simmer for 45 minutes or until the meat and vegetables are tender. Stir in peas; heat through.

YIELD: 9 servings.

the **ULTIMATE SOUP** cookbook

stuffed sweet pepper soup

1 pound lean ground beef (90% lean)
8 cups water
4 cups tomato juice
3 medium sweet red peppers, diced
1-1/2 cups chili sauce
1 cup uncooked long grain rice
2 celery ribs, diced
1 large onion, diced
2 teaspoons browning sauce, optional
3 teaspoons chicken bouillon granules
2 garlic cloves, minced
1/2 teaspoon salt

In a Dutch oven, over medium heat, cook beef until no longer pink; drain. Add the remaining ingredients; bring to a boil.

Reduce heat; simmer, uncovered, for 1 hour or until rice is tender.

YIELD: 16 servings.

joseph kendra
CORAOPOLIS, PENNSYLVANIA

I acquired my talents for all things culinary from my mom. This chunky soup filled with tomatoes, peppers, garlic and onions always evokes memories of her home-style cooking.

tomato mushroom soup

1 pound sliced fresh mushrooms
6 tablespoons butter, *divided*
2 medium onions, finely chopped
1 garlic clove, minced
2 medium carrots, chopped
3 celery ribs, finely chopped
3 tablespoons all-purpose flour
8 cups beef broth
2 medium tomatoes, peeled, seeded and chopped
1 can (15 ounces) tomato sauce
1 teaspoon salt
1/2 teaspoon pepper
3 tablespoons minced fresh parsley
Sour cream, optional

In a large kettle or Dutch oven, saute mushrooms in 4 tablespoons butter until tender. Remove the mushrooms with a slotted spoon; set aside and keep warm.

In the same kettle, saute the onions, garlic, carrots and celery in the remaining butter until tender. Stir in the flour until blended. Add the broth, tomatoes, tomato sauce, salt, pepper and half of the reserved mushrooms. Cover and allow to simmer for 30 minutes.

Stir in the parsley and remaining mushrooms; simmer, uncovered, for 5 minutes or until heated through. Garnish with sour cream if desired.

YIELD: 12 servings.

bonnie hawkins
ELKHORN, WISCONSIN

This soup recipe came about while I was experimenting with the fresh abundance of vegetables from my garden. I serve it often to my family, especially in the winter.

thyme for meatball soup

1 egg
1/4 cup dry bread crumbs
2 tablespoons minced fresh thyme *or* 2 teaspoons dried thyme, *divided*
1/2 teaspoon salt
1-1/2 pounds lean ground beef (90% lean)
1 small onion, chopped
2 medium carrots, chopped
3/4 pound fresh mushrooms, sliced
1 tablespoon olive oil
1-1/2 pounds red potatoes, cubed
2 cans (14-1/2 ounces *each*) beef broth
1 can (14-1/2 ounces) stewed tomatoes

In a large bowl, combine egg, bread crumbs, half of the thyme and salt. Crumble beef over mixture and mix well. Shape into 1-in. balls. In a Dutch oven or soup kettle, brown meatballs; drain and set aside.

In the same pan, saute the onion, carrots and mushrooms in oil until onion is tender. Stir in the potatoes, broth, tomatoes, meatballs and remaining thyme. Bring to a boil. Reduce heat; cover and simmer for 25-30 minutes or until potatoes are tender.

YIELD: 12 servings.

jennie freeman
LONG CREEK, OREGON

Thyme is one of my favorite herbs to grow. It adds a fresh spark to this hearty soup.

arlene lynn
LINCOLN, NEBRASKA

I take advantage of convenience items to prepare this hearty soup in a hurry. Bowls of the chunky mixture are chock-full of ground beef, noodles and vegetables.

ground beef

When browning ground beef or other ground meat, use a pastry blender to break up larger pieces shortly before the meat is completely cooked. This makes it much more suitable for soups, stews, chili and casseroles.

beef noodle soup

1 pound lean ground beef (90% lean)
1 can (46 ounces) V8 juice
1 envelope onion soup mix
1 package (3 ounces) beef ramen noodles
1 package (16 ounces) frozen mixed vegetables

In a large saucepan, cook the beef over medium heat until no longer pink; drain. Stir in the V8 juice, soup mix, contents of noodle seasoning packet and mixed vegetables.

Bring to a boil. Reduce heat; simmer, uncovered, for 6 minutes or until vegetables are tender. Return to a boil; stir in noodles. Cook for 3 minutes or until noodles are tender.

YIELD: 8 servings.

tracy thompson
CRANESVILLE, PENNSYLVANIA

Ready in minutes when I get home from work, this soup becomes part of a balanced meal with a tossed salad, rolls or fruit. For variation, try ground chicken, turkey or even venison instead of the ground beef.

stuffed pepper soup

1 package (8.8 ounces) ready-to-serve long grain and wild rice
1 pound lean ground beef (90% lean)

2 cups frozen chopped green peppers, thawed
1 cup chopped onion
1 jar (26 ounces) chunky tomato pasta sauce
1 can (14-1/2 ounces) Italian diced tomatoes, undrained
1 can (14 ounces) beef broth

Prepare the rice according to package directions. Meanwhile, in a large saucepan, cook the beef, green peppers and onion until the meat is no longer pink; drain. Stir in the pasta sauce, tomatoes, broth and prepared rice; heat through.

YIELD: 6-8 servings.

beefy vegetable soup

- 1 pound lean ground beef (90% lean)
- 1 medium onion, chopped
- 1 garlic clove, minced
- 2 cans (8 ounces *each*) tomato sauce
- 2 cans (16 ounces *each*) kidney beans, rinsed and drained, optional
- 1 package (10 ounces) frozen corn
- 1 cup shredded carrots
- 1 cup chopped green pepper
- 1 cup chopped sweet red pepper
- 1 cup chopped fresh tomato
- 1 tablespoon chili powder
- 1/2 teaspoon dried basil
- 1/2 teaspoon salt
- 1/4 teaspoon pepper
- Shredded cheddar cheese, sour cream and tortilla chips, optional

In a skillet, cook beef and onion over medium heat until the meat is no longer pink. Add garlic; cook 1 minute longer. Drain.

Transfer to a 5-qt. slow cooker. Stir in the tomato sauce, beans if desired, vegetables and seasonings. Cover and cook on low for 8 hours or until thick and bubbly, stirring occasionally. Serve with cheese, sour cream and chips if desired.

YIELD: 8-10 servings.

teresa king
CHAMBERSBURG, PENNSYLVANIA

I adapted this recipe from one I saw in a cookbook in an attempt to add more vegetables to our diet. When my young kids ate it without hesitation, I knew it was a keeper!

lively leftovers

Freeze soup in serving-size containers for quick, no-fuss meals. Whenever you crave something hot and hearty, just pull one out of the freezer and microwave for 3 to 5 minutes or until heated through. Lunch doesn't get any easier than that!

beef and tortellini soup

barbara kemmer
ROHNERT PARK, CALIFORNIA

If you're a fan of tomato soup, give my mom's recipe a try. My family loves it and so does everyone else who tries it.

5 tablespoons all-purpose flour, *divided*
1/2 pound beef top sirloin steak, cut into 1/2-inch cubes
3 teaspoons butter, *divided*
1 medium onion, chopped
1 celery rib, chopped
1 medium carrot, chopped
2 garlic cloves, minced
1 can (28 ounces) diced tomatoes, undrained
2 cans (14-1/2 ounces *each*) reduced-sodium beef broth
1-1/2 cups water, *divided*
1 teaspoon dried thyme
1/2 teaspoon white pepper
1/4 teaspoon salt
2 cups frozen beef tortellini

Place 2 tablespoons flour in a large resealable plastic bag. Add beef, a few pieces at a time, and shake to coat. In a nonstick Dutch oven, brown beef in 2 teaspoons butter; remove and keep warm.

In the same pan, saute the onion, celery and carrot in remaining butter until tender. Add garlic; cook 1 minute longer. Add the tomatoes, broth, 1 cup water, thyme, pepper, salt and reserved beef. Bring to a boil. Reduce heat; cover and simmer for 20 minutes. Add tortellini; cook 5-10 minutes longer or until tender.

Combine the remaining flour and water until smooth. Stir into the pan. Bring to a boil; cook and stir for 2 minutes or until thickened.

YIELD: 6 servings.

easy taco soup

1-1/2 pounds lean ground beef (90% lean)
1 large onion, chopped
1 can (15 ounces) pinto beans, rinsed and drained

1 can (14-1/2 ounces) stewed tomatoes
1 can (10 ounces) diced tomatoes and green chilies
1 can (10 ounces) chili without beans
1 pound process cheese (Velveeta), cubed
Salt, pepper and garlic powder to taste
2 cups (16 ounces) sour cream, *divided*

In a Dutch oven or soup kettle, cook beef and onion over medium heat until the meat is no longer pink; drain. Add the beans, tomatoes, chili, cheese and seasonings. Reduce the heat to low; cook and stir until cheese is melted. Stir in 1 cup sour cream; heat through (do not boil). Garnish with the remaining sour cream.

YIELD: 13 servings.

sue burton
FRANKFORT, KANSAS

This recipe is quick and easy. It's one of our standbys whenever we have a craving for something with a little Southwestern flair.

beef and bacon chowder

1 pound lean ground beef (90% lean)
2 cups chopped celery
1/2 cup chopped onion
4 cups milk
3 cups cubed peeled potatoes, cooked
2 cans (10-3/4 ounces *each*) condensed cream of mushroom soup, undiluted
2 cups chopped carrots, cooked
Salt and pepper to taste
12 bacon strips, cooked and crumbled

In a Dutch oven, cook the beef, celery and onion over medium heat until the meat is no longer pink; drain. Add the milk, potatoes, soup, carrots, salt and pepper; heat through. Stir in the crumbled bacon just before serving.

YIELD: 12 servings.

nancy schmidt
CENTER, COLORADO

Compliments are sure to come your way when you set bowls of this chunky chowder on the table. Crumbled bacon makes it even more indulgent.

spicy cheeseburger soup

1-1/2 cups water
2 cups cubed peeled potatoes
2 small carrots, grated
1 small onion, chopped
1/4 cup chopped green pepper
1 jalapeno pepper, seeded and chopped
1 garlic clove, minced
1 tablespoon beef bouillon granules
1/2 teaspoon salt
1 pound lean ground beef (90% lean), cooked and drained
2-1/2 cups milk, *divided*
3 tablespoons all-purpose flour
8 ounces process American cheese, cubed
1/4 to 1 teaspoon cayenne pepper, optional

1/2 pound sliced bacon, cooked and crumbled

In a large saucepan, combine the first nine ingredients; bring to a boil. Reduce the heat; cover and simmer for 15-20 minutes or until the potatoes are tender.

Stir in beef and 2 cups of milk; heat through. Combine flour and remaining milk until smooth; gradually stir into soup. Bring to a boil; cook and stir for 2 minutes or until thickened and bubbly. Reduce the heat; stir in the cheese until melted. Add the cayenne pepper if desired. Top with the bacon just before serving.

YIELD: 6-8 servings.

EDITOR'S NOTE: We recommend wearing disposable gloves when cutting hot peppers. Avoid touching your face.

lisa mast
WHITE CLOUD, MICHIGAN

This succulent soup brings my clan to the table in a hurry. I love the warming zip of cayenne, but it also tastes terrific without it if you prefer a mild flavor. Add a few simple side dishes, and you have a complete meal.

mrs. guy turnbull
ARLINGTON, MASSACHUSETTS

My beef lentil soup makes a great main course for a hearty lunch or dinner. It's also nice sipped from a mug when you're curled up in front of the fireplace on a cold winter evening.

frozen spinach

Use a salad spinner to thaw and remove the excess water in frozen spinach. Or, hold the spinach in a colander under running water and then squeeze the moisture out by hand.

beef lentil soup

1 pound lean ground beef (90% lean)
1 can (46 ounces) tomato *or* V8 juice
4 cups water
1 cup dried lentils, rinsed
2 cups chopped cabbage
1 cup sliced carrots
1 cup sliced celery
1 cup chopped onion
1/2 cup diced green pepper
1/2 teaspoon pepper
1/2 teaspoon dried thyme
1 bay leaf
1 teaspoon salt, optional
2 beef bouillon cubes, optional
1 package (10 ounces) frozen chopped spinach, thawed

In a large stockpot, cook beef over medium heat until no longer pink; drain. Add the tomato juice, water, lentils, cabbage, carrots, celery, onion, green pepper, pepper, thyme, bay leaf, salt and bouillon if desired.

Bring to a boil. Reduce heat; simmer, uncovered, for 1 to 1-1/2 hours or until the lentils and vegetables are tender. Add spinach and heat through. Remove bay leaf.

YIELD: 6 servings.

taste of home test kitchen
GREENDALE, WISCONSIN

Potatoes and roast beef come together in this rich and substantial soup. The result is a well-balanced, flavorful dish perfect for fall.

meat and potato soup

4 cups water
3 cups cubed cooked beef chuck roast
4 medium red potatoes, cubed
4 ounces sliced fresh mushrooms
1/2 cup chopped onion
1/4 cup ketchup
2 teaspoons beef bouillon granules
2 teaspoons cider vinegar
1 teaspoon brown sugar
1 teaspoon Worcestershire sauce
1/8 teaspoon ground mustard
1 cup coarsely chopped fresh spinach

In a Dutch oven, combine the first 11 ingredients. Bring to a boil. Reduce heat; cover and simmer for 14-18 minutes or until potatoes are tender. Stir in spinach; cook 1-2 minutes longer or until tender.

YIELD: 6 servings.

veggie meatball soup

1 package (12 ounces) frozen fully
  cooked Italian meatballs

1 can (28 ounces) diced tomatoes,
  undrained

3 cups beef broth

2 cups shredded cabbage

1 can (16 ounces) kidney beans, rinsed
  and drained

1 medium zucchini, sliced

1 cup fresh green beans, cut into 1-inch
  pieces

1 cup water

2 medium carrots, sliced

1 teaspoon dried basil

1/2 teaspoon minced garlic

1/4 teaspoon salt

1/8 teaspoon dried oregano

1/8 teaspoon pepper

1 cup uncooked elbow macaroni

1/4 cup minced fresh parsley

Grated Parmesan cheese, optional

In a 5-qt. slow cooker, combine the first 14
ingredients. Cover and cook on low for 5-6 hours or
until vegetables are almost tender.

Stir in macaroni and parsley; cook 30 minutes
longer or until the macaroni is tender. Serve with
cheese if desired.

YIELD: 6 servings.

penny fagan
MOBILE, ALABAMA

*Loaded with veggies,
meatballs and spices,
this meal-in-one soup can
warm up any winter day.
It's a recipe you'll make
time and again!*

meatball tortellini soup

sheryl little
SHERWOOD, ARKANSAS

This hearty soup with fast-cooking frozen meatballs is perfect for two. It became one of our favorite standbys after our son left home. My hubby can't get enough!

1 can (14-1/2 ounces) reduced-sodium beef broth

12 frozen fully cooked Italian meatballs (1/2 ounce *each*)

3/4 cup fresh baby spinach

3/4 cup stewed tomatoes

1 can (11 ounces) Mexicorn, drained

3/4 cup frozen cheese tortellini (about 20)

Dash salt and pepper

In a large saucepan, bring the broth to a boil. Add the meatballs. Reduce the heat; cover and simmer for 5 minutes.

Add the spinach, tomatoes and corn; cover and simmer for 5 minutes. Add the tortellini, salt and pepper; cover and simmer for 3 minutes or until tortellini is tender.

YIELD: 4 servings.

zesty taco soup

1 pound lean ground beef (90% lean)
1 medium onion, chopped
1 medium green pepper, chopped
1 envelope reduced-sodium taco seasoning
2/3 cup water
4 cups reduced-sodium V8 juice
1 cup chunky salsa

TOPPINGS:
3/4 cup shredded lettuce
6 tablespoons chopped fresh tomatoes
6 tablespoons shredded reduced-fat cheddar cheese
1/4 cup chopped green onions
1/4 cup fat-free sour cream
Tortilla chips, optional

In a large saucepan coated with cooking spray, cook the beef, onion and pepper over medium heat until meat is no longer pink; drain. Stir in taco seasoning and water; cook and stir for 5 minutes or until liquid is reduced.

Add V8 juice and salsa; bring to a boil. Reduce heat; simmer, uncovered, for 5 minutes or until heated through. Top each serving with 2 tablespoons of lettuce, 1 tablespoon of tomato and cheese, and 2 teaspoons of green onions and sour cream. Serve with tortilla chips if desired.

YIELD: 6 servings.

marylou von scheele
UNIVERSITY PLACE, WASHINGTON

Savory and satisfying, this thick, chili-like soup has a mild taco flavor and an eye-appealing color. It comes together quickly and can easily be doubled to feed a crowd.

barley peasant soup

1 pound beef stew meat, cut into 1/2- to 3/4-inch cubes
1 tablespoon olive oil
2 cups chopped onions
1 cup sliced celery
2 garlic cloves, minced
5 cups water
5 cups beef broth
2 cups sliced carrots
1-1/2 cups medium pearl barley
1 can (15 ounces) garbanzo beans *or* chickpeas, rinsed and drained
1 can (15 ounces) kidney beans, rinsed and drained
4 cups sliced zucchini
3 cups diced plum tomatoes
2 cups chopped cabbage
1/4 cup minced fresh parsley
1 teaspoon dried thyme
1-1/2 teaspoons Italian seasoning
Salt and pepper to taste
Grated Parmesan cheese, optional

In a large saucepan, brown meat in oil. Add onions and celery. Cook until beef is no longer pink. Add garlic and cook 1 minute longer. Add water and broth; bring to a boil. Add carrots and barley. Reduce heat; cover and simmer for 45-60 minutes or until barley is tender.

Add the beans, zucchini, tomatoes, cabbage, parsley and seasonings; simmer 15-20 minutes or until vegetables are tender. Top individual bowls with parmesan cheese if desired.

YIELD: 16-20 servings.

mary sullivan
SPOKANE, WASHINGTON

Barley brightens the broth of this soup that features a cornucopia of veggies. The recipe makes a savory lunch or dinner that will make you forget about the frightful weather outside.

too many tomatoes?

To quickly use up a huge supply of garden tomatoes, wash and core them, then puree in a blender with lemon juice, onion and celery to taste. This makes a great vegetable juice to drink or use as a base for soups.

debra baker
GREENVILLE, NORTH CAROLINA

You'll love my quick version of classic beef macaroni soup. Every spoonful is laden with veggies and pasta—it's as good as the original without all the fuss.

beef macaroni soup

1 pound lean ground beef (90% lean)
2 cups frozen mixed vegetables
1 can (14-1/2 ounces) diced tomatoes, undrained
1 can (14-1/2 ounces) beef broth
1/4 teaspoon pepper
1/2 cup uncooked elbow macaroni

In a large saucepan, cook beef over medium heat until no longer pink; drain. Stir in the mixed vegetables, tomatoes, broth and pepper. Bring to a boil; add macaroni. Reduce heat; cover and simmer for 8-10 minutes or until macaroni and vegetables are tender.

YIELD: 5 servings.

beef 'n' black bean soup

1 pound lean ground beef (90% lean)
2 cans (14-1/2 ounces *each*) chicken broth
1 can (14-1/2 ounces) diced tomatoes, undrained
8 green onions, thinly sliced
3 medium carrots, thinly sliced
2 celery ribs, thinly sliced
2 garlic cloves, minced
1 tablespoon sugar
1-1/2 teaspoons dried basil
1/2 teaspoon salt
1/2 teaspoon dried oregano
1/2 teaspoon ground cumin
1/2 teaspoon chili powder
2 cans (15 ounces *each*) black beans, rinsed and drained
1-1/2 cups cooked rice

In a skillet over medium heat, cook beef until no longer pink; drain. Transfer to a 5-qt. slow cooker. Add the next 12 ingredients. Cover and cook on high for 1 hour. Reduce heat to low; cook for 4-5 hours or until vegetables are tender. Add the beans and rice; cook 1 hour longer or until heated through.

YIELD: 10 servings.

vickie gibson
GARDENDALE, ALABAMA

I lead a busy life, so I'm always trying to come up with time-saving recipes. This colorful soup is one of my husband's favorites. It has been a hit at family gatherings, too.

holly dunkelberger
LA PORTE CITY, IOWA

Enjoy this impressive twist on an old favorite when you top each steaming bowl with herb dumplings.

tomato soup with herb dumplings

2 cans (14-1/2 ounces *each*) diced tomatoes, undrained
4 cups tomato juice
1/4 cup butter
1 teaspoon beef bouillon granules
1/4 teaspoon garlic powder
1/4 teaspoon salt
1/4 teaspoon pepper
1/4 teaspoon dried oregano
DUMPLINGS:
1-1/2 cups all-purpose flour
2 teaspoons baking powder
1/4 teaspoon salt
1/4 teaspoon poultry seasoning
1/4 teaspoon dried parsley flakes
1 egg
2/3 cup milk

In a Dutch oven, combine the first eight ingredients; bring to a boil. Reduce heat to simmer.

Meanwhile, for dumplings, combine the dry ingredients in a bowl. Beat egg and milk; stir into dry ingredients until a stiff dough forms. Drop by tablespoonfuls onto simmering soup.

Cover and simmer for 20 minutes or until toothpick inserted into a dumpling comes out clean (do not lift the cover while simmering). Serve immediately.

YIELD: 8 servings.

hearty split pea soup

1 package (16 ounces) dried split peas
8 cups water
2 medium potatoes, peeled and cubed
2 large onions, chopped
2 medium carrots, chopped
2 cups cubed cooked corned beef *or* ham
1/2 cup chopped celery
5 teaspoons chicken bouillon granules
1 teaspoon dried marjoram
1 teaspoon poultry seasoning
1 teaspoon rubbed sage
1/2 to 1 teaspoon pepper
1/2 teaspoon dried basil
1/2 teaspoon salt, optional

In a Dutch oven, combine all ingredients; bring to a boil. Reduce heat; cover and simmer for 1-1/4 to 1-1/2 hours or until peas and vegetables are tender.

YIELD: 12 servings.

barbara link
RANCHO CUCAMONGA, CALIFORNIA

Try my recipe if you're looking for a new spin on traditional split pea soup. The flavor is peppery rather than smoky, and the corned beef is an unexpected, tasty change of pace.

spicy chuck-wagon soup

kelly williams
MORGANVILLE, NEW JERSEY

Wish you could live like a cowboy on the range for a day? Give your taste buds a trip for the imagination with a steamy bowl of this robust, western-style soup. It's filled with tender potatoes, chunks of beef roast and cayenne pepper for a little kick—minus the cowboys' spurs.

2 tablespoons all-purpose flour

1 tablespoon paprika

1 teaspoon plus 1 tablespoon chili powder, *divided*

2 teaspoons salt

1 teaspoon garlic powder

1 boneless beef chuck roast (3 pounds), cut into 1-inch pieces

1/4 cup canola oil

2 medium onions, chopped

1 can (28 ounces) stewed tomatoes, undrained

1 can (10-1/2 ounces) condensed beef broth, undiluted

1 bay leaf

1/4 to 1/2 teaspoon cayenne pepper

5 medium red potatoes, cubed

4 medium carrots, sliced

1 can (11 ounces) whole kernel corn, drained

In a large resealable plastic bag, combine the flour, paprika, 1 teaspoon chili powder, salt and garlic powder. Add beef, a few pieces at a time, and shake to coat.

In a large soup kettle, brown beef in oil in batches. Stir in the onions, tomatoes, broth, bay leaf, cayenne and remaining chili powder. Bring to a boil. Reduce heat; cover and simmer for 30 minutes, stirring occasionally.

Add potatoes and carrots. Cover and simmer 35-40 minutes longer or until meat and vegetables are tender. Add corn and heat through. Discard the bay leaf before serving.

YIELD: 10 servings.

versatile beef barley soup

2 cups beef broth
8 cups water
2 cups chopped cooked roast beef
1/2 cup chopped carrots
3 celery ribs, chopped
1/2 cup chopped onion
1 can (14-1/2 ounces) diced tomatoes, undrained
1 cup quick-cooking barley
1 teaspoon dried oregano
1/2 teaspoon pepper
1 can (10-3/4 ounces) condensed tomato soup, undiluted
1/2 cup frozen or canned peas
1/2 cup frozen or canned cut green or wax beans
Seasoned salt to taste

In a stockpot, combine the first 10 ingredients; bring to a boil. Reduce heat; cover and simmer for 25 minutes, stirring occasionally. Add the soup, peas and beans. Simmer, uncovered, for 10 minutes. Add seasoned salt.

YIELD: 12-14 servings.

sharon kolenc
JASPER, ALBERTA

Whenever I make this beef barley soup, I tend to clean out the refrigerator by adding a combination of leftovers. My family says they have to watch out for the kitchen sink!

beef vegetable soup

1 pound lean ground beef (90% lean)
1 medium onion, chopped
2 garlic cloves, minced
4 cups spicy hot V8 juice
2 cups coleslaw mix
1 can (14-1/2 ounces) Italian stewed tomatoes
1 package (10 ounces) frozen corn
1 package (9 ounces) frozen cut green beans
2 tablespoons Worcestershire sauce
1 teaspoon dried basil
1/4 teaspoon pepper

In a large nonstick skillet, cook beef and onion over medium heat until meat is no longer pink. Add garlic; cook 1 minute longer. Drain. Transfer to a 5-qt. slow cooker. Stir in the remaining ingredients. Cover and cook on high for 4-5 hours or until heated through.

YIELD: 9 servings.

colleen jubl
DAYTON, OHIO

It's nice to come home to a simmering, ready-to-eat meal. This slow-cooked wonder goes well with a salad and breadsticks.

wintertime beef soup

1 pound lean ground beef (90% lean)
4 celery ribs, coarsely chopped
1 medium onion, coarsely chopped
1 medium green pepper, coarsely chopped
1 garlic clove, minced
2 cups water
2 cups reduced-sodium tomato juice
1 can (14-1/2 ounces) diced tomatoes, undrained
1 can (8 ounces) tomato sauce
2 teaspoons reduced-sodium beef bouillon granules
2 teaspoons chili powder
1/2 teaspoon salt
2 cans (16 ounces each) kidney beans, rinsed and drained
2 cups coarsely chopped cabbage

In a large saucepan or Dutch oven, cook the beef, celery, onion, green pepper and garlic over medium heat until meat is no longer pink; drain. Stir in the water, tomato juice, tomatoes, tomato sauce, bouillon, chili powder and salt. Bring to a boil. Reduce heat; cover and simmer for 30 minutes.

Stir in the kidney beans; return to a boil. Stir in cabbage. Reduce heat; cover and cook 12 minutes longer or until the cabbage is tender.

YIELD: 8 servings.

carol tupper
JOPLIN, MISSOURI

Kidney beans, ground beef, green pepper and chopped cabbage make this thick soup satisfying.

ruby williams
BOGALUSA, LOUISIANA

*Brimming with chunks
of beef, potatoes, carrots,
green beans and even
mushrooms, this
wonderfully satisfying
soup is a meal in itself,
and it's ready in no time.
I like to serve it with
warm corn bread and
a fruit salad.*

chunky vegetable beef soup

2 cans (14-1/2 ounces each) beef broth
1 tablespoon Worcestershire sauce
1 teaspoon ground mustard
1/2 teaspoon salt
1/4 teaspoon pepper
3 medium potatoes, peeled and cubed
6 medium carrots, cut into 1/2-inch
   slices
3 cups cubed cooked beef
2 cups frozen cut green beans, thawed
2 cups sliced fresh mushrooms
1 cup frozen peas, thawed
1 can (15 ounces) tomato sauce
2 tablespoons minced fresh parsley

In a Dutch oven, combine the broth, Worcestershire
sauce, mustard, salt and pepper. Stir in the potatoes
and carrots. Bring to a boil. Reduce the heat; cover

and simmer for 12 minutes or until the carrots are
crisp-tender.

Stir in the remaining ingredients. Return to a
boil. Reduce heat; simmer, uncovered, for 5 minutes
or until the vegetables are tender.

YIELD: 12 servings.

charla tinney
TYRONE, OKLAHOMA

*It's a snap to put together
this slow-cooked soup
before I leave for work.
I just add cooked pasta
when I get home and have
a few minutes to relax
before supper is ready.*

hearty veggie meatball soup

3 cups beef broth
2 cups frozen mixed vegetables, thawed
1 can (14-1/2 ounces) stewed tomatoes
12 frozen fully cooked Italian meatballs
   (1/2 ounce each), thawed
3 bay leaves
1/4 teaspoon pepper
1 cup spiral pasta, cooked and drained

In a 3-qt. slow cooker, combine the first six
ingredients. Cover and cook on low for 4-5 hours.
Just before serving, stir in pasta; heat through.
Discard bay leaves.

YIELD: 6 servings.

wild rice and cheddar dumpling soup

10 cups water
1 pound sliced fresh mushrooms
2 cups diced potatoes
2 cups chopped carrots
1-1/2 cups chopped celery
1 medium onion, chopped
3 chicken bouillon cubes
3 to 4 cups cubed cooked roast beef
2 cups cooked wild rice
3/4 cup all-purpose flour
3 cups milk
1/4 cup butter
1 tablespoon minced fresh parsley
2 to 3 teaspoons salt
3/4 teaspoon dried basil
3/4 teaspoon pepper

DUMPLINGS:

2 cups biscuit/baking mix
1 cup (4 ounces) shredded cheddar cheese
2/3 cup milk

Place the first seven ingredients in a stockpot. Bring to a boil. Reduce heat; cover and simmer for 10-15 minutes or until vegetables are tender. Add beef and rice.

In a small bowl, combine flour and milk until smooth. Stir into the soup. Bring to a boil; cook and stir for 2 minutes or until thickened. Stir in the butter and seasonings.

Combine the baking mix, cheese and milk. Drop by tablespoonfuls onto simmering soup. Cover and simmer for 12 minutes or until a toothpick inserted in a dumpling comes out clean (do not lift the cover while simmering).

YIELD: 14 servings.

teresa christensen
OSCEOLA, WISCONSIN

I'm a homemaker and love to brew up simmering soups and stews for my family. This thick and creamy delight is one of their all-time favorites.

wild rice

Wild rice is a dark-hulled, aquatic grass native to North America. It has a chewy texture and a nutty flavor. Grains expand 3 to 4 times their original size and some of the kernels may pop, exposing their white insides. Always rinse before cooking.

dana simmons
LANCASTER, OHIO

Even my father, who doesn't particularly like soup, enjoys my full-flavored version of traditional vegetable soup. He asked me to share the recipe with Mom, and I gladly obliged!

savory winter soup

2 pounds lean ground beef (90% lean)

3 medium onions, chopped

1 garlic clove, minced

3 cans (10-1/2 ounces *each*) condensed beef broth, undiluted

1 can (28 ounces) diced tomatoes, undrained

3 cups water

1 cup *each* diced carrots and celery

1 cup fresh *or* frozen cut green beans

1 cup cubed peeled potatoes

2 tablespoons minced fresh parsley *or* 2 teaspoons dried parsley flakes

1 teaspoon dried basil

1/2 teaspoon dried thyme

Salt and pepper to taste

In a large skillet, cook beef and onions over medium heat until the meat is no longer pink. Add the garlic; cook 1 minute longer. Drain.

Transfer to a 5-qt. slow cooker. Stir in the remaining ingredients. Cover and cook on high for 8 hours or until heated through.

YIELD: 14 servings.

EDITOR'S NOTE: To save chopping time, use frozen sliced carrots and frozen hash brown potatoes.

french onion tomato soup

4 cups thinly sliced onions
1 garlic clove, minced
2 tablespoons butter
1 can (46 ounces) tomato juice
2 teaspoons beef bouillon granules
3 tablespoons lemon juice
2 teaspoons dried parsley flakes
2 teaspoons brown sugar
6 slices French bread, toasted
2 cups (8 ounces) shredded part-skim mozzarella cheese

In a large saucepan, saute onions and garlic in butter until tender. Add the tomato juice, bouillon, lemon juice, parsley and brown sugar. Bring to a boil. Reduce heat; simmer, uncovered, for 10 minutes, stirring occasionally.

Ladle soup into 10-oz. ovenproof soup bowls or ramekins. Top with French bread; sprinkle with cheese. Broil 4-6 in. from the heat for 2-3 minutes or until cheese is bubbly.

YIELD: 6 servings.

clara honeyager
MUKWONAGO, WISCONSIN

Tomato juice lends a unique flavor sensation to typical French onion soup. I found the recipe in one of my mother's cookbooks and have made it many times since.

baked beefy onion soup

1-1/2 pounds meaty beef soup bones
2 quarts water
1 medium carrot, quartered
4 black peppercorns
3 teaspoons beef bouillon granules
2 sprigs fresh parsley
2 large onions, thinly sliced
1/4 cup butter
6 slices French bread (1/2 inch thick)
6 slices Swiss cheese

In a soup kettle, combine the first six ingredients. Bring to a boil over medium-high heat. Reduce heat; cover and simmer for 3 hours. Strain the broth, discarding soup bones, carrot and seasoning; skim fat.

Meanwhile, in a large skillet, saute the onions in butter over medium heat for 30 minutes or until golden brown. Divide the onions among six ovenproof bowls. Ladle about 1 cup broth onto each. Top each with a slice of bread and Swiss cheese. Bake at 350° for 50-55 minutes or until golden brown.

YIELD: 6 servings.

jeanne robinson
CINNAMINSON, NEW JERSEY

This onion soup recipe bakes up hot and bubbly like a casserole. It's great for parties and potlucks because it's easy to serve and can be made ahead.

hamburger minestrone

1 pound lean ground beef (90% lean)
1/2 cup chopped onion
1 garlic clove, minced
6 cups water
1 can (28 ounces) diced tomatoes, undrained

1-1/2 cups sliced zucchini
1 can (16 ounces) kidney beans, rinsed and drained
1-1/2 cups frozen whole kernel corn, thawed
1 cup shredded cabbage
1 celery rib with leaves, chopped
2 teaspoons beef bouillon granules
2 teaspoons Italian seasoning
3/4 teaspoon salt
1/2 cup uncooked elbow macaroni

In a Dutch oven, cook the beef, onion and garlic over medium heat until meat is no longer pink; drain. Add the water, tomatoes, zucchini, beans, corn, cabbage, celery, bouillon, Italian seasoning, salt and macaroni. Bring to a boil. Reduce heat; cover and simmer for 10-15 minutes or until macaroni is tender.

YIELD: 9 servings.

maudie breen
SALT LAKE CITY, UTAH

If you love minestrone, you'll love spooning up my classic version with Italian seasoning, vegetables, ground beef and macaroni.

italian seasoning

Italian seasoning can be found in the spice aisle of most grocery stores. It's also easy to mix up your own blend. Simply substitute 1/4 teaspoon each of basil, thyme, rosemary and oregano for each teaspoon of Italian seasoning called for in a recipe.

betty kennedy
ALEXANDRIA, VIRGINIA

Goulash is a popular European dish that I tried while teaching with the Defense Department in Germany. When I returned home, I created my own tasty version.

goulash defined

Any dish prepared by simmering food in liquid for a long period of time in a covered pot can be considered stew. Goulash is a kind of stew, usually a Hungarian stew, made with meat and vegetables and seasoned with paprika.

hungarian goulash soup

> 3 bacon strips, diced
> 1-1/2 pounds beef stew meat, cut into 1/2-inch cubes
> 1 small green pepper, seeded and chopped
> 2 medium onions, chopped
> 1 large garlic clove, minced
> 1 can (14-1/2 ounces) diced tomatoes
> 3 cups beef broth
> 2 tablespoons paprika
> 1-1/2 teaspoons salt
> Pepper to taste
> Dash sugar
> 2 large potatoes, peeled and diced
> 1/2 cup sour cream, optional

In a large kettle, cook bacon over medium heat until crisp. Remove to paper towels with a slotted spoon; drain, reserving 2 tablespoons drippings. Add beef cubes and brown on all sides. Add green pepper and onions; cook until tender. Add garlic; cook 1 minute longer. Stir in the tomatoes, broth, paprika, salt, pepper and sugar.

Cover and simmer for about 1-1/2 hours or until beef is tender. About 1/2 hour before serving, add the potatoes and reserved bacon; cook until potatoes are tender. Garnish each serving with a dollop of sour cream if desired.

YIELD: 8 servings.

deborah taylor
INKOM, IDAHO

If you love homemade meatballs, you'll love my comforting Swedish soup. I especially enjoy it alongside hot rolls, bread or muffins.

swedish meatball soup

> 1 egg
> 2 cups half-and-half cream, *divided*
> 1 cup soft bread crumbs
> 1 small onion, finely chopped
> 1-3/4 teaspoons salt, *divided*

> 1-1/2 pounds lean ground beef (90% lean)
> 1 tablespoon butter
> 3 tablespoons all-purpose flour
> 3/4 teaspoon beef bouillon granules
> 1/2 teaspoon pepper
> 1/8 to 1/4 teaspoon garlic salt
> 3 cups water
> 1 pound red potatoes, cubed
> 1 package (10 ounces) frozen peas, thawed

In a large bowl, beat egg; add 1/3 cup cream, bread crumbs, onion and 1 teaspoon of salt. Crumble beef over mixture and mix well. Shape into 1/2-in. balls.

In a Dutch oven, brown meatballs in butter in batches. Remove from the pan; set aside. Drain fat.

To pan, add the flour, bouillon, pepper, garlic salt and remaining salt; stir until smooth. Gradually stir in water; bring to a boil. Reduce heat; cook and stir for 2 minutes or until thickened. Add potatoes and meatballs.

Reduce heat; cover and simmer for 25 minutes or until the potatoes are tender. Stir in peas and remaining cream; heat through.

YIELD: 8 servings.

reuben chowder

- 1 small onion, sliced
- 1 tablespoon canola oil
- 2 cans (14 1/2 ounces *each*) vegetable broth
- 1 can (14-1/2 ounces) beef broth
- 2 teaspoons prepared horseradish
- 1 teaspoon Worcestershire sauce
- 1/2 teaspoon ground mustard
- 1/4 teaspoon celery salt
- 5 ounces deli corned beef, chopped
- 1 cup sauerkraut, rinsed and well drained
- 2 slices rye bread, cubed
- 4 slices Swiss cheese

In a small skillet, saute the onion in oil until tender. Meanwhile, in a large saucepan, bring the vegetable and beef broth to a boil; stir in the horseradish, Worcestershire sauce, mustard and celery salt. Add the corned beef, sauerkraut and onion. Reduce heat to low; cover and simmer for 10 minutes.

Ladle soup into four ovenproof bowls; top with bread cubes and Swiss cheese. Broil 3-4 in. from the heat for 2-3 minutes or until cheese is melted.

YIELD: 4 servings.

taste of home test kitchen
GREENDALE, WISCONSIN

Have a hankering for a Reuben? Enjoy all of your favorite sandwich ingredients in this delicious chowder. If you don't have rye bread on hand, cut the Swiss cheese into strips and place on top of the broth.

joann abbott
KERHONKSON, NEW YORK

My creamy soup is loaded with meatballs, barley, mushrooms, noodles and rice. Leftovers easily reheat for a fast, filling lunch or dinner.

meatball mushroom soup

1/2 pound lean ground beef (90% lean)
2 cans (10-3/4 ounces *each*) condensed cream of mushroom soup, undiluted
1-1/3 cups milk
1-1/3 cups water
1 teaspoon Italian seasoning
1 teaspoon dried minced onion
1/2 teaspoon dried minced garlic
1/4 cup quick-cooking barley
1/4 cup uncooked elbow macaroni
1/4 cup uncooked long grain rice
1 medium carrot, shredded
1 jar (4-1/2 ounces) sliced mushrooms, drained
2 tablespoons grated Parmesan cheese

Shape the beef into 1-in. balls; set aside. In a large saucepan, combine soup, milk and water; bring to a boil. Add Italian seasoning, onion, garlic, barley, macaroni and rice. Reduce heat; simmer, uncovered, for 15 minutes.

Meanwhile, brown meatballs in a nonstick skillet until no longer pink. Stir carrot into soup; cover and simmer for 5 minutes. Use a slotted spoon to transfer meatballs to soup. Stir in mushrooms and Parmesan cheese; heat through.

YIELD: 6 servings.

steak 'n' vegetable soup

1 pound beef top sirloin steak, cut into 1/2-inch cubes
1 cup chopped onion

2 teaspoons canola oil
2 cups cubed red potatoes
1 cup chopped carrots
1 cup frozen peas
1 can (14-1/2 ounces) beef broth
1 cup water
2 tablespoons balsamic vinegar
1 tablespoon minced fresh parsley
1 tablespoon minced chives
1-1/2 teaspoons minced fresh basil *or* 1/2 teaspoon dried basil
1 teaspoon minced fresh thyme *or* 1/4 teaspoon dried thyme
3/4 teaspoon salt
1/4 teaspoon pepper

In a large saucepan, cook beef and onion in oil until meat is no longer pink; drain. Stir in the potatoes, carrots and peas. Add the broth, water, vinegar, parsley, chives, basil, thyme, salt and pepper. Bring to a boil. Reduce heat; cover and simmer for 20-30 minutes or until meat and vegetables are tender.

YIELD: 6 servings.

edie despain
LOGAN, UTAH

This hearty soup calls for plenty of fresh herbs to enhance the flavor of the other ingredients. I like to serve steaming bowls alongside a crisp green salad and hot biscuits.

italian wedding soup

2 *eggs*, lightly beaten
1/2 cup seasoned bread crumbs
1 pound lean ground beef (90% lean)
1 pound bulk Italian sausage
3 medium carrots, sliced
3 celery ribs, diced
1 large onion, chopped
4-1/2 teaspoons olive oil
3 garlic cloves, minced
4 cans (14-1/2 ounces *each*) reduced-sodium chicken broth
2 cans (14-1/2 ounces *each*) beef broth
1 package (10 ounces) frozen chopped spinach, thawed and squeezed dry
1/4 cup minced fresh basil
1 envelope onion soup mix
4-1/2 teaspoons ketchup
1/2 teaspoon dried thyme
3 bay leaves
1-1/2 cups uncooked penne pasta

In a large bowl, combine eggs and bread crumbs. Crumble beef and sausage over mixture and mix well. Shape into 3/4-in. balls.

Place meatballs on a greased rack in a foil-lined 15-in. x 10-in. x 1-in. baking pan. Bake at 350° for 15-18 minutes or until no longer pink.

Meanwhile, in a Dutch oven, saute the carrots, celery and onion in oil until tender. Add garlic; cook 1 minute longer. Stir in the broth, spinach, basil, soup mix, ketchup, thyme and bay leaves.

Drain meatballs on paper towels. Bring soup to a boil; add the meatballs. Reduce the heat; simmer, uncovered, for 30 minutes. Add pasta; cook 13-15 minutes longer or until pasta is tender, stirring occasionally. Discard bay leaves.

YIELD: 10 servings.

noelle myers
GRAND FORKS, NORTH DAKOTA

I enjoyed a similar soup for lunch at work one day and decided to re-create it at home. I love the combination of meatballs, vegetables and pasta.

bread crumbs

It's a snap to make homemade seasoned bread crumbs. Simply break slices of dried bread into pieces and process in a blender or food processor until you have fine crumbs. Then season the crumbs to accommodate your family's tastes. A basic recipe may include dried basil and oregano, garlic and onion powder, grated Parmesan cheese, salt and paprika.

ginny perkins
COLUMIANA, OHIO

My hungry clan doesn't usually consider a bowl of soup "dinner." But after one taste of my comforting beef barley, they declared it a keeper! It's great garnished with sweet potato chips.

green peppers

A melon baller works great for quickly and easily scooping out the seeds and membranes from green peppers.

marilyn chesbrough
WAUTOMA, WISCONSIN

Old Man Winter sticks around for almost six months here in Wisconsin. A creamy soup like this one always heats us up around the dinner table.

beef barley soup

1-1/2 pounds beef stew meat
1 tablespoon canola oil
1 can (14-1/2 ounces) diced tomatoes
1 cup chopped onion
1 cup diced celery
1 cup sliced fresh carrots
1/2 cup chopped green pepper
4 cups beef broth
2 cups water
1 cup spaghetti sauce
2/3 cup medium pearl barley
1 tablespoon dried parsley flakes
2 teaspoons salt
1-1/2 teaspoons dried basil
3/4 teaspoon pepper

In a large skillet, brown meat in oil over medium heat; drain. Meanwhile, in a 5-qt. slow cooker, combine the vegetables, broth, water, spaghetti sauce, barley and seasonings. Stir in beef. Cover and cook on low for 9-10 hours or until meat is tender. Skim fat from cooking juices.

YIELD: 8 servings.

beefy wild rice soup

1 pound lean ground beef (90% lean)
1/2 teaspoon Italian seasoning
6 cups water, *divided*
2 large onions, chopped
3 celery ribs, chopped
1 cup uncooked wild rice

2 teaspoons beef bouillon granules
1/2 teaspoon pepper
1/4 teaspoon hot pepper sauce
3 cans (10-3/4 ounces *each*) condensed cream of mushroom soup, undiluted
1 can (4 ounces) mushroom stems and pieces, drained

In a Dutch oven, cook beef and Italian seasoning over medium heat until meat is no longer pink; drain. Add 2 cups water, onions, celery, rice, bouillon, pepper and hot pepper sauce; bring to a boil.

Reduce heat; cover and simmer for 45 minutes. Stir in the soup, mushrooms and remaining water. Cover and simmer for 30 minutes.

YIELD: 10-12 servings.

corny tomato dumpling soup

1 pound lean ground beef (90% lean)

3 cups fresh *or* frozen corn

1 can (28 ounces) diced tomatoes, undrained

2 cans (14-1/2 ounces *each*) beef broth

1 cup chopped onion

1 garlic clove, minced

1-1/2 teaspoons dried basil

1-1/2 teaspoons dried thyme

1/2 teaspoon dried rosemary, crushed

Salt and pepper to taste

CORN DUMPLINGS:

1 cup all-purpose flour

1/2 cup cornmeal

2-1/2 teaspoons baking powder

1/2 teaspoon salt

1 egg

2/3 cup milk

1 cup fresh *or* frozen corn

1/2 cup shredded cheddar cheese

1 tablespoon minced fresh parsley

In a large saucepan over medium heat, cook beef until no longer pink; drain. Stir in the corn, tomatoes, broth, onion, garlic and seasonings. Bring to a boil. Reduce heat; cover and simmer for 30-45 minutes.

For dumplings, combine the flour, cornmeal, baking powder and salt in a large bowl. In another large bowl, beat egg; stir in milk, corn, cheese and parsley. Stir into the dry ingredients just until moistened.

Drop by tablespoonfuls onto simmering soup. Cover and simmer for 15 minutes or until a toothpick inserted in a dumpling comes out clean (do not lift cover while simmering).

YIELD: 8 servings.

jackie ferris

TIVERTON, ONTARIO

We have a big garden on our farm and enjoy cooking with our harvest. Corn is the star ingredient in both the broth and dumplings. It lends a delicious, fresh-picked flavor to this savory tomato soup.

zesty macaroni soup

joan hallford
NORTH RICHLAND HILLS, TEXAS

The recipe for this thick, zippy soup caught my attention for two reasons— it calls for convenience ingredients and can be prepared in a jiffy. A chili macaroni mix lends a little spice, but I sometimes jazz it up even more with a can of chopped green chilies.

1 pound lean ground beef (90% lean)
1 medium onion, chopped
5 cups water
1 can (15 ounces) pinto beans, rinsed and drained
1 can (14-1/2 ounces) diced tomatoes, undrained
1 can (7 ounces) whole kernel corn, drained
1 can (4 ounces) chopped green chilies, optional
1/2 teaspoon ground mustard
1/2 teaspoon salt
1/8 teaspoon pepper
1 package (7-1/2 ounces) chili macaroni dinner mix
Salsa con queso dip

In a large saucepan, cook beef and onion over medium heat until meat is no longer pink; drain. Stir in the water, beans, tomatoes, corn and chilies if desired. Stir in the mustard, salt, pepper and contents of macaroni sauce mix. Bring to a boil. Reduce heat; cover and simmer for 10 minutes.

Stir in contents of macaroni packet. Cover and simmer 10-14 minutes longer or until macaroni is tender, stirring occasionally. Serve with salsa con queso dip.

YIELD: 8-10 servings.

EDITOR'S NOTE: This recipe was tested with Hamburger Helper brand chili macaroni. Salsa con queso dip can be found in the international food section or snack aisle of most grocery stores.

homemade beef broth

4 pounds meaty beef soup bones (beef shanks *or* short ribs)

3 medium carrots, cut into chunks

3 celery ribs, cut into chunks

2 medium onions, quartered

1/2 cup warm water

3 bay leaves

3 garlic cloves

8 to 10 whole peppercorns

3 to 4 sprigs fresh parsley

1 teaspoon *each* dried thyme, marjoram and oregano

3 quarts cold water

Place soup bones in a large roasting pan. Bake, uncovered, at 450° for 30 minutes. Add the carrots, celery and onions. Bake 30 minutes longer; drain the fat.

Using a slotted spoon, transfer the bones and vegetables to a large Dutch oven. Add warm water to the roasting pan; stir to loosen browned bits from the pan. Transfer the pan juices to kettle. Add seasonings and enough cold water just to cover. Slowly bring to a boil, about 30 minutes. Reduce the heat; simmer, uncovered, for 4-5 hours, skimming the surface as the foam rises. If necessary, add hot water during the first 2 hours to keep all of the ingredients covered.

Remove beef bones and set aside until cool enough to handle. If desired, remove meat from bones; discard bones and save meat for another use. Strain broth through a cheesecloth-lined colander, discarding vegetables and seasonings. If using immediately, skim fat or refrigerate for 8 hours or overnight; remove fat from surface. Broth can be covered and refrigerated for up to 3 days or frozen for 4-6 months.

YIELD: 10 servings.

BEEF MACARONI SOUP: Cook 1 pound ground beef over medium heat until no longer pink; drain. Stir in 2 cups frozen mixed vegetables, 1 can (14-1/2 ounces) diced tomatoes with juice, 1-3/4 cups Homemade Beef Broth and 1/4 teaspoon pepper. Bring to a boil; add 1/2 cup uncooked elbow macaroni. Reduce heat; cover and simmer for 8-10 minutes or until macaroni and vegetables are tender.

YIELD: 5 servings.

taste of home test kitchen
GREENDALE, WISCONSIN

Roasting the soup bones brings out delicious beefy flavors for this soup base. It refrigerates and freezes well to be used as needed.

add salt last

Add little or no salt, as well as other flavors, when making stock since it concentrates as it simmers and the liquid evaporates. Taste the soup when it is just about ready to be served and add enough salt to suit your tastes.

beef soup in a hurry

1 can (24 ounces) beef stew

1 can (14-1/2 ounces) stewed tomatoes, cut up

1 can (10-3/4 ounces) condensed vegetable beef soup, undiluted

1 can (8-3/4 ounces) whole kernel corn, drained

1/8 teaspoon hot pepper sauce

Combine all ingredients in a microwave-safe bowl. Cover and microwave on high for 2-3 minutes or until heated through, stirring once.

YIELD: 6 servings.

EDITOR'S NOTE: This recipe was tested in a 1,100-watt microwave.

loellen holley
TOPOCK, ARIZONA

I nicknamed my quick and easy beef soup recipe "throw-together soup" because it calls for just a few canned goods and stirs up fast in the microwave. Serve it with a green salad and hot rolls for a satisfying meal.

brenda jackson
GARDEN CITY, KANSAS

You'll be thankful for this simple-to-prepare soup when you have a busy day and need to make dinner in a hurry. It's chock-full of nutritious veggies, too!

pasta beef soup

1 pound lean ground beef (90% lean)

2 cans (14-1/2 ounces each) beef broth

1 package (16 ounces) frozen pasta with broccoli, corn and carrots in garlic-seasoned sauce

1-1/2 cups tomato juice

1 can (14-1/2 ounces) diced tomatoes, undrained

2 teaspoons Italian seasoning

1/4 cup shredded Parmesan cheese, optional

In a large saucepan, cook beef over medium heat until no longer pink; drain. Add the broth, pasta with vegetables, tomato juice, tomatoes and Italian seasoning; bring to a boil. Reduce heat; cover and simmer for 10 minutes or until the vegetables are tender. Serve with cheese if desired.

YIELD: 6 servings.

peggy linton
COBOURG, ONTARIO

Tender rice dumplings give a homemade touch to this hearty soup that takes advantage of canned goods, frozen vegetables and dry soup mix. It's a quick, nourishing all-in-one-pot meal.

dumpling vegetable soup

1/2 pound lean ground beef (90% lean)

4 cups water

1 can (28 ounces) diced tomatoes, undrained

1 package (10 ounces) frozen mixed vegetables

1 envelope onion soup mix

1/2 teaspoon dried oregano

1/4 teaspoon pepper

RICE DUMPLINGS:

1-1/4 cups all-purpose flour

1 teaspoon baking powder

1/2 teaspoon salt

1 tablespoon shortening

1/3 cup cooked rice, room temperature

1 tablespoon minced fresh parsley

1 egg, lightly beaten

1/2 cup milk

In a Dutch oven, cook beef over medium heat until no longer pink; drain. Add the water, tomatoes, vegetables, soup mix, oregano and pepper; bring to a boil. Reduce heat; cover and simmer for 30-40 minutes or until the vegetables are tender.

For dumplings, combine the flour, baking powder and salt in a bowl. Cut in shortening until the mixture resembles coarse crumbs. Add rice and parsley; toss. In a small bowl, combine egg and milk. Stir into rice mixture just until moistened.

Drop by teaspoonfuls onto simmering soup. Cover and simmer for 15 minutes or until a toothpick inserted in a dumpling comes out clean (do not lift the cover while simmering). Serve immediately.

YIELD: 6-8 servings.

easy hamburger soup

1-1/2 pounds lean ground beef (90% lean)
  1 medium onion, chopped
  1 can (28 ounces) diced tomatoes, undrained
  2 cans (14-1/2 ounces each) beef broth
  1 cup water
  4 celery ribs, thinly sliced
  4 large carrots, halved and thinly sliced
 10 whole peppercorns
  1 teaspoon dried thyme
1/2 teaspoon salt
1/2 cup quick-cooking barley
1/4 cup minced fresh parsley

In a large saucepan, cook the beef and onion over medium heat until meat is no longer pink; drain. Stir in the tomatoes, broth and water. Add the celery and carrots.

Place peppercorns on a double thickness of cheesecloth; bring up corners of cloth and tie with kitchen string to form a bag. Add to beef mixture. Stir in thyme and salt. Bring to a boil. Reduce heat; cover and simmer for 45 minutes or until vegetables are tender.

Return to a boil. Stir in the barley. Reduce heat; cover and simmer for 10-12 minutes or until barley is tender. Remove from the heat; stir in parsley. Let stand for 5 minutes. Discard spice bag.

YIELD: 8 servings.

mary prior
RUSH CITY, MINNESOTA

Lunch will be a little tastier when this beef and barley soup is in hand. It's easy to make and travels well in a thermos.

CHAPTER three

chicken & turkey

Comfort and tempt your family with one of these warming soups. There's an endless variety of ingredients, from noodles, rice and barley to carrots, beans and celery, to pique the appetites of your loved ones. As an added bonus, you can turn some of last night's chicken or leftover turkey into something that's good-tasting and good for you!

72   90   91

diane tayman

DIXON/GRAND DETOUR, ILLINOIS

Family and friends can't get enough of my healthy chicken soup. It's spicy, low in fat and filled with good-for-you ingredients.

spiced-up healthy soup

1 medium onion, chopped

1/3 cup medium pearl barley

4 garlic cloves, minced

2 tablespoons canola oil

5 cans (14-1/2 ounces *each*) reduced-sodium chicken broth

2 boneless skinless chicken breast halves (4 ounces *each*)

1 cup dried lentils, rinsed

1 jar (16 ounces) picante sauce

1 can (15 ounces) garbanzo beans *or* chickpeas, rinsed and drained

1/2 cup minced fresh cilantro

8 cups chopped fresh spinach

In a Dutch oven, saute onion and barley in oil until onion is tender. Add garlic; cook 1 minute longer. Add the broth, chicken and lentils; bring to a boil. Reduce heat; cover and simmer for 15 minutes or until chicken is no longer pink. Remove chicken and set aside.

Add the picante sauce, garbanzo beans and cilantro to the soup; cover and simmer 10 minutes longer or until barley and lentils are tender.

Shred chicken with two forks. Add spinach and chicken to soup. Simmer, uncovered, for 5 minutes or until spinach is wilted.

YIELD: 14 servings.

chicken tomato soup

1-1/2 cups water
3 cups frozen chopped broccoli
3/4 cup chopped onion
1 garlic clove, minced
3/4 pound boneless skinless chicken breast, cut into 1-inch chunks
1/2 teaspoon seasoned salt
1/4 teaspoon pepper
1 can (46 ounces) tomato juice
1 can (15-1/2 ounces) great northern beans, rinsed and drained
1 can (15 ounces) black beans, rinsed and drained
1 can (11 ounces) whole kernel corn, drained
1 tablespoon ketchup
1 teaspoon brown sugar
Crumbled bacon and shredded cheddar cheese, optional

In a Dutch oven, combine the water, broccoli, onion and garlic. Bring to a boil; boil for 8-10 minutes, stirring frequently.

Meanwhile, in a nonstick skillet, cook chicken until no longer pink, about 6 minutes. Sprinkle with seasoned salt and pepper. Add to broccoli mixture. stir in the tomato juice, beans, corn, ketchup and brown sugar; bring to a boil. Reduce heat; cover and simmer for 10-15 minutes, stirring occasionally. Garnish with bacon and cheese if desired.

YIELD: 12 servings.

connie johnson
SPRINGFIELD, MISSOURI

You'll love the variety of textures, colors and flavors in this crowd-pleasing soup. Its sweet tomato base boasts a delicious blend of chicken, broccoli, corn and a variety of beans. It's especially tasty garnished with shredded cheddar and crumbled bacon.

zesty chicken soup

1-1/4 pounds boneless skinless chicken breasts
4 cups water
1 medium onion, chopped
2 celery ribs, chopped
4 garlic cloves, minced
1 tablespoon canola oil
1 can (14-1/2 ounces) Mexican diced tomatoes
1 can (14-1/2 ounces) diced tomatoes
1 can (8 ounces) tomato sauce
1 cup medium salsa
3 medium zucchini, halved and sliced
2 medium carrots, sliced
1 cup frozen white corn
1 can (4 ounces) chopped green chilies
3 teaspoons ground cumin
2 teaspoons chili powder
1 teaspoon dried basil
Shredded cheddar cheese and tortilla chips, optional

Place chicken in a Dutch oven or soup kettle; add water. Bring to a boil; reduce heat. Cover and simmer for 10-15 minutes or until chicken juices run clear. Remove chicken; cut into 1/2-in. cubes. Return to cooking liquid.

In a large skillet, saute onion, celery and garlic in oil until tender; add to the Dutch oven. Stir in the tomatoes, tomato sauce, salsa, zucchini, carrots, corn, chilies, cumin, chili powder and basil. Bring to a boil. Reduce heat; cover and simmer for 20-25 minutes or until vegetables are tender.

Garnish with cheese and tortilla chips if desired. Soup may be frozen for up to 3 months.

YIELD: 10 servings.

gwen nelson
CASTRO VALLEY, CALIFORNIA

This south-of-the-border soup is chock-full of lean chicken and healthy vegetables. Add crispy tortilla chips on top for a pleasant crunch.

leftover tortilla chips

After a party, do you have leftover tortilla chips that are destined to go stale? Give those chips a second life by coarsely crushing them and adding them to spicy Mexican-style soups or chowders.

**taste of home
test kitchen**

GREENDALE, WISCONSIN

Chock-full of vegetables, chicken and pasta, this creamy creation from our Test Kitchen is sure to become a favorite at your home. No one will suspect it relies on leftover macaroni and cheese.

macaroni 'n' cheese soup

3-1/2 cups chicken broth
1-1/2 cups fresh broccoli florets
1 cup fresh cauliflowerets
1 cup sliced carrots
2 cups prepared macaroni and cheese
1 cup heavy whipping cream
1 cup cubed process cheese (Velveeta)
1 cup cubed cooked chicken
Pepper to taste

In a large saucepan, combine the broth, broccoli, cauliflower and carrots. Bring to a boil. Reduce heat; simmer, uncovered, for 10 minutes or until the vegetables are tender.

Add the macaroni and cheese, cream and process cheese. Cook and stir until cheese is melted. Add chicken and pepper; heat through.

YIELD: 8 servings.

sonali ruder

NEW YORK, NEW YORK

Sweet corn and cool sour cream help tame the smoky hot flavor of chipotle pepper in this well-balanced soup.

hearty chipotle chicken soup

1 large onion, chopped
1 tablespoon canola oil
4 garlic cloves, minced
4 cups reduced-sodium chicken broth
2 cans (15 ounces *each*) pinto beans, rinsed and drained

2 cans (14-1/2 ounces *each*) fire-roasted diced tomatoes, undrained
3 cups frozen corn
2 chipotle peppers in adobo sauce, seeded and minced
2 teaspoons adobo sauce
1 teaspoon ground cumin
1/4 teaspoon pepper
2 cups cubed cooked chicken breast
1/2 cup fat-free sour cream
1/4 cup minced fresh cilantro

In a Dutch oven, saute onion in oil until tender. Add garlic; cook 1 minute longer. Add the broth, beans, tomatoes, corn, chipotle peppers, adobo sauce, cumin and pepper. Bring to a boil. Reduce heat; simmer, uncovered, for 20 minutes.

Stir in chicken; heat through. Garnish with sour cream; sprinkle with cilantro.

YIELD: 8 servings.

cream of chicken noodle soup

2 medium onions
2 celery ribs
4 cups water
3 boneless skinless chicken breast halves (6 ounces each)
1-1/2 teaspoons salt
1/4 teaspoon pepper
2 tablespoons butter
1 can (14-1/2 ounces) chicken broth
1 large carrot, chopped
1 medium potato, peeled and chopped
2 teaspoons chicken bouillon granules
1-1/2 teaspoons dried basil
2 cups uncooked wide egg noodles
1-3/4 cups milk, *divided*
1/3 cup all-purpose flour

Chop one onion and one celery rib; set aside. Cut remaining onion and celery into chunks; place in a Dutch oven. Add the water, chicken, salt and pepper. Bring to a boil. Reduce the heat; cover and simmer for 25-30 minutes or until a meat thermometer reads 170°. Remove the chicken and strain broth; set both aside.

In the same pan, saute chopped onion and celery in butter until tender. Add the canned broth, carrot, potato, bouillon, basil and reserved broth. Bring to a boil. Reduce heat; cover and simmer for 20-30 minutes or until vegetables are tender.

Add the noodles. Return to a boil; cook for 6-8 minutes or until the noodles are tender. Cut chicken into chunks; add to the soup. Stir in 1-1/4 cups milk; heat through.

Combine flour and remaining milk until smooth; add to soup, stirring constantly. Bring to a boil; cook and stir for 2 minutes or until thickened.

YIELD: 8 servings.

donnie kingman
SAN JACINTO, CALIFORNIA

When we were at a restaurant, my husband remarked that I could make a better soup than they could. A challenge! We began discussing what we'd add and take out and quickly came up with this comforting soup.

cajun chicken & rice soup

lisa hammond

HIGGINSVILLE, MISSOURI

We enjoy this soothing, spicy soup frequently in our household. Its flavors stand out best when served with warm, fresh corn bread.

homemade poultry seasoning

If you don't have any poultry seasoning on hand, you can make your own with this simple recipe. Combine 3/4 teaspoon rubbed sage and 1/4 teaspoon dried thyme or marjoram. This yields 1 teaspoon of seasoning.

1 stewing chicken (about 6 pounds)
2 bay leaves
1 teaspoon salt
1 teaspoon poultry seasoning
1 teaspoon pepper
1 medium onion, chopped
2 celery ribs, chopped
1 tablespoon butter
12 garlic cloves, minced
1 can (10 ounces) diced tomatoes and green chilies, drained
3/4 cup orange juice
2 tablespoons minced fresh cilantro
2 teaspoons Cajun seasoning
1 teaspoon dried oregano
1/2 teaspoon dried thyme
1/2 teaspoon ground cumin
1/2 teaspoon paprika
2 cups cooked rice
1 can (15 ounces) pinto beans, rinsed and drained

Place chicken in a large stockpot; cover with water. Add the bay leaves, salt, poultry seasoning and pepper. Bring to a boil. Reduce heat; cover and simmer for 1-1/2 hours or until chicken is tender.

Remove chicken from broth; set aside to cool. Strain broth, discarding seasonings. Set aside 6 cups broth for the soup; save remaining broth for another use. Skim fat from soup broth. When cool enough to handle, remove chicken from bones; discard bones. Shred and set aside 3 cups chicken (save remaining chicken for another use).

In a large stockpot, saute onion and celery in butter until onion is crisp-tender. Add garlic; cook 1 minute longer. Stir in the tomatoes, orange juice, cilantro, seasonings and reserved broth. Bring to a boil. Reduce heat; cover and simmer for 15 minutes or until vegetables are tender. Stir in the rice, beans and reserved chicken; heat through.

YIELD: 12 servings.

southwestern chicken barley soup

1/2 cup chopped onion
1 teaspoon minced garlic
1 tablespoon olive oil
3 cups water
1 can (15-1/4 ounces) whole kernel corn, drained
1 can (15 ounces) black beans, rinsed and drained
1 can (15 ounces) tomato sauce
1 can (14-1/2 ounces) diced tomatoes, undrained
1 can (14-1/2 ounces) chicken broth
1/2 cup medium pearl barley
1 can (4 ounces) chopped green chilies, drained
1 tablespoon chili powder
1/2 to 1 teaspoon ground cumin
3 cups cubed cooked chicken

In a Dutch oven, saute onion and garlic in oil until tender. Add the water, corn, beans, tomato sauce, tomatoes, broth, barley, chilies, chili powder and cumin. Bring to a boil. Reduce the heat; cover and simmer for 45 minutes.

Stir in chicken; cook, uncovered, 15 minutes longer or until chicken is heated through and barley is tender.

YIELD: 12 servings.

kell ferrell
ALAMO, NORTH DAKOTA

My daily commute is about 80 miles round-trip, so I need quick, healthy dishes to fix for my family. If I don't have leftover chicken, I simply boil or poach some chicken breasts. I use the cooking liquid to replace part of the water in the recipe to add even more flavor.

classic turkey vegetable soup

6 cups turkey *or* chicken broth
3 medium potatoes, peeled and chopped
2 carrots, chopped
2 celery ribs, chopped
2 medium onions, chopped
2 cans (15 ounces *each*) cream-style corn
2 cans (8-1/2 ounces *each*) lima beans, drained
1 to 2 cups chopped cooked turkey
1/2 to 1 teaspoon chili powder
Salt and pepper to taste

In a large stockpot, combine the broth, potatoes, carrots, celery and onions. Bring to boil. Reduce heat; cover and simmer for 30 minutes or until the vegetables are tender.

Add the corn, lima beans, turkey, chili powder, salt and pepper. Cover and simmer 10 minutes longer.

YIELD: 12 servings.

bonnie smith
CLIFTON, VIRGINIA

This is one of my tried-and-true recipes that I always make after Thanksgiving when the turkey leftovers are just about used up. The carcass makes a wonderful broth, and it's amazing how much more meat is made available after boiling the bones!

lemony chicken noodle soup

1 small onion, chopped
2 tablespoons olive oil
1 tablespoon butter
1/4 pound boneless skinless chicken breast, cubed
1 garlic clove, minced
2 cans (14-1/2 ounces *each*) chicken broth
1 medium carrot, cut into 1/4-inch slices
1/4 cup fresh *or* frozen peas
1/2 teaspoon dried basil
2 cups uncooked medium egg noodles
1 to 2 tablespoons lemon juice

In a small saucepan, saute onion in oil and butter until tender. Add chicken; cook and stir until chicken is lightly browned and meat is no longer pink. Add garlic; cook 1 minute longer.

Stir in the broth, carrot, peas and basil. Bring to a boil. Reduce heat; cover and simmer for 5 minutes. Add the noodles. Cover and simmer for 8-10 minutes or until the noodles are tender. Stir in the lemon juice.

YIELD: 2 servings.

bill hilbrich
ST. CLOUD, MINNESOTA

This isn't Grandma's chicken soup, but it is comforting. The lemon juice gives this easy soup enough zip to make it interesting.

terry kuehn
WAUNAKEE, WISCONSIN

I cook most of my family's weekend meals, and my wife and I split weekday cooking duties. When it's my turn to be chef, I like to make this soup as a special treat for my family and neighbors, especially when they're feeling under the weather.

orzo vs. rice

Because of orzo's similar shape and mild flavor, it can be substituted for rice in many recipes. Nutritionally speaking, the two are similar as well. Ounce for ounce, rice and orzo contain similar amounts of fat, sugar, carbohydrates and sodium.

betty rench
EATON, INDIANA

For a surprising twist, I replace traditional noodles with orzo, small rice-like grains of pasta. It cooks up nicely with juicy chunks of chicken.

classic chicken noodle soup

- 1 stewing chicken (about 4 pounds), cut up
- 3 quarts water
- 2 cans (14-1/2 ounces *each*) chicken broth
- 5 celery ribs, coarsely chopped, *divided*
- 4 medium carrots, coarsely chopped, *divided*
- 2 medium onions, quartered, *divided*
- 2/3 cup coarsely chopped green pepper, *divided*
- 1-1/4 teaspoons pepper, *divided*
- 1 bay leaf
- 2 teaspoons salt
- 8 ounces uncooked medium egg noodles

In a large stockpot, combine the chicken, water, broth, half of the celery, carrots, onions and green pepper, 1/2 teaspoon pepper and the bay leaf. Bring to a boil. Reduce heat; cover and simmer for 2-1/2 hours or until chicken is tender. Chop the remaining onion; set aside.

Remove chicken from broth. When cool enough to handle, remove meat from bones and cut into bite-size pieces. Discard bones and skin; set aside.

Strain broth and skim fat; return broth to stockpot. Add the salt, chopped onion and remaining celery, carrots, green pepper and pepper. Bring to a boil. Reduce heat; cover and simmer for 10-12 minutes or until vegetables are crisp-tender. Add noodles and chicken. Cover and simmer for 12-15 minutes or until noodles are tender.

YIELD: 16 servings.

orzo chicken soup

- 1/2 cup chopped onion
- 1 tablespoon butter
- 3 cans (14-1/2 ounces *each*) reduced-sodium chicken broth, *divided*
- 1/2 cup sliced carrot
- 1/2 cup chopped celery
- 1 cup cubed cooked chicken breast
- 1/2 cup uncooked orzo pasta
- 1/4 teaspoon pepper
- Minced fresh parsley

In a large saucepan, saute onion in butter until tender. Add 1 can broth, carrot and celery; bring to a boil. Reduce the heat; cover and simmer for 15 minutes. Add the chicken, orzo, pepper and remaining broth; return to a boil. Reduce heat; cover and simmer for 25-30 minutes or until orzo and vegetables are tender. Sprinkle with parsley.

YIELD: 4 servings.

makeover curried chicken rice soup

1/4 cup butter, cubed

2 large carrots, finely chopped

2 celery ribs, finely chopped

1 small onion, finely chopped

3/4 cup plus 2 tablespoons all-purpose flour

1 teaspoon seasoned salt

1 teaspoon curry powder

2 cans (12 ounces *each*) fat-free evaporated milk

1 cup half-and-half cream

4-1/2 cups reduced-sodium chicken broth

3 cups cubed cooked chicken breast

2 cups cooked brown rice

In a Dutch oven, melt butter. Add the carrots, celery and onion; saute for 2 minutes. Sprinkle with flour; stir until blended. Stir in seasoned salt and curry. Gradually add milk and cream. Bring to a boil; cook and stir for 2 minutes or until thickened.

Gradually add broth. Stir in chicken and rice; return to a boil. Reduce heat; simmer, uncovered, for 10 minutes or until vegetables are tender.

YIELD: 11 servings.

rebecca cook

HELOTES, TEXAS

This lighter version of my family's favorite soup boasts all the hearty texture, warm comfort and delicious flavor of the original.

easy chicken cheese soup

lavonne lundgren
SIOUX CITY, IOWA

*Kids won't think twice
about eating their veggies
after they try this smooth,
cheesy concoction.*

4 cups cubed cooked chicken breast

3-1/2 cups water

2 cans (10-3/4 ounces *each*) condensed
cream of chicken soup, undiluted

1 package (16 ounces) frozen mixed
vegetables, thawed

1 can (14-1/2 ounces) diced potatoes,
drained

1 package (16 ounces) process cheese
(Velveeta), cubed

In a Dutch oven, combine the first five ingredients.
Bring to a boil. Reduce heat; cover and simmer for
8-10 minutes or until vegetables are tender. Stir in
cheese just until melted (do not boil).

YIELD: 7 servings.

turkey bean soup

1 pound ground turkey
1 cup chopped onion
1 cup chopped celery
1 tablespoon olive oil
1 can (49-1/2 ounces) chicken broth
2 cups frozen corn
1 can (15 ounces) white kidney *or* cannellini beans, rinsed and drained
1 cup frozen lima beans
1 can (4 ounces) chopped green chilies
1 teaspoon dried oregano
1 teaspoon ground cumin
1 teaspoon chili powder
1/2 teaspoon salt
Shredded cheddar cheese, optional

In a Dutch oven, cook the turkey, onion and celery in oil over medium heat until meat is no longer pink. Add the broth, corn, beans, chilies, oregano, cumin, chili powder and salt. Bring to a boil. Reduce heat; cover and simmer for 30 minutes or until heated through. Serve with cheese if desired.

YIELD: 8 servings.

taste of home test kitchen
GREENDALE, WISCONSIN

Substitute your favorite beans if cannellini and lima beans are not to your family's taste. To keep costs down, stock up on ground turkey when it's on sale.

vegetable chicken soup

3 quarts water
2 large carrots, sliced
1 cup chopped onion
3 celery ribs, sliced
2 cups fresh broccoli florets
2 cups fresh cauliflowerets
2 garlic cloves, minced
3 tablespoons chicken bouillon granules
3 tablespoons picante sauce
2-1/4 teaspoons minced fresh thyme *or* 3/4 teaspoon dried thyme
2-1/4 teaspoons minced fresh basil *or* 3/4 teaspoon dried basil
1 teaspoon minced fresh rosemary *or* 1/2 teaspoon dried rosemary, crushed
1/4 teaspoon cayenne pepper, optional
2 cups cubed cooked chicken breast
3-1/2 cups egg noodles, cooked and drained

In a large soup kettle, combine the water, carrots, onion and celery. Bring to a boil. Reduce heat; cover and simmer for 20 minutes or until the vegetables are tender.

Add the broccoli, cauliflower, garlic, bouillon, picante sauce and seasonings. Cover and simmer for 20 minutes or until the broccoli and cauliflower are tender.

Add chicken and noodles. Cover and simmer for 5 minutes or until heated through.

YIELD: 12 servings.

betty kline
PANORAMA VILLAGE, TEXAS

I work hard to stick to a low-fat diet, and my husband loves a tasty, filling soup, so this recipe fits the bill for both of us.

cooling veggie soup

If your children say that their soup is too hot to eat, add a few frozen vegetables to their bowls instead of ice cubes. The soup cools a bit as the veggies quickly thaw to a perfect tenderness, and the kids get some extra vitamins.

heather ewald
BOTHELL, WASHINGTON

Creamy peanut butter and pureed tomatoes flavor the tender chicken in this unique soup. I got the recipe from my aunt who served as a missionary in Africa for 45 years. "Soup" is the Nigerian word for "gravy."

peanutty chicken soup

1 broiler/fryer chicken (3 to 4 pounds), cut up
4 tablespoons peanut oil, *divided*
2 tablespoons soy sauce
Dash salt
1 cup water
4 medium tomatoes, cut into wedges
3 large sweet red peppers, cut into wedges
1 large onion, cut into wedges
1 cup creamy peanut butter

In a Dutch oven, brown chicken in 2 tablespoons oil; drain. Brush chicken with soy sauce; sprinkle with salt. Add water. Bring to a boil. Reduce heat; cover and simmer for 30-35 minutes or until chicken juices run clear.

Meanwhile, in a food processor, combine the tomatoes, red peppers and onion. Cover and process until blended.

In a large saucepan, heat remaining oil over medium heat; add tomato mixture. Bring to a boil. Reduce heat; cook and stir for 5-7 minutes or until thickened. Remove from the heat; stir in peanut butter until blended. Add to the chicken mixture; heat through.

YIELD: 4 servings.

june sangrey
MANHEIM, PENNSYLVANIA

With this recipe, you can make the most of even the smallest pieces of leftover meat on your holiday turkey. This soup balances its wonderful rich flavor with a creamy broth full of rice and vegetables.

homemade turkey soup

1 leftover turkey carcass (from a 10– to 12-pound turkey)
2 quarts water
1 medium onion, halved
1/2 teaspoon salt
2 bay leaves
1 cup chopped carrots
1 cup uncooked long-grain rice
1/3 cup chopped celery
1/4 cup chopped onion
1 can (10-3/4 ounces) condensed cream of chicken *or* cream of mushroom soup, undiluted

Place the turkey carcass in a stockpot; add the water, onion, salt and bay leaves. Slowly bring to a boil over low heat; cover and simmer for 2 hours.

Remove carcass; cool. Strain broth and skim off fat. Discard onion and bay leaves. Return broth to the pan. Add the carrots, rice, celery and chopped onion; cover and simmer until rice and vegetables are tender.

Remove turkey from bones; discard bones and cut turkey into bite-size pieces. Add turkey and cream soup to broth; heat through.

YIELD: 8-10 servings.

the **ULTIMATE SOUP** cookbook

mexican chicken soup

1-1/2 pounds boneless skinless chicken breasts, cubed

2 teaspoons canola oil

1/2 cup water

1 envelope reduced-sodium taco seasoning

1 can (32 ounces) V8 juice

1 jar (16 ounces) salsa

1 can (15 ounces) black beans, rinsed and drained

1 package (10 ounces) frozen corn, thawed

6 tablespoons reduced-fat cheddar cheese

6 tablespoons reduced-fat sour cream

2 tablespoons minced fresh cilantro

In a large nonstick skillet, saute chicken in oil until no longer pink. Add water and taco seasoning; simmer, uncovered, until chicken is well coated.

Transfer to a 5-qt. slow cooker. Stir in the V8 juice, salsa, beans and corn. Cover and cook on low for 3-4 hours or until heated through. Serve with cheese, sour cream and cilantro.

YIELD: 6 servings.

marlene kane
LAINESBURG, MICHIGAN

This zesty dish is loaded with chicken, corn and black beans in a mildly spicy red broth. As a busy mom, I'm always looking for dinner recipes that I can prepare in the morning. My kids love the taco-like taste of this soup, and I love its ease of preparation.

roasted veggie and meatball soup

sandy lund
BROOKINGS, SOUTH DAKOTA

I make this appetizing soup almost every Sunday during our frigid South Dakota winters. A variety of roasted vegetables and turkey meatballs perk up the broth.

 5 medium red potatoes, cubed
 4 large carrots, cut into 1/2-inch slices
 1 large red onion, halved and cut into wedges
 4 tablespoons canola oil, *divided*
1-1/4 teaspoons salt, *divided*
 3 tablespoons minced fresh basil
 3 garlic cloves, crushed
 1 egg, lightly beaten
1/2 cup seasoned bread crumbs
1/4 cup grated Parmesan cheese
1/4 cup minced fresh parsley
1/2 teaspoon pepper
 1 pound ground turkey
 1 carton (32 ounces) reduced-sodium chicken broth
 2 cups water
 1 can (14-1/2 ounces) diced tomatoes, undrained

In a large bowl, combine the potatoes, carrots, onion, 2 tablespoons oil and 1/2 teaspoon salt. Place in a single layer in two greased 15-in. x 10-in. x 1-in. baking pans.

Bake at 425° for 20 minutes. Add basil and garlic; toss to coat. Bake 10-15 minutes longer or until vegetables are tender.

In a large bowl, combine the egg, bread crumbs, cheese, parsley, 1/2 teaspoon salt and pepper. Crumble turkey over mixture and mix well. Shape into 1-in. balls.

In a Dutch oven, brown meatballs in remaining oil in batches; drain and set aside.

In the same pan, combine the broth, water, tomatoes, roasted vegetables and remaining salt. Return meatballs to pan. Bring to a boil. Reduce heat; cover and simmer for 45-55 minutes or until meatballs are no longer pink.

YIELD: 8 servings.

turkey soup

- 1 leftover turkey breast carcass (from an 8-pound turkey breast)
- 3 quarts water
- 4 teaspoons chicken bouillon granules
- 2 bay leaves
- 1/2 cup uncooked instant rice
- 1/2 cup uncooked quick-cooking barley
- 1-1/2 cups sliced carrots
- 1 cup chopped onion
- 1 cup sliced celery
- 1 garlic clove, minced
- 1 teaspoon salt
- 1/4 teaspoon pepper
- 1 cup cubed cooked turkey
- 2 tablespoons minced fresh parsley or 2 teaspoons dried parsley flakes

Place carcass, water, bouillon and bay leaves in a Dutch oven; bring to a boil. Reduce heat; cover and simmer for 1-1/2 hours. Remove carcass; cool.

Remove meat from bones and cut into bite-size pieces; set meat aside. Discard bones. Strain broth and skim fat; discard bay leaves. Add rice and barley to broth; bring to a boil. Reduce heat; cover and simmer for 30 minutes.

Stir in the carrots, onion, celery, garlic, salt and pepper; cover and simmer 20-25 minutes longer or until the vegetables are tender. Add cubed turkey, parsley and reserved turkey; heat through.

YIELD: 12 servings.

myrna sisel
GREEN BAY, WISCONSIN

I make the most of my turkey by simmering the carcass to create this warm and comforting soup. The golden broth is full of rice, barley and colorful veggies.

chunky chicken rice soup

- 2 cans (14-1/2 ounces each) chicken broth
- 1 cup water
- 1 package (16 ounces) frozen mixed vegetables, thawed
- 1 package (6 ounces) grilled chicken strips, cut into 1/2-inch cubes
- 1/2 teaspoon poultry seasoning
- 1/4 teaspoon pepper
- 2 cups uncooked instant rice
- 1 tablespoon minced fresh parsley

In a large saucepan, combine the first six ingredients; bring to a boil over medium heat. Reduce heat; cover and simmer for 5 minutes. Stir in rice and parsley. Remove from heat; cover and let stand for 5 minutes.

YIELD: 6 servings.

jacquie olson
WEST LINN, OREGON

This is a simple and satisfying soup that my family enjoys. It goes great with a sandwich.

perked up rice soup

For a change of pace, replace the white rice called for in Chunky Chicken Rice Soup with a long-grain and wild rice mix. The aroma and flavor will perk up a cold winter day.

emily fast
LEAVENWORTH, KANSAS

A good friend gave me her black bean soup recipe a few years ago, and I've been making it ever since. My family loves Mexican food, and bowls of this pack enough flavor to please us all.

southwestern chicken black bean soup

1 pound boneless skinless chicken breasts, cubed
1 tablespoon canola oil
1 tablespoon chopped onion
1 jalapeno pepper, seeded and finely chopped
3 garlic cloves, minced
2 cans (14-1/2 ounces *each*) reduced-sodium chicken broth
3 cups fresh corn *or* frozen corn
1 can (15-1/2 ounces) black beans, rinsed and drained
2 tablespoons lime juice
1/2 teaspoon salt
1/2 teaspoon hot pepper sauce
1/4 teaspoon pepper
1/2 cup minced fresh cilantro

16 baked tortilla chip scoops, crumbled
1/2 cup shredded reduced-fat cheddar cheese

In a Dutch oven, saute the chicken in oil until no longer pink. Remove with a slotted spoon and set aside. In the same pan, saute the onion and jalapeno pepper until tender. Add the garlic and saute; cook 1 minute longer.

Stir in the broth, corn, beans, lime juice, salt, hot pepper sauce, pepper and reserved chicken; bring to a boil. Reduce the heat; simmer, uncovered, for 30 minutes.

Stir in cilantro. Top each serving with crumbled tortilla chips and cheese.

YIELD: 8 servings.

elissa armbruster
MEDFORD, NEW JERSEY

Traditional chicken soup gets an interesting twist from a dumpling-like broth-stretcher called rivels. Chock-full of chicken, vegetables and herbs, you won't be able to resist it!

chicken corn soup with rivels

1 cup chopped carrots
1 celery rib, chopped
1 medium onion, chopped
2 teaspoons canola oil
2 cans (14-1/2 ounces *each*) reduced-sodium chicken broth
2 cups fresh *or* frozen corn
2 cups cubed cooked chicken breast

1/2 teaspoon minced fresh parsley
1/4 teaspoon salt
1/4 teaspoon dried tarragon
1/4 teaspoon pepper
3/4 cup all-purpose flour
1 egg, beaten

In a large saucepan, saute the carrots, celery and onion in oil until tender. Add the broth, corn, chicken, parsley, salt, tarragon and pepper. Bring to a boil.

Meanwhile, for rivels, place the flour in a bowl; cut in egg with a fork until crumbly. Drop dough by teaspoonfuls into boiling soup, stirring constantly. Cook and stir for 1-2 minutes or until rivels are cooked through.

YIELD: 7 servings.

old-fashioned turkey noodle soup

BROTH:

1 leftover turkey carcass
   (from a 12– to 14-pound turkey)

2 cooked turkey wings, meat removed

2 cooked turkey drumsticks, meat removed

1 turkey neck bone

1 medium unpeeled onion, cut into wedges

2 small unpeeled carrots, cut into chunks

6 to 8 garlic cloves, peeled

4 quarts plus 1 cup cold water, *divided*

SOUP:

3 quarts water

5 cups uncooked egg noodles

2 cups diced carrots

2 cups diced celery

3 cups cubed cooked turkey

1/4 cup minced fresh parsley

2-1/2 teaspoons salt

2 teaspoons dried thyme

1 teaspoon pepper

Place the turkey carcass, bones from wings and drumsticks, neck bone, onion, carrots and garlic in a 15-in. x 10-in. x 1-in. baking pan coated with cooking spray. Bake, uncovered, at 400° for 1 hour, turning once.

Transfer the carcass, bones and vegetables to an 8-qt. soup kettle. Add 4 qts. cold water; set aside. Pour remaining cold water into baking pan, stirring to loosen browned bits. Add to kettle. Bring to a boil. Reduce heat; cover and simmer for 3-4 hours.

Cool slightly. Strain broth; discard bones and vegetables. Set soup kettle in an ice-water bath until cooled, stirring occasionally. Cover and refrigerate overnight.

Skim fat from broth. Cover and bring to a boil. Reduce heat to a simmer. Meanwhile, in a Dutch oven, bring 3 qts. water to a boil. Add noodles and carrots; cook for 4 minutes. Add celery; cook 5-7 minutes longer or until noodles and vegetables are tender. Drain; add to simmering broth. Add cubed turkey; heat through. Stir in the parsley, salt, thyme and pepper.

YIELD: 10 servings.

taste of home test kitchen

GREENDALE, WISCONSIN

Our Test Kitchen created this down-home soup to make the most of leftover turkey. Roasting the turkey bones, garlic and vegetables adds richness and depth to the flavor without additional fats.

transporting soup

Whenever you're bringing a soup, stew or chili to a party or potluck dinner, you'll find it can be easily transported in a 5-quart slow cooker.

harold tartar
WEST PALM BEACH, FLORIDA

This slow cooker recipe brings people back for seconds. Made with just the right amounts of chicken, corn, tomatoes, peppers and chilies, the savory soup puts a little zip in mealtime.

southwestern chicken soup

1-1/4 pounds boneless skinless chicken breasts, cut into thin strips

1 to 2 tablespoons canola oil

2 cans (14-1/2 ounces *each*) chicken broth

1 package (16 ounces) frozen corn, thawed

1 can (14-1/2 ounces) diced tomatoes, undrained

1 medium onion, chopped

1 medium green pepper, chopped

1 medium sweet red pepper, chopped

1 can (4 ounces) chopped green chilies

1-1/2 teaspoons seasoned salt, optional

1 teaspoon ground cumin

1/2 teaspoon garlic powder

In a large skillet, saute the chicken in oil until lightly browned. Transfer to a 5-qt. slow cooker with a slotted spoon. Stir in the remaining ingredients. Cover and cook on low for 6-8 hours or until the chicken and vegetables are tender. Stir the soup before serving.

YIELD: 10 servings.

turkey noodle soup

2 cups water
3/4 cup cubed cooked turkey breast
1 celery rib with leaves, sliced
1/4 cup chopped onion
2 garlic cloves, minced
1/2 teaspoon salt
1/8 teaspoon dried marjoram
1/8 teaspoon pepper
1 bay leaf
1/2 cup cubed peeled potatoes
1/4 cup frozen peas
1/4 cup uncooked yolk-free wide noodles
Dash browning sauce, optional

In a large saucepan, combine the first nine ingredients; bring to a boil. Reduce heat; cover and simmer for 10 minutes or until celery is tender.

Add the potato, peas and noodles; cover and simmer 15 minutes longer or until potatoes are tender. Discard bay leaf. Stir in browning sauce if desired.

YIELD: 2 servings.

doris nehoda
COOS BAY, OREGON

My husband follows a low-fat diet, so I'm always looking for delicious recipes that meet his dietary requirements. This easy and economical recipe is perfect for two.

italian chicken rice soup

1 can (49-1/2 ounces) chicken broth
1 jar (26 ounces) meatless spaghetti sauce
1-1/2 cups cubed cooked chicken
2 tablespoons minced fresh parsley
1/2 to 1 teaspoon dried thyme
3 cups cooked rice
1 teaspoon sugar

In a soup kettle or Dutch oven, combine the broth, spaghetti sauce, chicken, parsley and thyme. Bring to a boil. Reduce heat; simmer, uncovered, for 10 minutes. Stir in rice and sugar. Simmer, uncovered, for 10 minutes or until heated through.

YIELD: 10 servings.

wendy sorensen
LOGAN, UTAH

I created this soup so my family and I could enjoy a satisfying sit-down meal on busy nights. It's ready in no time but tastes like it simmered all day. Try adding fresh zucchini or using leftover turkey instead of chicken.

turkey vegetable soup

1 pound lean ground turkey
1 cup chopped celery
1/2 cup chopped onion
2 to 3 garlic cloves, minced
2 cans (14-1/2 ounces each) reduced-sodium beef broth
2-1/2 cups reduced-sodium tomato juice
1 can (14-1/2 ounces) diced tomatoes, drained
1 cup sliced fresh mushrooms
3/4 cup frozen French-style green beans
1/2 cup sliced carrots
1-1/2 teaspoons Worcestershire sauce
1 teaspoon dried parsley flakes
1 teaspoon dried thyme
1/2 teaspoon sugar
1/2 teaspoon dried basil
1/4 teaspoon pepper
1 bay leaf

In a Dutch oven coated with cooking spray, saute the turkey, celery and onion until meat is no longer pink. Add garlic; cook 1 minute longer. Drain.

Stir in remaining ingredients. Bring to a boil. Reduce heat; cover and simmer for 1 hour or until vegetables are tender. Discard bay leaf. Soup may be frozen for up to 3 months.

YIELD: 4 servings.

bonnie lebarron
FORESTVILLE, NEW YORK

Low-sodium ingredients don't diminish the full flavor of this brothy soup. The ground turkey gives it a heartiness everyone will welcome on a cold day.

freezing celery

When you have some spare time, chop a few stalks of celery or a few onions. After sauteing them in butter, spoon them into ice cube trays, freeze, then pop the frozen "veggie cubes" into a labeled freezer bag to store. The veggies are an invaluable addition to soups when you're in a hurry.

kim seeger
BROOKLYN PARK, MINNESOTA

I tried a tortilla soup at a restaurant and decided to create my own easy version. This recipe perfectly captures the flavor so I can enjoy the tasty dish at home.

garnishes for soups

Dress up a soup with a sprinkle of nuts, chopped fresh herbs, vegetable slices, croutons, tortilla strips, shredded cheese or crumbled bacon.

becky christman
BRIDGETON, MISSOURI

You wouldn't guess that this quick and simple soup is low in fat, too. Since my husband loves spicy foods, I sometimes use medium or hot salsa in this recipe for extra heat.

taste of home test kitchen
GREENDALE, WISCONSIN

Rich in chicken flavor, this traditional broth is lightly seasoned with herbs. Besides making wonderful chicken soups, it can be used in casseroles, rice dishes and other recipes that call for chicken broth.

chicken tortilla soup

1-1/4 pounds boneless skinless chicken breasts
1 cup chopped onion
1 teaspoon minced garlic
2 cans (14-1/2 ounces *each*) reduced-sodium chicken broth
1 can (28 ounces) crushed tomatoes
1 can (16 ounces) kidney beans, rinsed and drained
1 can (8 ounces) tomato sauce
1 can (6 ounces) tomato paste
1 can (4 ounces) chopped green chilies
2 teaspoons chili powder
1 teaspoon ground cumin
3/4 teaspoon dried oregano
1/2 teaspoon sugar
1/4 teaspoon salt
1/4 teaspoon pepper
3 corn tortillas (6 inches), cut into 1/2-inch strips

Broil chicken breasts 3-4 in. from the heat for 5-6 minutes on each side or until a meat thermometer reads 170°.

In a Dutch oven coated with cooking spray, cook onion until tender. Add garlic; cook 1 minute longer. Stir in the broth, tomatoes, beans, tomato sauce, tomato paste, chilies and seasonings. Shred chicken with two forks; add to soup. Bring to a boil. Reduce heat; simmer, uncovered, for 10-15 minutes.

Meanwhile, place tortilla strips on an ungreased baking sheet. Bake at 350° for 12-15 minutes or until crisp. Serve with soup.

YIELD: 8 servings.

salsa chicken soup

1/2 pound boneless skinless chicken breasts, cubed
1 can (14-1/2 ounces) chicken broth
1-3/4 cups water
1 to 2 teaspoons chili powder
1 cup frozen corn
1 cup salsa
Shredded Monterey Jack cheese *or* pepper Jack cheese, optional

In a large saucepan, combine the chicken, broth, water and chili powder. Bring to a boil. Reduce heat; cover and simmer for 5 minutes. Add corn; return to a boil. Reduce heat; simmer, uncovered, for 5 minutes or until chicken is no longer pink and corn is tender. Add salsa and heat through. Garnish with cheese if desired.

YIELD: 6 servings.

homemade chicken broth

2-1/2 pounds bony chicken pieces
2 celery ribs with leaves, cut into chunks
2 medium carrots, cut into chunks
2 medium onions, quartered
2 bay leaves
1/2 teaspoon dried rosemary, crushed
1/2 teaspoon dried thyme
8 to 10 whole peppercorns
2 quarts cold water

Place all ingredients in a soup kettle or Dutch oven. Slowly bring to a boil; reduce heat. Skim foam. Cover and simmer for 2 hours.

Set chicken aside until cool enough to handle. Remove meat from bones. Discard bones; save meat for another use. Strain broth, discarding vegetables and seasonings. Refrigerate for 8 hours or overnight. Skim fat from surface.

YIELD: 6 servings.

turkey pasta soup

1 cup uncooked small pasta shells
1 pound lean ground turkey
2 medium onions, chopped
2 garlic cloves, minced
3 cans (14-1/2 ounces *each*) reduced-sodium chicken broth
2 cans (15 ounces *each*) white kidney *or* cannellini beans, rinsed and drained
2 cans (14-1/2 ounces *each*) Italian stewed tomatoes
2 teaspoons dried oregano
2 teaspoons dried basil
1 teaspoon fennel seed, crushed
1 teaspoon pepper
1/2 teaspoon salt
1/4 teaspoon crushed red pepper flakes

Cook pasta according to the package directions. Meanwhile, in a large stock pot, cook turkey and onions over medium heat until meat is no longer pink. Add garlic; cook 1 minute longer. Drain. Stir in the broth, beans, tomatoes and seasonings. Bring to a boil. Reduce heat; simmer, uncovered, for 10 minutes.

Drain pasta and add to the soup. Cook 5 minutes longer or until heated through.

YIELD: 10 servings.

marie ewert
RICHMOND, MICHIGAN

This quick soup has such a great flavor that everyone I've shared it with has added the recipe to their list of favorites. It also simmers up well in a slow cooker.

esther nafziger

LA JUNTA, COLORADO

One taste of this traditional curry-flavored soup, and folks will know it didn't come from a can! It fills your kitchen with a wonderful aroma while it simmers on its own.

mulligatawny soup

1 medium tart apple, peeled and diced

1/4 cup *each* chopped carrot, celery and onion

1/4 cup butter, cubed

1/3 cup all-purpose flour

1 teaspoon curry powder

1/2 teaspoon sugar

1/2 teaspoon salt

1/8 teaspoon pepper

1/8 teaspoon ground mace

6 cups chicken *or* turkey broth

1 cup cubed cooked chicken *or* turkey

1 medium tomato, peeled, seeded and chopped

1/2 cup chopped green pepper

2 whole cloves

1 tablespoon minced fresh parsley

1 cup cooked rice

In a Dutch oven or soup kettle, saute the apple, carrot, celery and onion in butter for 5 minutes or until tender. Stir in the flour, curry, sugar, salt, pepper and mace until blended. Gradually add the broth.

Bring to a boil. Cook and stir for 2 minutes or until thickened. Add the chicken, tomato, green pepper, cloves and parsley; return to a boil. Reduce heat; cover and simmer for 20-30 minutes. Add rice; heat through. Discard cloves before serving.

YIELD: 8 servings.

turkey meatball soup

1 package (12 ounces) refrigerated fully cooked Italian turkey meatballs
1 can (49-1/2 ounces) chicken broth
2 cups uncooked egg noodles
2 cups cut fresh green beans
1 cup sliced fresh carrots
1 cup chopped celery
1 cup chopped onion
1 tablespoon dried parsley flakes
1 teaspoon garlic powder
1 teaspoon dried oregano
1 teaspoon dried basil
1/4 teaspoon pepper

In a Dutch oven, combine all ingredients. Bring to a boil. Reduce heat; simmer, uncovered, for 20-25 minutes or until noodles are tender.

YIELD: 6 servings.

taste of home test kitchen
GREENDALE, WISCONSIN

Cooked Italian turkey meatballs can be found in the refrigerated section of your local grocery stores. You can also substitute frozen beef meatballs.

chicken noodle soup

1 broiler/fryer chicken (2 to 3 pounds)
2-1/2 quarts water
1/2 medium onion, chopped
3 teaspoons salt
2 teaspoons chicken bouillon granules
1/8 teaspoon pepper
1/4 teaspoon dried marjoram
1/4 teaspoon dried thyme
1 bay leaf
1-1/2 cups uncooked fine egg noodles
1 cup chopped celery
1 cup chopped carrots

In a stockpot, combine the first 9 ingredients; bring to a boil. Reduce heat; cover and simmer for 1-1/2 hours. Remove chicken; allow to cool. Strain broth; discard bay leaf.

Skim fat. Debone chicken and cut into chunks; return chicken and broth to pan. Add the noodles, celery and carrots; bring to a boil. Reduce heat; cover and simmer for 25-30 minutes or until noodles and vegetables are tender.

YIELD: 8-10 servings.

diane edgecomb
HUMBOLDT, SOUTH DAKOTA

I like making homemade noodles for this recipe. And I'll often toss in potatoes and corn to make it stick to our ribs and keep my family full.

add the noodles last

Chicken noodle soup may yield a better flavor if the soup is made and refrigerated without the noodles. When it's time to serve, add the noodles to the amount of soup you're going to use and cook until tender.

**taste of home
test kitchen**

GREENDALE, WISCONSIN

Bring a bit of the Southwest to your table with this spirit-warming soup. Loaded with tender chicken, diced tomatoes and a fiesta of seasonings, it's sure to be requested time and again.

flavorful chicken tortilla soup

1 cup chopped onion

1 teaspoon minced garlic

3 cups chicken broth

1 can (14-1/2 ounces) Mexican diced tomatoes

1/2 teaspoon chili powder

1/4 teaspoon ground cumin

1-1/2 pounds boneless skinless chicken breast, cubed

2 tablespoons cornstarch

1/4 cup cold water

1/4 cup shredded Mexican cheese blend

1 tablespoon minced fresh cilantro

Tortilla chips, optional

In a large saucepan, combine the first six ingredients; bring to a boil. Add chicken. Reduce heat; cover and simmer for 4-6 minutes or until chicken is no longer pink. Combine cornstarch and water until smooth; gradually stir into soup.

Bring to a boil; cook and stir for 1 minute or until thickened. Top servings with cheese and cilantro. Serve with tortilla chips if desired.

YIELD: 6 servings.

katherine preiss

PENFIELD, PENNSYLVANIA

This chunky soup is full of flavor and zip! Eliminate the jalapeno pepper if you don't want as much zing. To make it vegetarian, I omit the turkey and add a small can of garbanzo beans in the last few minutes of cooking.

zesty turkey tomato soup

1/4 pound lean ground turkey

1 small zucchini, diced

1 small onion, chopped

1 can (14-1/2 ounces) reduced-sodium chicken broth

1 cup canned Mexican diced tomatoes

1/3 cup uncooked whole wheat spiral pasta

1/2 teaspoon minced fresh basil

1/4 teaspoon ground cumin

1/8 teaspoon pepper

1 tablespoon chopped jalapeno pepper, optional

Shredded fat-free cheddar cheese, optional

In a large saucepan, cook the turkey, zucchini and onion over medium heat until meat is no longer pink; drain.

Stir in the broth, tomatoes, pasta, basil, cumin, pepper and jalapeno if desired. Bring to a boil. Reduce heat; simmer, uncovered, for 13-15 minutes or until pasta is tender. Garnish with the cheese if desired.

YIELD: 3 servings.

chicken soup with potato dumplings

1/4 cup chopped onion
1 tablespoon canola oil
2 garlic cloves, minced
6 cups chicken broth
2 cups cubed cooked chicken
2 celery ribs, chopped
2 medium carrots, sliced
1/4 teaspoon dried sage leaves

DUMPLINGS:

1-1/2 cups biscuit/baking mix
1 cup cold mashed potatoes
(with added milk)
1/4 cup milk
1 tablespoon chopped green onion
1/8 teaspoon pepper

In a large saucepan, saute onion in oil for 3-4 minutes or until tender. Add garlic; cook 1 minute longer. Stir in the broth, chicken, celery, carrots and sage. Bring to a boil. Reduce heat; cover and simmer for 10-15 minutes or until vegetables are tender.

In a small bowl, combine the dumpling ingredients. Drop heaping tablespoonfuls of batter onto simmering soup. Cover and simmer for 20 minutes or until a toothpick inserted in a dumpling comes out clean (do not lift the cover while the soup is simmering).

YIELD: 5 servings.

marie mcconnell
SHELBYVILLE, ILLINOIS

Our family calls this comforting, old-fashioned soup our "Sunday dinner soup" because it's almost a complete dinner in a bowl. You'll love the flavor!

julia thornely
LAYTON, UTAH

*Here is my favorite cream
of mushroom soup recipe. It
gets its tang from a splash
of hot pepper sauce.*

zippy chicken mushroom soup

1/2 pound fresh mushrooms, chopped
1/4 cup *each* chopped onion, celery and carrot
1/4 cup butter, cubed
1/2 cup all-purpose flour
5-1/2 cups chicken broth
1 teaspoon pepper
1/2 teaspoon white pepper
1/4 teaspoon dried thyme
Pinch dried tarragon
1/2 teaspoon hot pepper sauce
3 cups half-and-half cream
2-1/2 cups cubed cooked chicken
1 tablespoon minced fresh parsley
1-1/2 teaspoons lemon juice
1/2 teaspoon salt

In a Dutch oven, saute the mushrooms, onion, celery and carrot in butter until tender. Stir in flour until blended. Gradually add the broth and seasonings. Bring to a boil. Reduce heat; simmer, uncovered, for 10 minutes.

Stir in the cream, chicken, parsley, lemon juice and salt; heat through (do not boil).

YIELD: 11 servings.

chunky chicken veggie soup

8 cups chicken broth
6 medium carrots, sliced
2 medium onions, chopped
2 small zucchini, chopped
4 garlic cloves, minced
6 cups cubed cooked chicken
2 cans (28 ounces *each*) crushed
  tomatoes
1 can (14-1/2 ounces) diced tomatoes,
  undrained
1 can (10 ounces) diced tomatoes with
  green chilies, undrained
1 can (8 ounces) tomato sauce
4 teaspoons sugar

1 teaspoon salt
1 teaspoon celery salt
1 teaspoon Creole seasoning
1/2 teaspoon pepper

In a large stockpot, bring the broth, carrots and onions to a boil. Reduce heat; simmer, uncovered, for 5 minutes. Add zucchini and garlic; simmer 5 minutes longer or until vegetables are crisp-tender. Stir in the remaining ingredients; heat through.

YIELD: 20 servings.

EDITOR'S NOTE: The following spices may be substituted for 1 teaspoon Creole seasoning: 1/4 teaspoon *each* of dried thyme, ground cumin and cayenne pepper.

sundra hauck
BOGALUSA, LOUISIANA

Catering to a Christmas crowd or a huddle of hungry football fans? Try my hot, savory soup loaded with veggies, chicken and seasonings. Serve with warm bread for a stick-to-your-ribs meal in a bowl.

basic turkey soup

TURKEY BROTH:
1 leftover turkey carcass
8 cups water
1 teaspoon chicken bouillon granules
1 celery rib with leaves
1 small onion, halved
1 carrot
3 whole peppercorns
1 garlic clove
1 teaspoon seasoned salt
1 teaspoon dried thyme
TURKEY VEGETABLE SOUP:
8 cups turkey broth
2 teaspoons chicken bouillon granules
1/2 to 3/4 teaspoon pepper

4 cups sliced carrots, celery, green
  beans *and/or* other vegetables
3/4 cup chopped onion
4 cups diced cooked turkey

Place all broth ingredients in a large stockpot; cover and bring to a boil. Reduce heat; simmer for 25 minutes. Strain broth; discard bones and vegetables. Cool; skim fat. Use immediately for turkey vegetable soup or refrigerate and use within 24 hours.

For soup, combine the broth, bouillon, pepper, vegetables and onion in a large stockpot. Cover and simmer for 15-20 minutes or until the vegetables are tender. Add turkey and heat through.

YIELD: 8-10 servings.

katie koziolek
HARTLAND, MINNESOTA

I simmer a rich broth using the turkey carcass then add my favorite vegetables to this soup.

chicken barley soup

1 broiler/fryer chicken (2 to 3 pounds),
  cut up
8 cups water
1-1/2 cups chopped carrots
1 cup chopped celery
1/2 cup medium pearl barley
1/2 cup chopped onion
1 teaspoon chicken bouillon granules
1 teaspoon salt, optional
1 bay leaf
1/2 teaspoon poultry seasoning

1/2 teaspoon pepper
1/2 teaspoon rubbed sage

In a large stockpot, cook chicken in water until tender. Cool broth and skim off fat. Set chicken aside until cool enough to handle. Remove meat from bones; discard bones and cut meat into cubes. Return meat to pan along with remaining ingredients. Bring to a boil. Reduce the heat; cover and simmer for 1 hour or until vegetables and barley are tender. Discard bay leaf.

YIELD: 5 servings.

diana costello
MARION, KANSAS

Try my recipe the next time you're looking for a chicken soup that is so filling it can serve as the main course. I've shared the recipe many times.

patty d'amore

GLENDORA, CALIFORNIA

It's a tradition in our house to serve my pumpkin soup on Halloween. The fragrant blend hits the spot on a cool autumn afternoon.

mincing fresh garlic

To mince fresh garlic, crush a garlic clove with the blade of a chef's knife. Peel away the skin. Mince as directed.

curry chicken pumpkin soup

4 bacon strips, diced
1/4 cup chopped onion
2 cups cubed peeled pie pumpkin
2 cups chicken broth
1 can (14-1/2 ounces) diced tomatoes, undrained
1 teaspoon curry powder
3/4 cup cubed cooked chicken breast
1/3 cup frozen corn
1/3 cup cooked small pasta shells

In a large saucepan, cook bacon and onion over medium heat until bacon is crisp; drain. Add the pumpkin, broth, tomatoes and curry; bring to a boil. Reduce heat; cover and simmer for 8-10 minutes or until pumpkin is tender. Stir in the chicken, corn and pasta; heat through.

YIELD: 4 servings.

denise kilgore

LINO LAKES, MINNESOTA

This low-calorie tomato soup is quick to prepare and filled with a bounty of good-for-you ingredients.

turkey barley tomato soup

1 pound lean ground turkey
3/4 cup sliced *or* baby carrots
1 medium onion, chopped
1 celery rib, chopped
1 garlic clove, minced
1 envelope reduced-sodium taco seasoning, *divided*
3-1/2 cups water
1 can (28 ounces) Italian diced tomatoes, undrained
3/4 cup quick-cooking barley
1/2 teaspoon minced fresh oregano *or* 1/8 teaspoon dried oregano

In a Dutch oven, cook the turkey, carrots, onion, celery, garlic and 1 tablespoon taco seasoning over medium heat until meat is no longer pink. Stir in the water, tomatoes and remaining taco seasoning; bring to a boil. Reduce heat; cover and simmer for 20 minutes. Add barley; cover and simmer for 15-20 minutes longer or until the barley is tender. Stir in the oregano.

YIELD: 6 servings.

amish chicken corn soup

12 cups water

2 pounds boneless skinless chicken breasts, cubed

1 cup chopped onion

1 cup chopped celery

1 cup shredded carrots

3 chicken bouillon cubes

2 cans (14-3/4 ounces *each*) cream-style corn

2 cups uncooked egg noodles

1/4 cup butter

1 teaspoon salt

1/4 teaspoon pepper

In a Dutch oven, combine the water, chicken, onion, celery, carrots and bouillon. Bring to a boil. Reduce the heat; simmer, uncovered, for 30 minutes or until the chicken is no longer pink and the vegetables are tender.

Stir in the corn, noodles and butter; cook 10 minutes longer or until noodles are tender. Season with salt and pepper.

YIELD: 16 servings.

beverly hoffman
SANDY LAKE, PENNSYLVANIA

Cream-style corn and butter add richness to traditional Amish soup. The recipe yields a big batch, but it freezes well for future meals.

nancy clow
MALLORYTOWN, ONTARIO

I'm a busy mom who relies on my slow cooker for fast, nutritious meals with minimal prep time and cleanup. I knew this recipe was a keeper when I didn't have any leftovers and my husband asked me to make it a second time.

chunky chicken soup

1-1/2 pounds boneless skinless chicken breasts, cut into 2-inch strips

2 teaspoons canola oil

2/3 cup finely chopped onion

2 medium carrots, chopped

2 celery ribs, chopped

1 cup frozen corn

2 cans (10-3/4 ounces each) condensed cream of potato soup, undiluted

1-1/2 cups chicken broth

1 teaspoon dill weed

1 cup frozen peas

1/2 cup half-and-half cream

In a large skillet over medium-high heat, brown chicken in oil or until no longer pink. With a slotted spoon, transfer to a 5-qt. slow cooker. Add the onion, carrots, celery and corn. In a large bowl, whisk the soup, broth and dill until blended; stir into slow cooker. Cover and cook on low for 4 hours or until vegetables are tender. Stir in peas and cream.

Cover and cook 30 minutes longer or until heated through.

YIELD: 7 servings.

chicken vegetable soup

1 medium onion, chopped
1 celery rib, chopped

2 teaspoons canola oil
1 garlic clove, minced
1-1/2 cups chicken broth
1 cup chopped tomatoes
1 cup cubed cooked chicken
1/4 teaspoon dried marjoram
1/4 teaspoon dried thyme
1/8 teaspoon pepper
1 bay leaf

In a large saucepan, saute onion and celery in oil until tender. Add garlic; cook 1 minute longer. Stir in the broth, tomatoes, chicken, marjoram, thyme, pepper and bay leaf. Bring to a boil. Reduce heat; cover and simmer for 30 minutes or until heated through. Discard bay leaf.

YIELD: 2 servings.

ruby williams
BOGALUSA, LOUISIANA

Every grandmother knows that nothing cures a cold better than homemade soup. I find this recipe nicely accommodates my great-grandson and me.

freeze cubed chicken

When chicken pieces are on sale, purchase several packages and bake all the chicken, skin side up, on foil-lined pans. Once cool, remove the skin and bones, cube the meat and freeze in measured portions to use in soups, stews and chowders.

spicy chicken tomato soup

2 cans (14-1/2 ounces *each*) chicken broth
3 cups cubed cooked chicken
2 cups frozen corn
1 can (10-3/4 ounces) tomato puree
1 can (10 ounces) diced tomatoes and green chilies
1 large onion, finely chopped
2 garlic cloves, minced
1 bay leaf
1 to 2 teaspoons ground cumin
1 teaspoon salt
1/2 to 1 teaspoon chili powder

1/8 teaspoon pepper
1/8 teaspoon cayenne pepper
4 white *or* yellow corn tortillas (6 inches), cut into 1/4-inch strips

In a 5-qt. slow cooker, combine the first 13 ingredients. Cover and cook on low for 4 hours.

Place the tortilla strips on an ungreased baking sheet. Bake at 375° for 5 minutes; turn. Bake 5 minutes longer. Discard bay leaf from soup. Serve with tortilla strips.

YIELD: 8 servings.

margaret bailey
COFFEEVILLE, MISSISSIPPI

Cumin, chili powder and cayenne pepper give my slow-cooked specialty its kick. I serve bowls with crunchy tortilla strips that bake up in no time. Any leftover soup freezes well for those nights I don't feel like cooking.

basil turkey soup

2 cups beef broth
2-1/2 cups frozen mixed vegetables
1 can (14-1/2 ounces) diced tomatoes, undrained
3/4 cup uncooked small shell pasta
3/4 teaspoon dried basil
3/4 teaspoon pepper
2-1/2 cups cubed cooked turkey
2-1/2 teaspoons dried parsley flakes

In a large saucepan, combine the first six ingredients. Bring to a boil. Reduce heat; cover and simmer for 7-10 minutes or until the pasta and vegetables are tender. Stir in turkey and parsley; heat through.

YIELD: 6 servings.

taste of home test kitchen
GREENDALE, WISCONSIN

After a busy day, it's easy to put together this soup with leftover turkey and frozen vegetables. It tastes like it's simmered all day!

morgan byers

BERKLEY, MICHIGAN

Looking for a true classic to serve for dinner? Give my chicken and dumpling soup a try. My husband loves it so much he says he could eat it every day of the week.

easy dumplings

Use flour tortillas to make quick and easy dumplings for soup. Use a sharp knife to cut a stack of tortillas into strips. Add them to the simmering soup mixture and let them thicken. They are simple, fast and taste just as yummy as dumplings made from biscuit mix.

taste of home test kitchen

GREENDALE, WISCONSIN

This tasty soup has a surprisingly short simmering time. Leftover turkey has never tasted so good!

chicken and dumpling soup

3/4 pound boneless skinless chicken breasts, cut into 1-inch cubes
1/4 teaspoon salt
1/8 teaspoon pepper
2 teaspoons olive oil
1/4 cup all-purpose flour
4 cups reduced-sodium chicken broth, *divided*
1 cup water
2 cups frozen French-cut green beans
1-1/2 cups sliced onions
1 cup coarsely shredded carrots
1/4 teaspoon dried marjoram
2/3 cup reduced-fat biscuit/baking mix
1/3 cup cornmeal
1/4 cup shredded reduced-fat cheddar cheese
1/3 cup fat-free milk

Sprinkle chicken with salt and pepper. In a nonstick skillet, saute chicken in oil until browned and no longer pink.

In a large saucepan, combine flour and 1/2 cup broth until smooth. Stir in water and remaining broth. Add the beans, onions, carrots, marjoram and chicken. Bring to a boil. Reduce heat; simmer, uncovered, for 10 minutes.

Meanwhile, in a small bowl, combine the biscuit mix, cornmeal and cheese. Stir in the milk just until moistened. Drop the batter in 12 mounds onto simmering soup. Cover and simmer for 15 minutes or until a toothpick inserted in a dumpling comes out clean (do not lift the cover while simmering).

YIELD: 4 servings.

turkey rice soup

1/2 cup sliced fresh mushrooms
1/2 cup chopped onion
2 teaspoons canola oil
2 cans (14-1/2 ounces *each*) chicken broth
2 cups water
1/2 cup apple juice, optional
1 package (6 ounces) long grain and wild rice mix
2-1/2 cups cubed cooked turkey
2 cups frozen mixed vegetables

In a large saucepan, saute mushrooms and onion in oil for 3 minutes. Stir in the broth, water and apple juice if desired. Bring to a boil. Stir in rice mix. Reduce heat; cover and simmer for 20 minutes.

Stir in turkey and vegetables; cook 5 minutes longer or until rice and vegetables are tender.

YIELD: 6 servings.

lemon-chicken velvet soup

2 tablespoons butter
2 tablespoons all-purpose flour
1 can (14-1/2 ounces) chicken broth
3 tablespoons lemon juice
1-1/2 cups cubed cooked chicken breast
10 fresh *or* frozen sugar snap peas
2 tablespoons minced fresh parsley
1 teaspoon grated lemon peel
3 tablespoons heavy whipping cream

In a small saucepan, melt the butter. Stir in the flour until smooth; gradually add the broth and lemon juice. Bring to a boil; cook and stir for 1-2 minutes or until thickened.

Stir in the chicken, peas, parsley and lemon peel; cook 2-3 minutes longer or until chicken is heated through and peas are crisp-tender. Stir in cream; heat through (do not boil).

YIELD: 2 servings.

celeste buckley
REDDING, CALIFORNIA

Here's the perfect antidote to a chilly spring day. The lively flavor of lemon perks up this rich, brothy soup accented with fresh sugar snap peas.

deborah lou mitchell

CLARKSVILLE, INDIANA

I incorporated this chicken soup as part of my heart-healthy diet, and I lost 67 pounds in six months! It's a light and tasty soup that is guaranteed to please.

chilly-day chicken soup

1/4 pound boneless skinless chicken breast, cut into small pieces

1/4 cup chopped onion

2 teaspoons butter

1 cup diced red potatoes

1 medium carrot, grated

1 can (14-1/2 ounces) reduced-sodium chicken broth

1/2 cup water

1/4 teaspoon pepper

2 tablespoons uncooked instant rice

1/8 teaspoon salt

In a small nonstick saucepan, saute chicken and onion in butter until chicken is no longer pink. Stir in the potatoes, carrot, broth, water and pepper. Bring to a boil. Reduce heat; cover and simmer for 10-12 minutes or until potatoes are tender.

Return to a boil; stir in rice and salt. Remove from the heat. Cover and let stand for 5 minutes or until the rice is tender.

YIELD: 2 servings.

hearty turkey vegetable soup

- 1 pound lean ground turkey
- 1 medium onion, chopped
- 2 small zucchini, quartered lengthwise and sliced
- 1 large carrot, cut into 1-inch julienne strips
- 3 cans (14 ounces *each*) reduced-sodium beef broth
- 1 jar (26 ounces) garden-style pasta sauce *or* meatless spaghetti sauce
- 1 can (16 ounces) kidney beans, rinsed and drained
- 1 can (15-1/2 ounces) great northern beans, rinsed and drained
- 1 can (14-1/2 ounces) Italian diced tomatoes, undrained
- 1 tablespoon dried parsley flakes
- 2 teaspoons dried oregano
- 1 teaspoon pepper
- 1 teaspoon hot pepper sauce
- 1 cup uncooked small shell pasta

In a Dutch oven coated with cooking spray, cook turkey and onion over medium heat until meat is no longer pink; drain. Add zucchini and carrot; cook and stir 1 minute longer. Stir in the broth, pasta sauce, beans, tomatoes, parsley, oregano, pepper and hot pepper sauce.

Bring to a boil. Reduce heat; cover and simmer for 45 minutes. Meanwhile, cook the pasta according to the package directions; drain. Just before serving, stir in the pasta.

YIELD: 10 servings.

julie anderson
BLOOMINGTON, ILLINOIS

I love turkey vegetable soup, but most recipes I come across are too high in fat. I experimented until I found the perfect blend of nutritious ingredients for this low-fat version.

low-sodium soup secrets

To keep the sodium in your soup du jour on the lighter side, stir additional herbs or a salt-free seasoning blend into your soup instead of salt. When recipes call for canned chicken broth, replace it with reduced-sodium broth.

turkey dumpling soup

- 1 meaty leftover turkey carcass (from an 11-pound turkey)
- 6 cups chicken broth
- 6 cups water
- 2 celery ribs, cut into 1-inch slices
- 1 medium carrot, cut into 1-inch slices
- 1 tablespoon poultry seasoning
- 1 bay leaf
- 1/2 teaspoon salt
- 1/2 teaspoon pepper

SOUP INGREDIENTS:

- 1 medium onion, chopped
- 2 celery ribs, chopped
- 2 medium carrots, sliced
- 1 cup fresh *or* frozen cut green beans
- 1 package (10 ounces) frozen corn
- 1 package (10 ounces) frozen peas
- 2 cups biscuit/baking mix
- 2/3 cup milk

In a large soup kettle or Dutch oven, combine the first nine ingredients. Bring to a boil. Reduce heat; cover and simmer for 3 hours.

Remove carcass and allow to cool. Remove meat and set aside 4 cups for soup (refrigerate any remaining meat for another use); discard bones. Strain broth, discarding vegetables and bay leaf.

Return broth to kettle; add onion, celery, carrots and beans. Bring to a boil. Reduce heat; cover and simmer for 10 minutes or until the vegetables are tender. Add corn, peas and reserved turkey. Bring to a boil; reduce heat.

Combine the biscuit mix and milk. Drop by teaspoonfuls onto simmering broth. Cover and simmer for 10 minutes or until a toothpick inserted in a dumpling comes out clean (do not lift the cover while simmering).

YIELD: 16 servings.

debbie wolf
MISSION VIEJO, CALIFORNIA

Simmering up a big pot of soup is one of my holiday traditions. This is a variation on a recipe my mom made while I was growing up. My husband and kids can't get enough of the tender dumplings.

pork, ham & sausage

Here, you'll find everything your meat-loving taste buds can handle! From spicy Italian sausage to smoky bacon and everything in between, delicious comfort awaits in these soups that feature pork and its family of meats. So go ahead, fire up the stove and delight your family tonight.

114　　　118　　　125

eleanor niska
TWIN FALLS, IDAHO

My daughter created this soup to use up some leftover pork. Use more water for a thin soup or less water for a noodle dish. Mushroom-flavored ramen noodles also yield good results.

pork noodle soup

1/2 cup chopped celery
1/2 cup chopped onion
1 tablespoon olive oil
1/2 teaspoon minced garlic
7 cups water
1-1/2 cups cut fresh asparagus (1-inch pieces)
1/2 cup chopped cabbage
1-1/2 teaspoons minced fresh parsley
3/4 teaspoon dried tarragon
Dash cayenne pepper, optional
2 packages (3 ounces *each*) pork ramen noodles
2 cups cubed cooked pork

In a Dutch oven, saute celery and onion in oil until tender. Add garlic; cook 1 minute longer. Stir in the water, asparagus, cabbage, parsley, tarragon and cayenne if desired. Bring to a boil.

Coarsely crush the noodles. Add the noodles with the contents of the seasoning packets to the pan. Bring to a boil. Reduce heat; simmer, uncovered, for 3-5 minutes or until the noodles and vegetables are tender. Add pork; heat through.

YIELD: 10 servings.

pizza soup

1-1/4 cups sliced fresh mushrooms
1/2 cup finely chopped onion
1 teaspoon canola oil
2 cups water
1 can (15 ounces) pizza sauce
1 cup chopped pepperoni
1 cup chopped fresh tomatoes
1/2 cup cooked Italian sausage
1/4 teaspoon Italian seasoning
1/4 cup grated Parmesan cheese
Shredded part-skim mozzarella cheese

In a large saucepan, saute mushrooms and onion in oil for 2-3 minutes or until tender. Add the water, pizza sauce, pepperoni, tomatoes, sausage and Italian seasoning. Bring to a boil over medium heat. Reduce heat; cover and simmer for 20 minutes, stirring occasionally.

Before serving, stir in Parmesan cheese. Garnish with mozzarella cheese.

YIELD: 4 servings.

donna britsch
TEGA CAY, SOUTH CAROLINA

Anyone who loves pizza won't be able to get enough of my soup. The kids help themselves to a big bowl whenever I set this specialty on the table.

kielbasa potato chowder

1/2 pound smoked kielbasa *or* Polish sausage, cut into 1/2-inch pieces
3 bacon strips, diced
1 small onion, finely chopped
1 garlic clove, minced
1-1/2 cups reduced-sodium chicken broth
1-1/2 cups water
2 medium potatoes, peeled and cubed
1/2 teaspoon chicken bouillon granules
1/8 teaspoon pepper
2 kale leaves, torn *or* 1/3 cup chopped fresh spinach
1/2 cup heavy whipping cream *or* 2% milk

In a large nonstick skillet, brown kielbasa and bacon; drain, reserving 1 teaspoon drippings. Add onion; cook over medium heat for 2-3 minutes or until onion is tender. Add garlic; 1 minute longer.

In a large saucepan, bring broth and water to a boil. Add the potatoes, bouillon and pepper. Cook for 10 minutes or until potatoes are tender.

Add the meat mixture and kale; cook over medium heat for 2 minutes or until kale is wilted. Reduce heat. Add the cream; cook 1 minute longer or until heated through.

YIELD: 4 servings.

misty chandler
LAWTON, OKLAHOMA

There's just the right touch of comfort in this sensational sausage chowder. My husband and I make a meal of it with some warm bread.

ham and corn chowder

2 celery ribs, chopped
1/4 cup chopped onion
1 jalapeno pepper, seeded and chopped
2 tablespoons butter
2 tablespoons all-purpose flour
3 cups whole milk

2 cups cubed fully cooked ham
2 cups cubed cooked potatoes
1-1/2 cups fresh *or* frozen corn
1 can (14-3/4 ounces) cream-style corn
3/4 teaspoon minced fresh thyme *or* 1/4 teaspoon dried thyme
1/8 to 1/4 teaspoon cayenne pepper
1/8 teaspoon salt

In a large saucepan, saute the celery, onion and jalapeno in butter until vegetables are tender. Stir in flour until blended; gradually add milk. Bring to a boil; cook and stir for 2 minutes or until thickened. Stir in the remaining ingredients. Bring to a boil. Reduce heat; cover and simmer for 10 minutes or until heated through.

YIELD: 8 servings.

EDITOR'S NOTE: We recommend wearing disposable gloves when cutting hot peppers. Avoid touching your face.

sharon price
CALDWELL, IDAHO

My husband and I love soup, so I'm always looking for easy recipes. This chowder gets a little kick from cayenne and chopped jalapeno pepper.

jeannie klugh
LANCASTER, PENNSYLVANIA

This soup is so versatile. You can use leftover meatballs instead of hot dogs or fresh corn in place of frozen. Feel free to toss in any cheese blend you have on hand.

hot dog potato soup

2 cans (18.8 ounces *each*) ready-to-serve chunky baked potato with cheddar and bacon bits soup

4 hot dogs, halved lengthwise and sliced

1 cup (4 ounces) shredded cheddar-Monterey Jack cheese

1 cup frozen corn

1 cup whole milk

In a large microwave-safe bowl, combine all the ingredients. Cover and microwave on high for 8-10 minutes or until heated through, stirring every 2 minutes.

YIELD: 5 servings.

nancy tafoya
FORT COLLINS, COLORADO

My husband is not a "soup-for-dinner" kind of guy, but he loves this chunky, stick-to-your-ribs creation. I always serve it with a warm loaf of homemade bread.

italian sausage tortellini soup

1/3 pound bulk hot Italian sausage

1/3 cup chopped onion

1 garlic clove, minced

1-3/4 cups beef broth

1-1/4 cups water

3/4 cup chopped tomatoes

1/2 cup chopped green pepper

1/3 cup sliced fresh carrot

1/3 cup dry red wine *or* additional beef broth

1/3 cup tomato sauce

1/4 cup tomato paste

1/4 teaspoon dried oregano

1/4 teaspoon dried basil

3/4 cup frozen cheese tortellini

1/2 cup sliced quartered zucchini

2 tablespoons minced fresh parsley

Crumble sausage into a large saucepan; cook over medium heat until no longer pink. Remove with a slotted spoon to paper towels. In the drippings, saute the onion until tender. Add the garlic; cook 1 minute longer.

Stir in the broth, water, tomatoes, green pepper, carrot, wine, tomato sauce, tomato paste, oregano and basil. Bring to a boil. Reduce heat; simmer, uncovered, for 30 minutes.

Skim fat. Stir in the sausage, tortellini, zucchini and parsley. Cover and simmer 10-15 minutes longer or until tortellini is tender.

YIELD: 2 servings.

minestrone with italian sausage

linda reis
SALEM, OREGON

1 pound bulk Italian sausage

1 large onion, chopped

2 large carrots, chopped

2 celery ribs, chopped

1 medium leek (white portion only), chopped

1 medium zucchini, cut into 1/2-inch pieces

1/4 pound fresh green beans, trimmed and cut into 1/2-inch pieces

3 garlic cloves, minced

6 cups beef broth

2 cans (14-1/2 ounces each) diced tomatoes with basil, oregano and garlic

3 cups shredded cabbage

1 teaspoon dried basil

1 teaspoon dried oregano

1/4 teaspoon pepper

1 can (15 ounces) garbanzo beans or chickpeas, rinsed and drained

1/2 cup uncooked small pasta shells

3 tablespoons minced fresh parsley

1/3 cup grated Parmesan cheese

In a Dutch oven, cook sausage and onion over medium heat until meat is no longer pink; drain. Stir in the carrots, celery and leek; cook for 3 minutes. Add the zucchini, green beans and garlic; cook 1 minute longer.

Stir in the broth, tomatoes, cabbage, basil, oregano and pepper. Bring to a boil. Reduce heat; cover and simmer for 45 minutes.

Return to a boil. Stir in the garbanzo beans, pasta and parsley. Cook for 6-9 minutes or until pasta is tender. Serve with cheese.

YIELD: 11 servings.

I make this satisfying soup all the time because it's my dad's favorite. The recipe makes a big batch, so I often have leftovers to freeze. It tastes just as great reheated.

sharon rose brand
STAYTON, OREGON

I like to experiment with recipes to shake up the flavors. I sometimes omit the bacon and butter in this chowder, and I have used canned corn and creamed corn with good results, too. We like this with big, soft, hot pretzels instead of crackers.

versatile ham and corn chowder

8 bacon strips, cut into 1-inch pieces
1 medium onion, finely chopped
1 cup sliced celery
1/2 cup diced green pepper
3 cups cubed peeled potatoes (about 3 medium)
3 cups chicken broth
4 cups whole milk, *divided*
4 cups fresh *or* frozen whole kernel corn, *divided*
2 cups cubed fully cooked ham
2 tablespoons butter
3 tablespoons minced fresh parsley
1 teaspoon salt
1/8 teaspoon pepper
1/8 teaspoon hot pepper sauce, optional

In a large saucepan, cook bacon until crisp. Remove bacon to paper towel to drain, reserving 1/4 cup drippings in pan. Saute the onion, celery and green pepper in drippings for 5 minutes. Add potatoes and broth. Reduce heat; cover and simmer for 10 minutes.

Place 1/2 cup milk and 2 cups corn in a blender; cover and process until pureed. Pour into saucepan. Add the ham and remaining corn; simmer for 10 minutes or until the vegetables are tender. Stir in the butter, parsley, salt, pepper, pepper sauce if desired and remaining milk; heat through. Garnish with bacon.

YIELD: 10-12 servings.

sausage cabbage soup

1 medium onion, chopped
1 tablespoon canola oil
1 tablespoon butter
2 medium carrots, thinly sliced and halved
1 celery rib, thinly sliced
1 teaspoon caraway seeds
2 cups water
2 cups chopped cabbage
1/2 pound fully cooked smoked kielbasa or Polish sausage, halved and cut into 1/4-inch slices
1 can (14-1/2 ounces) diced tomatoes, undrained
1 tablespoon brown sugar
1 can (15 ounces) white kidney beans, rinsed and drained
1 tablespoon white vinegar
1 teaspoon salt
1/4 teaspoon pepper
Minced fresh parsley

In a 3-qt. saucepan, saute onion in oil and butter until tender. Add carrots and celery; saute for 3 minutes. Add caraway; cook and stir 1 minute longer. Stir in the water, cabbage, sausage, tomatoes and brown sugar; bring to a boil. Reduce heat; cover and simmer for 15-20 minutes or until vegetables are tender.

Add the beans, vinegar, salt and pepper. Simmer, uncovered, for 5-10 minutes or until heated through. Sprinkle with parsley.

YIELD: 6 servings.

stella garrett
ORLANDO, FLORIDA

My family often requests this satisfying soup. I serve it for lunch or as a cold-weather Sunday supper. It adds to a delicious, balanced meal with a tossed green salad and a crusty loaf of bread.

stir-fried pork soup

2/3 pound boneless pork loin, cut into thin strips
1 cup sliced fresh mushrooms
1 cup chopped celery
1/2 cup diced carrots
2 tablespoons canola oil
6 cups chicken broth
1/2 cup chopped fresh spinach
2 tablespoons cornstarch
3 tablespoons cold water
1 egg, lightly beaten
Pepper to taste

In a 3-qt. saucepan, stir fry pork, mushrooms, celery and carrots in oil until the pork is browned and vegetables are tender. Add broth and spinach.

Combine cornstarch and water to make a thin paste; stir into soup. Return to a boil; boil for 1 minute. Quickly stir in the egg. Add the pepper. Serve immediately.

YIELD: 4-6 servings.

louise johnson
HARRIMAN, TENNESSEE

Are you a fan of Asian cuisine? Then you will love my stir-fried soup starring pork. Serve it with fried noodles or rice.

italian zucchini soup

1 pound bulk Italian sausage
1 cup chopped onion
2 cups chopped celery
1 medium green pepper, chopped
2 to 4 tablespoons sugar
2 teaspoons salt
1/2 teaspoon dried basil
1/2 teaspoon dried oregano
1/2 teaspoon pepper
4 cups diced tomatoes, undrained
4 cups diced zucchini
Grated Parmesan cheese, optional

In a Dutch oven, brown sausage with onion; drain excess fat. Add the next eight ingredients; cover and simmer 1 hour. Stir in the zucchini and simmer 10 minutes. Sprinkle with cheese if desired.

YIELD: 8 servings.

clara mae chambers
SUPERIOR, NEBRASKA

My neighbor gave me her cherished recipe for Italian zucchini soup. Quick and simple, it's a great way to enjoy an abundance of fresh garden veggies.

joyce lulewicz
BRUNSWICK, OHIO

My hubby's grandmother used to make her own homemade sausage and tortellini for her tortellini soup. Even though I don't make those ingredients from scratch, folks love mine just as much!

classic tortellini soup

- 1/2 pound bulk Italian sausage
- 1 small onion, thinly sliced
- 1 garlic clove, minced
- 1 can (14-1/2 ounces) reduced-sodium chicken broth
- 1/2 cup water
- 1-1/2 cups torn fresh spinach
- 3/4 cup refrigerated cheese tortellini
- 2 tablespoons shredded Parmesan cheese

In a small saucepan, cook sausage over medium heat until no longer pink; drain. Add onion; cook and stir until tender. Add garlic; cook 1 minute longer. Stir in broth and water; bring to a boil. Reduce heat; simmer, uncovered, for 10 minutes.

Return to a boil. Reduce heat, add spinach and tortellini; cook for 7-9 minutes or until tortellini is tender. Sprinkle with cheese.

YIELD: 2 servings.

laurie todd
COLUMBUS, MISSISSIPPI

This old-fashioned favorite is a snap to make, and it's economical, too. Carrots, celery and onion accent the subtle flavor of the split peas, while a ham bone adds a meaty touch. It's sure to replace autumn's chill with a much cozier feeling.

split pea soup

- 1 package (16 ounces) dried green split peas
- 1 meaty ham bone
- 1 large onion, chopped
- 1 teaspoon salt
- 1/2 teaspoon pepper
- 1/2 teaspoon dried thyme
- 1 bay leaf
- 1 cup chopped carrot
- 1 cup chopped celery

Sort peas and rinse with cold water. Place peas in a Dutch oven; add water to cover by 2 in. Bring to a boil; boil for 2 minutes. Remove from heat; cover and let stand for 1 to 4 hours or until peas are softened. Drain and rinse peas, discarding liquid.

Return peas to Dutch oven. Add 2-1/2 qts. water, ham bone, onion, salt, pepper, thyme and bay leaf. Bring to a boil. Reduce heat; cover and simmer for 1-1/2 hours, stirring occasionally.

Remove the ham bone; when cool enough to handle, remove meat from bone. Discard bone; dice meat and return to soup. Add carrots and celery. Simmer, uncovered, for 45-60 minutes or until soup reaches desired thickness and the vegetables are tender. Discard bay leaf.

YIELD: 10 servings.

pasta sausage soup

1-1/2 pounds hot *or* sweet Italian
    sausage links
1 medium onion, chopped
1 medium green pepper, cut into strips
1 garlic clove, minced
1 can (28 ounces) diced tomatoes,
    undrained
6 cups water
2 to 2-1/2 cups uncooked bow tie pasta
1 tablespoon sugar
1 tablespoon Worcestershire sauce
2 teaspoons chicken bouillon granules
1 teaspoon salt
1 teaspoon dried basil
1 teaspoon dried thyme

Remove casings from sausage; cut into 1-in. pieces.
In a Dutch oven, brown sausage over medium heat.
Remove sausage with a slotted spoon; drain,
reserving 2 tablespoons drippings. Saute onion and
green pepper in drippings until tender. Add garlic;
cook 1 minute longer.

    Return sausages to the pan; stir in the remaining
ingredients. Bring to a boil. Reduce heat. Simmer,
uncovered, for 15-20 minutes or until pasta is
tender, stirring occasionally.

YIELD: 12 servings.

alice rabe
BEEMER, NEBRASKA

*We have a few amazing
sausage makers in our
town, so this soup often
makes an appearance on
my menus. It has a rich
flavor and is even tastier
the next day. If you are
unable to find bow tie
pasta, you can substitute
another macaroni product.*

janice thompson

LANSING, MICHIGAN

A little bit of this thick and hearty soup goes a long way, so it's terrific to take to potlucks. Be sure to bring copies of the recipe, too!

hearty meatball soup

2 eggs
1 cup soft bread crumbs
1 teaspoon salt
1/2 teaspoon pepper
1 pound lean ground beef (90% lean)
1 pound ground pork
1/2 pound ground turkey
4 cups beef broth
1 can (46 ounces) tomato juice
2 cans (14-1/2 ounces *each*)
    stewed tomatoes
8 cups shredded cabbage
1 cup thinly sliced celery
1 cup thinly sliced carrots
8 green onions, sliced
3/4 cup uncooked long grain rice

2 teaspoons dried basil
3 tablespoons minced fresh parsley
2 tablespoons soy sauce

In a large bowl, combine the eggs, bread crumbs, salt and pepper. Crumble meat over mixture and mix well. Shape into 1-in. balls.

In a stockpot, bring broth to a boil. Carefully add the meatballs. Add the tomato juice, tomatoes, vegetables, rice and basil. Bring to a boil. Reduce heat; cover and simmer for 30 minutes.

Add the parsley and soy sauce. Simmer, uncovered, for 10 minutes or until meatballs are no longer pink and vegetables are tender.

YIELD: 22 servings.

ham 'n' chickpea soup

1/2 cup uncooked orzo pasta
1 small onion, chopped
2 teaspoons canola oil
1 cup cubed fully cooked lean ham
2 garlic cloves, minced

1 teaspoon dried rosemary, crushed
1 teaspoon rubbed sage
2 cups reduced-sodium beef broth
1 can (14-1/2 ounces) diced tomatoes, undrained
1 can (15 ounces) chickpeas or garbanzo beans, rinsed and drained
4 tablespoons shredded Parmesan cheese
1 tablespoon minced fresh parsley

Cook orzo according to the the package directions. Meanwhile, in a large saucepan, saute onion in oil for 3 minutes. Add the ham, garlic, rosemary and sage; saute 1 minute longer. Stir in the broth and tomatoes. Bring to a boil. Reduce heat; simmer, uncovered, for 10 minutes.

Drain orzo; stir into the soup. Add chickpeas; heat through. Sprinkle each serving with the cheese and parsley.

YIELD: 4 servings.

linda arnold
EDMONTON, ALBERTA

Swimming with ham, vegetables, chickpeas and orzo pasta, my special soup is loaded with good-for-you ingredients and mouthwatering flavor.

chickpeas

Chickpeas (also known as garbanzo beans) have a delicious nutlike taste and a buttery texture. They provide a concentrated source of protein that can be enjoyed year-round and are available either dried or canned.

italian sausage orzo soup

1/4 pound bulk Italian sausage
1/2 cup sliced fresh mushrooms
1/2 cup sliced zucchini
1/4 cup chopped onion
1 teaspoon olive oil
1 garlic clove, minced
1-1/4 cups reduced-sodium chicken broth
1 cup canned diced tomatoes, undrained
1/2 teaspoon dried basil
1/8 teaspoon pepper
3 tablespoons uncooked orzo or small shell pasta
1 tablespoon minced fresh parsley

In a large saucepan, cook the sausage, mushrooms, zucchini and onion in oil over medium heat until meat is no longer pink; drain. Add garlic; cook 1 minute longer. Add the broth, tomatoes, basil and pepper. Bring to a boil. Stir in pasta. Reduce heat; cover and simmer for 15-20 minutes or until pasta is tender. Sprinkle with parsley.

YIELD: 2 servings.

deborah redfield
BUENA PARK, CALIFORNIA

I always look for recipes high in taste and nutrition but low on prep time and fat. This chunky soup fits the bill and is such a family favorite that I serve it at least once a month!

deborah amrine
FORT MYERS, FLORIDA

I created my special bean soup to warm my family up on chilly winter days when we lived along the shore of Lake Michigan. We've since moved to Florida—but my gang still can't get enough!

shaker bean soup

1 pound dried great northern beans
1 meaty ham bone *or* 2 smoked
   ham hocks
8 cups water
1 large onion, chopped
3 celery ribs, diced
2 medium carrots, shredded
Salt to taste
1/2 teaspoon pepper
1/2 teaspoon dried thyme
1 can (28 ounces) crushed tomatoes
   in puree
2 tablespoons brown sugar
1-1/2 cups finely shredded fresh spinach

Sort and rinse beans. Place in a Dutch oven; cover with water and bring to a boil. Boil 2 minutes. Remove from heat; let stand 1 hour. Drain beans and discard liquid.

In the same pan, add the ham bone, water and beans. Bring to a boil. Reduce heat; cover and simmer for 1-1/2 hours or until meat easily falls from the bone.

Remove bone from broth; cool. Trim the meat from the bone. Discard the bone. Add the ham, onion, celery, carrots, salt, pepper and thyme to bean mixture. Cover and simmer for 1 hour or until the beans are tender.

Add the tomatoes and brown sugar. Cook for 10 minutes. Just before serving, add spinach.

YIELD: 20 servings.

onion soup with sausage

sundra hauck
BOGALUSA, LOUISIANA

With a yummy slice of mozzarella cheese bread on top, this hearty broth makes an impressive luncheon or light supper. It looks great and tastes simply wonderful.

1/2 pound pork sausage links, cut into
   1/2-inch pieces
1 pound sliced fresh mushrooms
1 cup sliced onion
2 cans (14-1/2 ounces *each*) beef broth
4 slices Italian bread
1/2 cup shredded part-skim mozzarella
   cheese

In a large saucepan, cook sausage over medium heat until no longer pink; drain. Add mushrooms and onion; cook for 4-6 minutes or until tender. Stir in the broth. Bring to a boil. Reduce heat; simmer, uncovered, for 4-6 minutes or until heated through.

Ladle into four 2-cup ovenproof bowls. Top each with a slice of bread; sprinkle with cheese. Broil until cheese is melted.

YIELD: 4 servings.

sausage wild rice soup

9 cups water, *divided*

1 cup uncooked wild rice

2 pounds bulk Italian sausage

2 large onions, chopped

2 teaspoons olive oil

6 garlic cloves, minced

3 cartons (32 ounces *each*) chicken broth

1 can (28 ounces) diced tomatoes, undrained

1 can (6 ounces) tomato paste

2 teaspoons dried basil

2 teaspoons dried oregano

1 package (6 ounces) fresh baby spinach, coarsely chopped

1/2 teaspoon salt

1/2 teaspoon pepper

In a large saucepan, bring 3 cups water to a boil. Stir in rice. Reduce heat; cover and simmer for 55-60 minutes or until tender.

Meanwhile, in a stockpot, cook sausage over medium heat until no longer pink; drain. Remove and set aside. In the same pan, saute onions in oil until tender. Add garlic; cook 1 minute longer. Stir in the broth, tomatoes, tomato paste, basil, oregano and remaining water. Return sausage to the pan. Bring to a boil. Reduce heat; simmer, uncovered, for 20 minutes.

Stir in the spinach, salt, pepper and wild rice; heat through.

YIELD: 13 servings.

tonya schaffer
HURON, SOUTH DAKOTA

Here's a recipe that yields a big batch. I often divide leftovers into containers to freeze for future meals or to pull out when I'm called upon to bring a dish to a party or church supper.

bacon veggie chowder

sheena hoffman
NORTH VANCOUVER,
BRITISH COLUMBIA

When the temperature tumbles, I whip up comfort foods like my bacon veggie chowder. It's easy to prepare, and the aroma makes mouths water.

4 bacon strips, diced
1/2 cup chopped onion
2 medium red potatoes, cubed
2 small carrots, halved lengthwise and thinly sliced
1 cup water
1-1/2 teaspoons chicken bouillon granules
2 cups whole milk
1-1/3 cups frozen corn
1/4 teaspoon pepper
2 tablespoons all-purpose flour
1/4 cup cold water
1-1/4 cups shredded cheddar cheese

In a large saucepan, cook bacon over medium heat until crisp. Remove to paper towels with a slotted spoon; drain, reserving 2 teaspoons drippings. Saute onion in drippings until tender. Add the potatoes, carrots, water and bouillon. Bring to a boil. Reduce heat; cover and simmer for 15-20 minutes or until the vegetables are almost tender.

Stir in the milk, corn and pepper. Cook 5 minutes longer. Combine flour and cold water until smooth; gradually stir into soup. Bring to a boil; cook and stir for 1-2 minutes or until thickened. Remove from the heat; stir in the cheese until melted. Sprinkle with the bacon.

YIELD: 4 servings.

ham 'n' swiss soup

4-1/2 teaspoons butter
4-1/2 teaspoons all-purpose flour
  1 can (14-1/2 ounces) reduced-sodium chicken broth
  1 cup chopped broccoli
  2 tablespoons chopped onion
  1 cup cubed fully cooked ham
1/2 cup heavy whipping cream
1/8 teaspoon dried thyme
3/4 cup shredded Swiss cheese

In a large saucepan, melt butter; stir in flour until smooth; gradually add broth. Bring to a boil; cook and stir for 2 minutes or until thickened. Add broccoli and onion; cook and stir until crisp-tender. Add the ham, cream and thyme; heat through. Stir in the cheese until melted.

YIELD: 2 servings.

taste of home test kitchen
GREENDALE, WISCONSIN

Loaded with ham and broccoli, our flavorful soup is sure to warm spirits. Add buttermilk biscuits and a simple spinach salad for a complete meal.

sausage potato soup

1/2 pound smoked kielbasa, diced
  6 medium potatoes, peeled and cubed
  2 cups frozen corn
1-1/2 cups chicken broth
  1 celery rib, sliced
1/4 cup sliced carrot
1/2 teaspoon garlic powder
1/2 teaspoon onion powder
1/2 teaspoon salt
1/4 teaspoon pepper
1-1/2 cups whole milk
2/3 cup shredded cheddar cheese
  1 teaspoon minced fresh parsley

In a large saucepan, brown the sausage; drain. Set the sausage aside. In the same pan, combine the potatoes, corn, broth, celery, carrot and seasonings. Bring to a boil.

Reduce heat; cover and simmer for 15 minutes or until vegetables are tender. Add the milk, cheese, parsley and sausage. Cook and stir over low heat until cheese is melted and soup is heated through.

YIELD: 6 servings.

jennifer lefevre
HESSTON, KANSAS

After a full day of teaching and coaching, I'm often too tired to spend a lot of time preparing dinner. So I rely on this thick, chunky blend that I can have on the table in 30 minutes. We all enjoy the flavor of the smoked sausage.

ham and bean soup

3/4 pound fully cooked ham, cubed
  1 medium onion, chopped
  2 garlic cloves, minced
  2 tablespoons butter
  2 cans (15-1/2 ounces *each*) great northern beans, rinsed and drained

  3 cups chicken broth
  2 cups water
  1 cup diced peeled potatoes
3/4 cup diced carrots
3/4 cup diced celery
1/4 teaspoon pepper
1/2 cup frozen peas
  2 tablespoons minced fresh parsley

In a large saucepan, saute the ham, onion and garlic in butter until the onion is tender. Add the next seven ingredients; cover and simmer for 30 minutes or until vegetables are tender. Add peas and cook for 5 minutes longer or until heated through. Stir in the parsley.

YIELD: 8 servings.

mary detweiler
MIDDLEFIELD, OHIO

I spent many years as a restaurant cook, and this was hands down our best-selling soup. One taste and your family will agree it's a winner!

linda lohr
LITITZ, PENNSYLVANIA

Our county is proud to boast a rich German heritage. Dishes that include sauerkraut, potatoes and sausage are famous around here. I simmer up this slow-cooked specialty as soon as winter arrives.

sauerkraut

Did you know that sauerkraut is an excellent source of fiber and other essential nutrients, including iron, vitamin K and vitamin C? In fact, in the 18th century, sailors ate sauerkraut on long voyages to prevent scurvy, a disease caused by vitamin C deficiency.

slow-cooked sauerkraut soup

- 1 medium potato, cut into 1/4-inch cubes
- 1 pound smoked kielbasa, cut into 1/2-inch cubes
- 1 can (32 ounces) sauerkraut, rinsed and well drained
- 4 cups chicken broth
- 1 can (10-3/4 ounces) condensed cream of mushroom soup, undiluted
- 1/2 pound fresh mushrooms, sliced
- 1 cup cubed cooked chicken
- 2 medium carrots, cut into 1/4-inch slices
- 2 celery ribs, sliced
- 2 tablespoons white vinegar
- 2 teaspoons dill weed
- 1/2 teaspoon pepper
- 3 to 4 bacon strips, cooked and crumbled

In a 5-qt. slow cooker, combine the first 12 ingredients. Cover and cook on high for 5-6 hours or until the vegetables are tender. Skim fat. Garnish with bacon.

YIELD: 10-12 servings.

dave bock
AUBURN, WASHINGTON

I concocted this hefty and full-flavored meal-in-a-bowl one cool autumn day. It's a fast and fuss-free family favorite!

vegetable pork soup

- 1 boneless pork loin chop (4 ounces), cut into 1/2-inch cubes
- 1/4 pound smoked kielbasa *or* Polish sausage, chopped
- 1/4 cup chopped onion
- 1 celery rib, chopped
- 1 small carrot, chopped
- 1 teaspoon butter
- 1 garlic clove, minced
- 1/4 teaspoon paprika
- 2 cups reduced-sodium chicken broth
- 1 small tart apple, chopped
- 1 small red potato, chopped
- 1/4 teaspoon Chinese five-spice powder
- 1 teaspoon honey

In a large saucepan, cook the pork, sausage, onion, celery and carrot in butter over medium-high heat for 5 minutes or until pork is no longer pink and vegetables are tender. Add garlic and paprika; cook 1 minute longer.

Stir in the broth, apple, potato and five-spice powder. Bring to a boil. Reduce the heat; cover and simmer for 12-15 minutes or until the pork is tender. Stir in the honey; cook for 2 minutes or until heated through.

YIELD: 4 servings.

creamy cauliflower and bacon soup

1 medium head cauliflower (2 pounds),
  cut into florets
2 cups half-and-half cream, *divided*
1/2 cup shredded Asiago cheese
1/2 teaspoon salt
1/2 teaspoon ground nutmeg
1/8 teaspoon pepper
1/2 to 1 cup water
4 bacon strips, cooked and crumbled

Place cauliflower in a steamer basket; place in a large saucepan over 1 in. of water. Bring to a boil; cover and steam for 8-10 minutes or until tender. Cool slightly.

Place cauliflower and 1/2 cup cream in a food processor; cover and process until pureed. Transfer to a large saucepan.

Stir in the cheese, salt, nutmeg, pepper and remaining cream. Add enough water to reach desired consistency; heat through. Sprinkle each serving with bacon.

YIELD: 4 servings.

mildred caruso
BRIGHTON, TENNESSEE

You won't need to serve a lot of side dishes with my rich soup because it's filling all on its own. For a simple garnish, add a drop of hot sauce to the top and swirl it with a butter knife to blend.

ham 'n' veggie soup

barbara thompson
LANSDALE, PENNSYLVANIA

The addition of ham to this veggie-filled broth makes the colorful dish a complete meal.

1 medium onion, thinly sliced and separated into rings

1 medium zucchini, cubed

1 tablespoon olive oil

1 pound sliced fresh mushrooms

3 cups fresh *or* frozen corn

3 cups cubed fully cooked ham

6 medium tomatoes, peeled, seeded and chopped

1/2 cup chicken broth

1-1/2 teaspoons salt

1/2 teaspoon garlic powder

1/2 teaspoon pepper

Shredded part-skim mozzarella cheese

In a large saucepan, saute onion and zucchini in oil for 5 minutes or until onion is tender. Add the mushrooms, corn and ham; cook and stir for 5 minutes.

Stir in the tomatoes, broth, salt, garlic powder and pepper. Bring to a boil. Reduce heat; cover and simmer for 5 minutes. Uncover; simmer 5-8 minutes longer. Garnish with mozzarella cheese.

YIELD: 8-10 servings.

baked potato soup

4 large baking potatoes
(about 2-3/4 pounds)
2/3 cup butter
2/3 cup all-purpose flour
3/4 teaspoon salt
1/4 teaspoon white pepper
6 cups milk
1 cup (8 ounces) sour cream
1/4 cup thinly sliced green onions
10 bacon strips, cooked and crumbled
1 cup (4 ounces) shredded cheddar
cheese

Bake potatoes at 350° for 65-75 minutes or until tender; cool completely. Peel and cube potatoes.

In a large saucepan, melt butter; stir in flour, salt and pepper until smooth. Gradually add milk. Bring to a boil; cook and stir for 2 minutes or until thickened. Remove from the heat; whisk in sour cream. Add potatoes and green onions. Garnish with bacon and cheese.

YIELD: 10 servings.

joann goetz
GENOA, OHIO

My husband and I enjoyed a delicious potato soup at a restaurant while on vacation, and I came home determined to duplicate it. It took me five years to get the taste just right!

creamed cabbage soup

2 cans (14-1/2 ounces *each*)
chicken broth
2 celery ribs, chopped
1 medium head cabbage
(3 pounds) , shredded
1 medium onion, chopped
1 medium carrot, chopped
1/4 cup butter
3 tablespoons all-purpose flour
1 teaspoon salt
1/4 teaspoon pepper
2 cups half-and-half cream
1 cup whole milk
2 cups cubed fully cooked ham
1/2 teaspoon dried thyme
Minced fresh parsley

In a large Dutch oven, combine the broth, celery, cabbage, onion and carrot; bring to a boil. Reduce heat; cover and simmer for 15-20 minutes or until vegetables are tender.

Meanwhile, melt butter in a small saucepan. Stir in the flour, salt and pepper until blended. Combine cream and milk; gradually add to flour mixture. Bring to a boil; cook and stir for 2 minutes or until thickened. Gradually stir into vegetable mixture. Add the ham and thyme and heat through. Garnish with parsley.

YIELD: 8-10 servings.

laurie harms
GRINNELL, IOWA

My favorite summer activity is to plant my own vegetables, watch them grow, and add them to delicious recipes like my cabbage soup.

sausage chicken soup

3/4 pound boneless skinless chicken
breasts
2 medium potatoes, peeled and cut into
1/4-inch cubes
1 can (14-1/2 ounces) chicken broth
1 medium onion, diced
1 medium sweet red pepper, diced
1 medium green pepper, diced
1 garlic clove, minced
3/4 cup picante sauce
3 tablespoons all-purpose flour
3 tablespoons water
1/2 pound smoked sausage, diced
Sliced habanero peppers, optional

Place chicken in a greased microwave-safe dish. Cover and microwave on high for 3-6 minutes or until a meat thermometer reads 170°, turning every 2 minutes. Cut into cubes; set aside.

Place the potatoes and broth in a 2-1/2-qt. microwave-safe bowl. Cover and microwave on high for 3-1/2 minutes. Add the onion, peppers and garlic; cook 3-1/2 minutes longer or until potatoes are tender. Stir in the picante sauce.

In a small bowl, combine flour and water until smooth. Gradually add to potato mixture. Cover and cook on high for 2-3 minutes or until thickened. Add chicken and sausage; cook 1-2 minutes longer or until heated through. Sprinkle with habaneros if desired.

YIELD: 6 servings.

EDITOR'S NOTE: This recipe was tested in a 1,100-watt microwave.

helen macdonald
LAZO, BRITISH COLUMBIA

I've been making this satisfying soup for years and still see my hubby's eyes light up whenever I set it on the table. It's loaded with slices of smoked sausage, chunks of chicken, fresh peppers and hearty potatoes.

marcia wolff
ROLLING PRAIRIE, INDIANA

A good friend brought samples of her kielbasa soup to a tasting class sponsored by our local homemakers club. The mixture of sausage, apples and vegetables creates an unexpected, enticing flavor combination.

kielbasa cabbage soup

- 3 cups coleslaw mix
- 2 medium carrots, chopped
- 1/2 cup chopped onion
- 1/2 cup chopped celery
- 1/2 teaspoon caraway seeds
- 2 tablespoons butter
- 1 carton (32 ounces) chicken broth
- 3/4 to 1 pound smoked kielbasa *or* Polish sausage, cut into 1/2-inch pieces
- 2 medium unpeeled Golden Delicious apples, chopped
- 1/4 teaspoon pepper
- 1/8 teaspoon salt

In a large saucepan, saute the coleslaw mix, carrots, onion, celery and caraway seeds in butter for

5-8 minutes or until vegetables are crisp-tender. Stir in the remaining ingredients.

Bring to a boil. Reduce heat; simmer, uncovered, for 20-30 minutes, stirring occasionally.

YIELD: 6 servings.

heather persch
HUDSONVILLE, MICHIGAN

I'm always searching for new and interesting soup recipes. I came across this gem in a church cookbook and changed up a few ingredients to perfect the flavor for my family.

sausage tortellini soup

- 1 pound bulk Italian sausage
- 2 cups water
- 2 cups chopped cabbage
- 1 can (14-1/2 ounces) Italian stewed tomatoes, undrained and cut up
- 1 can (14-1/2 ounces) beef broth
- 1 can (10-1/2 ounces) condensed French onion soup
- 1 package (9 ounces) refrigerated cheese tortellini
- 1/2 cup grated Parmesan cheese

In a large saucepan, cook sausage over medium heat until no longer pink; drain. Stir in the water, cabbage, tomatoes, broth and soup. Bring to a boil. Reduce heat; simmer, uncovered, for 8 minutes. Stir in tortellini; cook 7-9 minutes longer or until pasta is tender. Sprinkle with cheese.

YIELD: 10 servings.

smoked sausage soup

2 cups chopped onions

2 tablespoons butter

2 cups cubed cooked chicken

1 pound smoked sausage,
  cut into bite-size pieces

3 cups sliced celery

3 cups sliced summer squash

2 cups chicken broth

1 can (8 ounces) tomato sauce

1/4 cup minced fresh parsley

2 tablespoons cornstarch

2 tablespoons poultry seasoning

1 teaspoon dried oregano

1 teaspoon ground cumin

1 teaspoon Liquid Smoke, optional

1/2 teaspoon pepper

In a small skillet, saute onions in butter until tender.
Transfer to a 3-qt. slow cooker. Stir in the remaining
ingredients. Cook on high for 5-6 hours or until the
vegetables are tender.

YIELD: 6-8 servings.

rachel lyn grasmick
ROCKY FORD, COLORADO

*My rich soup is packed
with vegetables, sausage
and chicken. I guarantee
that, bite after bite, it's
unlike any soup you've
ever tasted.*

beef and sausage soup

darlene dickinson

LEBEC, CALIFORNIA

Folks enjoy my beef and sausage soup. Whenever I bring it to a potluck or church supper, I never leave without sharing the recipe!

  1 pound beef stew meat, cut into 1/2-inch cubes
  1 tablespoon canola oil
  1 pound bulk Italian sausage, shaped into balls
  1 can (28 ounces) diced tomatoes, undrained
3-1/2 cups water
  1 cup chopped onion
  1 tablespoon Worcestershire sauce
  1 teaspoon salt
1/2 teaspoon Italian seasoning
  2 cups cubed peeled potatoes
  1 cup sliced celery

In a Dutch oven over medium-high heat, brown beef in oil on all sides. Remove with a slotted spoon and set aside. Brown sausage on all sides; drain. Return beef to the pan. Add the tomatoes, water, onion and seasonings. Bring to a boil. Reduce heat; cover and simmer for 1-1/2 hours or until the beef is tender. Add the potatoes and celery. Cover and simmer for 30 minutes or until vegetables are tender.

YIELD: 6-8 servings.

hearty corn chowder

1/2 pound sliced bacon
1 cup chopped celery
1/2 cup chopped onion
2 cups cubed peeled potatoes
1 cup water
2 cups frozen corn
1 can (14-3/4 ounces) cream-style corn
1 can (12 ounces) evaporated milk
6 ounces smoked sausage links, cut into
   1/4-inch slices
1 teaspoon dill weed

In a large saucepan, cook bacon over medium heat until crisp. Remove to paper towels with a slotted spoon; drain, reserving 2 tablespoons drippings. Crumble bacon and set aside.

Saute celery and onion in drippings until onion is lightly browned. Add potatoes and water. Cover and cook over medium heat for 10 minutes. Stir in corn, milk, sausage, dill and bacon. Cook until potatoes are tender, about 30 minutes.

YIELD: 4-6 servings.

mark twiest
ALLENDALE, MICHIGAN

Everyone in my wife's family is a corn lover, so her mom devised this chowder to satisfy their appetites. You can also add chicken if you like.

bacon

Use kitchen shears to easily slice uncooked bacon. Always check the date stamp on packages of vacuum-sealed bacon to make sure it's fresh. The date reflects the last date of sale. Once the package is opened, bacon should be used within a week. For long-term storage, freeze bacon for up to 1 month.

mexican leek soup

1 can (15 ounces) pinto beans, rinsed
   and drained
2 medium leeks (white portion only),
   chopped
1/2 cup water
3/4 cup coarsely chopped fresh spinach
1 cup (4 ounces) shredded cheddar
   cheese
2 tablespoons grated Parmesan cheese
2 tablespoons grated Romano cheese
1/2 teaspoon ground cumin
1/2 teaspoon coarsely ground pepper
1/4 teaspoon cayenne pepper
1/8 teaspoon salt
1/4 cup heavy whipping cream
1/4 cup french-fried onions
2 bacon strips, cooked and crumbled

Place the beans, leeks and water in a 1-qt. microwave-safe bowl. Cover and microwave on high for 4-5 minutes or until tender.

In a blender, process bean mixture and spinach until smooth. Return to the bowl; add cheeses and seasonings. Whisk in cream. Cover and cook for 2-3 minutes or until heated through, stirring once. Sprinkle with onions and bacon.

YIELD: 2 servings.

donna ahnert
SCOTIA, NEW YORK

You can enjoy my south-of-the-border creation morning, noon or night. Add a fried egg on top for breakfast or a generous splash of hot sauce for a spicy lunch or dinner.

marilyn lee
MANHATTAN, KANSAS

I tasted a sausage tomato soup at a local restaurant. So when I came across a similar recipe, I made a few easy changes to create my own yummy version.

italian sausage

Not sure if a recipe calling for Italian sausage means sweet or hot? Any Taste of Home recipe that calls for Italian sausage always refers to sweet Italian sausage. Recipes using hot Italian sausage specifically call for that type.

sausage tomato soup

1/2 pound bulk Italian sausage
1 medium onion, chopped
1 small green pepper, chopped
1 can (28 ounces) diced tomatoes, undrained
1 can (14-1/2 ounces) beef broth
1 can (8 ounces) tomato sauce
1/2 cup picante sauce
1-1/2 teaspoons sugar
1 teaspoon dried basil
1/2 teaspoon dried oregano
1/2 to 3/4 cup shredded part-skim mozzarella cheese

In a saucepan, cook the sausage, onion and green pepper over medium heat until meat is no longer pink; drain. Stir in the tomatoes, broth, tomato sauce, picante sauce, sugar, basil and oregano. Bring to a boil. Reduce heat; cover and simmer for 10 minutes. Sprinkle with cheese.

YIELD: 6 servings.

erin walstead
ORANGE, CALIFORNIA

Here's a black-eyed pea soup that is delicious and requires little fuss. After one taste, it will become one of your favorites.

easy black-eyed pea soup

3 bacon strips, diced
1 medium onion, finely chopped
1 garlic clove, minced
2 cans (14-1/2 ounces each) beef broth
1 can (10 ounces) diced tomatoes and green chilies, undrained
1/4 teaspoon salt
1/4 teaspoon pepper
2 cans (15-1/2 ounces each) black-eyed peas, rinsed and drained

In a large saucepan, cook bacon over medium heat until crisp. Using a slotted spoon, remove to paper towels to drain.

In the drippings, saute onion until tender. Add garlic; cook 1 minute longer. Stir in the broth, tomatoes, salt and pepper. Bring to a boil. Stir in black-eyed peas and bacon; heat through.

YIELD: 6 servings.

tortellini soup

2 packages (7 ounces *each*) pork breakfast sausage links

2 cans (14-1/2 ounces *each*) Italian stewed tomatoes

2 cups water

1 cup chopped onion

1/2 cup chopped celery

1 garlic clove, minced

1 teaspoon dried oregano

1/8 to 1/4 teaspoon cayenne pepper

1/8 to 1/4 teaspoon hot pepper sauce

1 bay leaf

3/4 cup refrigerated tortellini

In a 3-qt. saucepan, brown sausage; drain and cut into bite-size pieces. Return to pan; stir in the next nine ingredients.

Bring to a boil. Reduce heat; simmer, uncovered, for 15 minutes. Add tortellini. Bring to a boil. Reduce heat; simmer, uncovered, for 5 minutes or until pasta is tender. Discard bay leaf.

YIELD: 8 servings.

karen shiveley
SPRINGFIELD, MINNESOTA

My rich and spicy tortellini soup brings a little Italian flair to the table. You won't believe how easy it is to make.

sauerkraut sausage soup

yvonne kett
APPLETON, WISCONSIN

My husband and I make our own sauerkraut and grow many of the veggies that star in this easy slow cooker soup. It cooks all day and smells delicious when we come home from a long day at work.

4 cups chicken broth
1 pound smoked Polish sausage, cut into 1/2-inch slices
1 can (16 ounces) sauerkraut, rinsed and well drained
2 cups sliced fresh mushrooms
1-1/2 cups cubed peeled potatoes
1 can (10-3/4 ounces) condensed cream of mushroom soup, undiluted
1-1/4 cups chopped onions
2 large carrots, sliced

2 celery ribs, chopped
2 tablespoons white vinegar
2 teaspoons dill weed
1 teaspoon sugar
1/4 teaspoon pepper

In a 5-qt. slow cooker, combine all the ingredients. Cover and cook on low for 5-6 hours or until the vegetables are tender.

YIELD: 10 servings.

hearty black-eyed pea soup

1/4 cup sliced celery
1/4 cup chopped onion
1-1/2 teaspoons butter
1 can (15-1/2 ounces) black-eyed peas, rinsed and drained
1 cup water
3/4 cup Italian stewed tomatoes, cut up
1/2 cup cubed fully cooked ham
1/2 teaspoon Italian seasoning
1/8 teaspoon pepper
Pinch salt

In a large saucepan, saute celery and onion in butter until tender. Add the peas, water and tomatoes. Bring to a boil. Stir in the ham, Italian seasoning, pepper and salt. Reduce heat; simmer, uncovered, for 20 minutes or until heated through.

YIELD: 2 servings.

yvonne peterson
MOUNTAIN VIEW, MISSOURI

This recipe for black-eyed pea soup will be one you go back to again and again. Omit the cubed ham to make it meatless.

sausage mushroom soup

1 pound bulk Italian sausage
2 cans (14-1/2 ounces *each*) beef broth
2 jars (4-1/2 ounces *each*) sliced mushrooms
1 cup finely chopped celery
1/2 cup quick-cooking barley
1/3 cup shredded carrot

In a large saucepan, cook sausage over medium heat until no longer pink; drain. Add the remaining ingredients. Bring to a boil. Reduce heat; cover and simmer for 10 minutes or until the vegetables and barley are tender.

YIELD: 6 servings.

twila maxwell
FORT MYERS, FLORIDA

My easy sausage soup is a breeze to make. It calls for only six ingredients and takes less than half an hour from preparation to dinner table.

barley

Barley absorbs a lot of soup broth. If you like barley in your soup but the leftovers are too thick, add extra chicken, beef or vegetable broth to the extras while reheating to achieve desired consistency.

beverlee deberry

HEMPSTEAD, TEXAS

Here's a delicious soup that won't leave you hungry. Combined with a loaf of French bread, it's a complete meal.

🥄 **peeling potatoes**

Cut potatoes in half before you peel them. This way, you'll know if one has gone bad and should be discarded before you spend time peeling the entire potato.

rebecca clark

HAMMOND, LOUISIANA

I created this recipe years ago when I had a surplus of fresh sweet corn. The soup is easy to make and always disappears quickly from the table.

kielbasa potato soup

    1 medium leek, (white portion only), halved and sliced
    1 tablespoon butter
1-3/4 cups chicken broth
    1 medium potato, peeled and diced
  1/3 pound fully cooked kielbasa *or* Polish sausage, cut into bite-size pieces
  1/4 cup heavy whipping cream
  1/8 teaspoon *each* caraway and cumin seeds, toasted
  1/3 cup thinly sliced fresh spinach

In a large saucepan, saute leek in butter until tender. Add broth and potato; bring to a boil. Reduce heat; cover and simmer for 15-20 minutes or until potato is tender.

Stir in the sausage, cream, caraway and cumin; heat through (do not boil). Just before serving, add the spinach.

YIELD: 2 servings.

corn and sausage soup

2-1/2 cups chopped onions
  1/2 cup *each* chopped green pepper, sweet red pepper and celery
    6 tablespoons butter
1-1/2 pounds fully cooked smoked sausage, cut into 1/4-inch pieces
    3 garlic cloves, minced
    4 cans (15 ounces *each*) Italian-style tomato sauce
    3 packages (16 ounces *each*) frozen corn
    2 cans (14-1/2 ounces *each*) Italian diced tomatoes, undrained
    2 cups water
    3 bay leaves
1-1/2 teaspoons *each* dried basil, oregano and thyme
  1/2 teaspoon pepper
  1/4 teaspoon dried marjoram
  1/4 teaspoon hot pepper sauce, optional

In a Dutch oven or soup kettle, saute the onions, peppers and celery in butter until tender. Add the sausage and garlic; cook for 8-10 minutes or until heated through.

Stir in the remaining ingredients. Bring to a boil. Reduce heat; simmer, uncovered, for 1 hour, stirring occasionally. Discard bay leaves before serving.

YIELD: 16-18 servings.

spinach sausage soup

1 pound bulk Italian sausage

4 cans (14-1/2 ounces *each*) chicken broth

8 small red potatoes, quartered and thinly sliced

1 envelope Italian salad dressing mix

2 cups fresh spinach *or* frozen chopped spinach

In a large skillet, brown sausage over medium heat until no longer pink. Meanwhile, in a Dutch oven, combine the broth, potatoes and salad dressing mix. Bring to a boil; cover and simmer for 10 minutes or until potatoes are tender.

Drain sausage. Add sausage and spinach to broth mixture; heat through.

YIELD: 10 servings.

bonita krugler
ANDERSON, INDIANA

Chock-full of potatoes, Italian sausage and spinach, here's a soup that will disappear fast. Adjust the amount of broth to suit your tastes.

CHAPTER **five**

meatless

Hearty, satisfying, delicious and good for you—the recipes in this chapter prove that you don't need meat to make wonderful soups. Loaded with vegetables, grains, pasta and beans, this section is full of change-of-pace menu ideas. And, as an added bonus, most of the dishes that follow are economical as well.

136   140   160

carrot broccoli soup

sandy smith
LONDON, ONTARIO

I turn to this soup when I need to whip up dinner in a jiffy. It's so nutritious filled to the brim with carrots and broccoli!

1 medium onion, chopped
2 medium carrots, chopped
2 celery ribs, chopped
1 tablespoon butter
3 cups fresh broccoli florets
3 cups fat-free milk, *divided*
3/4 teaspoon salt
1/2 teaspoon dried thyme
1/8 teaspoon pepper
3 tablespoons all-purpose flour

In a large saucepan coated with cooking spray, cook the onion, carrots and celery in butter for 3 minutes. Add the broccoli; cook 3 minutes longer. Stir in 2-3/4 cups milk, salt, thyme and pepper.

Bring to a boil. Reduce heat; cover and simmer for 5-10 minutes or until vegetables are tender. Combine the flour and remaining milk until smooth; gradually stir into the soup. Bring to a boil; cook 2 minutes longer or until thickened.

YIELD: 4 servings.

vegetable broth

2 tablespoons olive oil
2 medium onions, cut into wedges
2 celery ribs, cut into 1-inch pieces
1 whole garlic bulb, separated into cloves and peeled
3 medium leeks, white and light green parts only, cleaned and cut into 1-inch pieces
3 medium carrots, cut into 1-inch pieces
8 cups water
1/2 pound fresh mushrooms, quartered
1 cup packed fresh parsley sprigs
4 sprigs fresh thyme
1 teaspoon salt
1/2 teaspoon whole peppercorns
1 bay leaf

Heat oil in a stockpot over medium heat until hot. Add the onions, celery and garlic. Cook and stir for 5 minutes or until tender. Add leeks and carrots; cook and stir 5 minutes longer. Add the water, mushrooms, parsley, thyme, salt, peppercorns and bay leaf; bring to a boil. Reduce heat; simmer, uncovered, for 1 hour.

Remove from the heat. Strain through a cheesecloth-lined colander; discard vegetables. If using immediately, skim fat, or refrigerate for 8 hours or overnight; remove fat from surface. Broth can be covered and refrigerated for up to 3 days or frozen for up to 4 to 6 months.

YIELD: 5-1/2 servings.

taste of home test kitchen
GREENDALE, WISCONSIN

The pleasant flavors of celery and mushroom shine through in this homemade vegetable broth. Feel free to use it as a substitute for chicken broth in meatless recipes.

freezing soup

Many broth-based soups freeze well for up to 3 months. Thaw in the refrigerator before reheating. It's best not to freeze soups prepared with potatoes, fruit, cheese, sour cream, yogurt, eggs or milk.

pear squash bisque with cinnamon cream

3/4 cup sour cream
1-1/2 teaspoons maple syrup
1/2 teaspoon ground cinnamon
2 medium butternut squash (3 pounds *each*)
1 tablespoon butter, melted
1-1/2 teaspoons Caribbean jerk seasoning
4-1/2 cups vegetable broth
4 medium pears, peeled and chopped
1/2 cup packed brown sugar
1-1/2 teaspoons ground cinnamon
1/2 teaspoon salt
1/2 teaspoon ground ginger
1/4 teaspoon ground nutmeg
1/4 teaspoon ground cloves
3/4 cup heavy whipping cream

For cinnamon cream, in a small bowl, combine the sour cream, maple syrup and cinnamon. Cover and refrigerate until serving.

Peel squash. Scoop out seeds and pulp; rinse and pat seeds dry. In a small bowl, combine the squash seeds, butter and jerk seasoning. Spread onto a greased 15-in. x 10-in. x 1-in. baking pan. Bake at 375° for 12-15 minutes or until lightly browned, stirring once. Cool on a wire rack.

Meanwhile, cut squash into cubes. In a large saucepan, combine squash, broth and pears; bring to a boil. Reduce heat; cover and simmer for 10-15 minutes or until squash is tender. Cool slightly.

In a blender, process squash mixture in batches until smooth. Return all to the pan. Add brown sugar and seasonings. Gradually stir in whipping cream. Garnish soup with cinnamon cream and spiced seeds.

YIELD: 12 servings.

elaine sweet
DALLAS, TEXAS

Looking for something out of the ordinary to include on your Thanksgiving Day menu? Guests will rave about this delicately sweet and fruity squash soup.

winter squash

The most common varieties of winter squash are butternut, acorn, hubbard, spaghetti and turban. Look for squash that feel heavy for their size and have hard, deep-colored rinds free of blemishes. Unwashed winter squash can be stored in a dry, cool, well-ventilated place for up to 1 month.

vera bathurst
ROGUE RIVER, OREGON

This fresh-tasting soup is packed with colorful, nutritious vegetables. I've recommended it to my friends for years.

speedy vegetable soup

2 cans (one 49 ounces, one 14-1/2 ounces) reduced-sodium vegetable broth *or* chicken broth
2 celery ribs, thinly sliced
1 medium green pepper, chopped
1 medium onion, chopped
2 medium carrots, chopped
1 envelope onion soup mix
1 bay leaf
1/4 teaspoon garlic powder
1/4 teaspoon pepper
1 can (14-1/2 ounces) diced tomatoes, undrained

In a Dutch oven, combine the first nine ingredients; bring to a boil over medium heat. Reduce the heat; cover and simmer for 15-20 minutes or until vegetables are tender. Add tomatoes; heat through. Discard bay leaf.

YIELD: 11 servings.

jane ward
CHURCHVILLE, MARYLAND

The addition of sugar puts a sweet spin on classic tomato soup. It's great on a cold winter day served alongside your favorite grilled sandwich.

quick tomato soup

1/4 cup butter
1/4 cup all-purpose flour
1 teaspoon curry powder
1/4 teaspoon onion powder
1 can (46 ounces) tomato juice
1/4 cup sugar
Oyster crackers, optional

In a large saucepan, melt butter. Stir in flour, curry powder and onion powder until smooth. Gradually add tomato juice and sugar. Cook, uncovered, until thickened and heated through, about 5 minutes. Serve with crackers if desired.

YIELD: 6 servings.

linda rose proudfoot
HUNTINGTON, CONNECTICUT

This heavenly golden soup is as pretty as it is satisfying. Add an extra garlic bulb to intensify the flavor if you'd like.

butternut squash soup

3 pounds unpeeled butternut squash, halved and seeded
2 large unpeeled onions
1 small garlic bulb
1/4 cup olive oil
2 tablespoons minced fresh thyme *or* 2 teaspoons dried thyme
3 to 3-1/2 cups vegetable broth *or* chicken broth
1/2 cup heavy whipping cream
3 tablespoons minced fresh parsley
1/2 teaspoon salt
1/4 teaspoon pepper
Sprigs fresh thyme, optional

Cut squash into eight large pieces. Place cut side up in a 15-in. x 10-in. x 1-in. baking pan. Cut 1/4 in. off tops of onion and garlic bulbs (the end that comes to a closed point). Place cut side up in baking pans.

Brush vegetables with oil; sprinkle with thyme. Cover tightly with foil and bake at 350° for 1-1/2 to 2 hours or until vegetables are very tender. Uncover and let stand until lukewarm.

Remove peel from squash and onions; remove soft garlic from skins. In a large bowl, combine the vegetables, broth and cream. Puree in small batches in a blender until smooth; transfer mixture to a large saucepan. Add the parsley, salt and pepper; heat through (do not boil). Garnish the soup with thyme if desired.

YIELD: 8 servings.

vegetable soup with dumplings

1-1/2 cups chopped onions

4 medium carrots, sliced

3 celery ribs, sliced

2 tablespoons canola oil

3 cups vegetable broth

4 medium potatoes, peeled and sliced

4 medium tomatoes, chopped

2 garlic cloves, minced

1/2 teaspoon salt

1/2 teaspoon pepper

1/4 cup all-purpose flour

1/2 cup water

1 cup chopped cabbage

1 cup frozen peas

CARROT DUMPLINGS:

2-1/4 cups reduced-fat biscuit/baking mix

1 cup shredded carrots

1 tablespoon minced fresh parsley

1 cup cold water

10 tablespoons shredded reduced-fat cheddar cheese

In a Dutch oven, cook the onions, carrots and celery in oil for 6-8 minutes or until crisp-tender. Stir in the broth, potatoes, tomatoes, garlic, salt and pepper. Bring to a boil. Reduce heat; cover and simmer for 15-20 minutes or until vegetables are tender.

In a small bowl, combine flour and water until smooth; stir into vegetable mixture. Bring to a boil; cook and stir for 2 minutes or until thickened. Stir in cabbage and peas.

For dumplings, in a small bowl, combine baking mix, carrots and parsley. Stir in water until moistened. Drop in 10 mounds onto simmering soup. Cover and simmer for 15 minutes or until a toothpick inserted in a dumpling comes out clean (do not lift cover while simmering). Garnish with cheese.

YIELD: 10 servings.

karen mau

JACKSBORO, TENNESSEE

Not only is this my clan's favorite meatless soup, but it's a complete meal-in-one. It's loaded with vegetables, and the fluffy carrot dumplings are a great change of pace.

simple soup

Looking for a quick and easy way to make a delicious, hearty meal out of canned tomato or vegetable soup? Simply dilute the concentrate with tomato juice instead of water, then top the bubbling mixture with homemade dumplings.

**taste of home
test kitchen**
GREENDALE, WISCONSIN

*If you enjoy cream of
tomato soup, try making
it with purchased roasted
red peppers. Using jarred
peppers keeps preparation
simple and pureeing the
soup in a blender yields
a smooth texture.*

roasted red pepper soup

1 large sweet onion, chopped

2 teaspoons butter

2 garlic cloves, minced

2 jars (15-1/2 ounces *each*) roasted
   sweet red peppers, drained

2 cups vegetable broth

1/2 teaspoon dried basil

1/4 teaspoon salt

1 cup half-and-half cream

In a large saucepan, saute onion in butter for
2-3 minutes or until tender. Add garlic; cook
1 minute longer. Stir in the red peppers, broth, basil
and salt. Bring to a boil. Reduce heat; cover and
simmer for 20 minutes. Cool slightly.

In a blender, cover and process soup in batches
until smooth. Remove 1 cup to a small bowl; stir in
cream. Return remaining puree to pan. Stir in the
cream mixture; heat through (do not boil).

YIELD: 6 servings.

cream of vegetable soup

2 cups chopped sweet onions
1-1/2 cups chopped carrots
1 cup chopped celery
2 tablespoons canola oil
4 cups cubed peeled potatoes
1 large head cauliflower, broken into florets
3 cans (14-1/2 ounces *each*) reduced-sodium vegetable broth *or* chicken broth
2 teaspoons salt
2 teaspoons white pepper
1/2 cup half-and-half cream
Fresh basil

In Dutch oven, saute the onions, carrots and celery in oil until onions are tender. Add potatoes and cauliflower; saute 5-6 minutes longer. Add the broth, salt and pepper. Bring to a boil. Reduce heat; cover and simmer for 10-12 minutes or until vegetables are tender. Let stand until cool.

Puree vegetable mixture in a blender or food processor in batches. Return all to the pan. Stir in cream; heat through. (Do not boil.) Garnish with fresh basil.

YIELD: 11 servings.

vicki kamstra
SPOKANE, WASHINGTON

The texture of this soup is creamy and smooth, making it easy to get my daily dose of veggies!

red pepper tomato soup

2 medium sweet red peppers
2 cups water
10 plum tomatoes
1 Anaheim pepper, seeded and chopped
2 garlic cloves, minced
1 cup vegetable broth *or* chicken broth
2 tablespoons rice vinegar
2 tablespoons minced fresh basil
1/2 cup shredded part-skim mozzarella cheese

Broil red peppers 4 in. from the heat until skins blister. With tongs, rotate peppers a quarter turn. Broil and rotate until all sides are blistered and blackened. Immediately place peppers in a bowl; cover and let stand for 15-20 minutes. Peel off and discard charred skin. Remove stems and seeds. Finely chop peppers.

In a large saucepan, bring water to a boil. Add tomatoes; cover and boil for 3 minutes. Drain and immediately place tomatoes in ice water. Drain and pat dry.

In the same pan, combine the roasted peppers, tomatoes, Anaheim pepper and garlic; heat through. Stir in the broth and vinegar; heat through. Stir in basil. Cool slightly.

In small batches, puree soup in a blender. Return to the pan and heat through. Garnish with cheese.

YIELD: 5 servings.

EDITOR'S NOTE: We recommend wearing disposable gloves when cutting hot peppers. Avoid touching your face.

jane shapton
IRVINE, CALIFORNIA

Vine-ripened plum tomatoes punched up with peppers, garlic and rice vinegar make my zippy creation a summer standout. Serve with cheesy garlic breadsticks and a tossed salad.

harvest sweet potato soup

1 cup chopped celery
1/2 cup chopped onion
1 tablespoon canola oil
3 medium sweet potatoes (about 1 pound), peeled and cubed
3 cups vegetable broth *or* chicken broth
1 bay leaf
1/2 teaspoon dried basil
1/4 teaspoon salt, optional

In a Dutch oven, saute celery and onion in oil until tender. Add remaining ingredients; bring to a boil over medium heat. Reduce heat; simmer for 25-30 minutes or until potatoes are tender.

Discard bay leaf. Cool slightly. In a blender, process soup in batches until smooth. Return all to pan and heat through.

YIELD: 4 servings.

gayle becker
MT. CLEMENS, MICHIGAN

My family loves leftovers of my sweet potato soup, so I always double the recipe. They prefer it warm, but it can also be served chilled.

melissa fitzgerald
JEANETTE, PENNSYLVANIA

Portobello mushrooms are a fun addition to classic French onion soup. Pair a simmering bowl with a fresh garden salad for a filling meal.

portobello mushroom onion soup

5 cups thinly sliced halved onions
4 fresh thyme sprigs
3 tablespoons butter, *divided*
1-1/2 pounds sliced baby portobello mushrooms
3 tablespoons brandy, optional

3 garlic cloves, minced
8 cups vegetable broth
1 cup white wine *or* additional vegetable broth
1/4 teaspoon pepper
13 slices French bread
13 slices provolone cheese

In a Dutch oven or soup kettle, saute onions and thyme in 1 tablespoon butter until onions are tender, about 8 minutes. Reduce heat; cook, uncovered, over low heat for 20 minutes or until onions are golden brown, stirring occasionally. Remove onions to a bowl.

In the same pan, melt remaining butter. Add mushrooms, brandy if desired and garlic; saute for 1 minute. Return onions to pan. Add broth, wine or additional broth and pepper; bring to a boil. Reduce heat; cover and simmer for 40-45 minutes or until onions are very tender.

Meanwhile, place French bread slices on a baking sheet; top each slice with provolone cheese. Broil 4-6 inches from the heat for 1-2 minutes or until cheese is melted. Discard thyme sprigs from soup; top soup with cheese-topped bread.

YIELD: 13 servings.

michelle kaiser
BOZEMAN, MONTANA

My mom often made her thick corn chowder when I was growing up. Once I started college, she passed the recipe to me with a special recipe box she created. That was over 10 years ago, and the soup is still one of my favorites.

parmesan corn chowder

2 cups water
2 cups cubed peeled potatoes
1/2 cup sliced carrots
1/2 cup sliced celery

1/4 cup chopped onion
1/4 cup butter
1/4 cup all-purpose flour
1 teaspoon salt
1/2 teaspoon pepper
2 cups whole milk
1 can (14-3/4 ounces) cream-style corn
1-1/2 cups (6 ounces) shredded Parmesan cheese

In a large saucepan, combine the first five ingredients; bring to a boil. Reduce heat; cover and simmer for 12-15 minutes or until the vegetables are tender (do not drain).

Meanwhile, in a small saucepan, melt butter. Stir in the flour, salt and pepper until smooth; gradually stir in milk. Bring to a boil; cook and stir for 2 minutes or until thickened. Stir into the vegetable mixture. Add corn and cheese. Cook 10 minutes longer or until heated through.

YIELD: 7 servings.

tomato spinach soup

2 large yellow onions, cubed

2 tablespoons olive oil

1 can (28 ounces) diced tomatoes, undrained

1 quart water

4 beef bouillon cubes

1 cup sliced fresh mushrooms

3/4 teaspoon Italian seasoning

1/2 teaspoon dried basil

1/2 teaspoon salt

1/8 teaspoon pepper

4 cups loosely packed spinach leaves

Grated Parmesan *or* shredded cheddar cheese, optional

In a Dutch oven or soup kettle, saute onions in oil over medium heat for 10 minutes or until tender. Add the next eight ingredients; bring to a boil. Reduce heat; cover and simmer for 30 minutes. Stir in spinach; simmer for 3-5 minutes or until tender. Garnish individual servings with cheese if desired.

YIELD: 8-10 servings.

erna ketchum

SAN JOSE, CALIFORNIA

My first experience with tomato spinach soup was in a local cafe. After some experimentation with the ingredients, I created a combination my family preferred to the original.

meatless tortellini soup

donna morgan

HEND, TENNESSEE

I top bowls of this succulent soup with a sprinkling of grated Parmesan and serve it with crusty bread to round out the meal.

2 garlic cloves, minced

1 tablespoon butter

3 cans (14-1/2 ounces *each*) reduced-sodium vegetable broth *or* chicken broth

1 package (9 ounces) refrigerated cheese tortellini

1 can (14-1/2 ounces) diced tomatoes with green chilies, undrained

1 package (10 ounces) frozen chopped spinach, thawed

In a large saucepan, saute the garlic in butter for 1 minute. Stir in the broth. Bring to a boil. Add tortellini; cook for 7-9 minutes or until tender. Stir in the tomatoes and spinach; heat through.

YIELD: 5 servings.

roasted pepper potato soup

2 medium onions, chopped

2 tablespoons canola oil

1 jar (7 ounces) roasted sweet red peppers, undrained and chopped

1 can (4 ounces) chopped green chilies, drained

2 teaspoons ground cumin

1 teaspoon salt

1 teaspoon ground coriander

3 cups diced peeled potatoes

3 cups vegetable broth

2 tablespoons minced fresh cilantro

1 tablespoon lemon juice

1/2 cup reduced-fat cream cheese, cubed

In a large saucepan, saute onions in oil until tender. Stir in the roasted peppers, chilies, cumin, salt and coriander. Cook and stir for 2 minutes. Stir in potatoes and broth; bring to a boil.

Reduce the heat; cover and simmer for 10-15 minutes or until potatoes are tender. Stir in cilantro and lemon juice. Cool slightly. In a blender, process the cream cheese and half of the soup until smooth. Return all to pan and heat through.

YIELD: 6 servings.

hollie powell
ST. LOUIS, MISSOURI

I have a penchant for this rich potato soup, which is more flavorful than most others I've tried. I like the lemon and cilantro, but you can adjust any of the ingredients or seasonings to suit your tastes.

garlic-basil tortellini soup

2 garlic cloves, minced

1 teaspoon butter

2 cans (14-1/2 ounces each) reduced-sodium vegetable broth or chicken broth

1/2 cup water

1/3 cup minced fresh basil

1/4 teaspoon pepper

2-1/2 cups frozen cheese tortellini

1 can (19 ounces) white kidney beans or cannellini beans, rinsed and drained

2 tablespoons balsamic vinegar

1/4 cup shredded Parmesan cheese

In a large saucepan, saute garlic in butter until tender. Stir in the broth, water, basil and pepper. Bring to a boil. Stir in tortellini. Reduce heat; simmer, uncovered, for about 3 minutes or until tortellini begins to float. Stir in beans and vinegar; heat through. Sprinkle with Parmesan cheese.

YIELD: 4 servings.

linda kees
BOISE, IDAHO

My soup is so tasty and filling, it can be eaten as a main dish. The balsamic vinegar adds an extra dimension to the flavor.

out of garlic?

When a recipe calls for a clove of garlic and you're out of fresh bulbs, substitute about 1/4 teaspoon of garlic powder for each clove. And the next time you're shopping, look for convenient jars of fresh minced garlic in the produce section. Use 1/2 teaspoon of minced garlic for each clove.

marge hill
GLENSIDE, PENNSYLVANIA

When my husband and I visit farmers markets, we often come home with more vegetables than we can eat. I lightened up this tarragon-flavored soup to make use of the fresh broccoli we buy. We like it with crusty bread, a salad or a sandwich.

broccoli cheese soup

1/2 cup chopped sweet onion
3 garlic cloves, minced
2 tablespoons all-purpose flour
1 can (14-1/2 ounces) reduced-sodium vegetable broth *or* chicken broth
4 cups fresh broccoli florets
1/4 to 1/2 teaspoon dried tarragon
1/4 teaspoon dried thyme
1/8 teaspoon pepper
1-1/2 cups 1% milk
1-1/4 cups shredded reduced-fat cheddar cheese, *divided*

In a large nonstick saucepan coated with cooking spray, saute onion until tender. Add garlic; cook 1 minute longer. Stir in flour until blended. Gradually whisk in broth. Bring to a boil; cook and stir for 1-2 minutes or until slightly thickened.

Add the broccoli, tarragon, thyme and pepper; return to a boil. Reduce heat; cover and simmer for 10 minutes or until broccoli is tender. Add milk; cook, uncovered, 5 minutes longer. Remove from heat; cool to room temperature.

In a blender, process soup in batches until smooth. Return all to the pan; heat through. Reduce heat. Add 1 cup of cheese; stir just until melted. Serve immediately. Garnish with remaining cheese.

YIELD: 4 servings.

lucille franck
INDEPENDENCE, IOWA

Feel free to toss in whatever veggies you have on hand for this delicious recipe.

mixed vegetable soup

2 small carrots, grated
2 celery ribs, chopped
1 small onion, chopped
1/2 cup chopped green pepper
1/4 cup butter, cubed
2 cans (14-1/2 ounces *each*) reduced-sodium vegetable *or* chicken broth
2 cans (14-1/2 ounces *each*) no-salt-added diced tomatoes, undrained
1 tablespoon sugar
1/4 teaspoon pepper
1/4 cup all-purpose flour

In a large saucepan, saute the carrots, celery, onion and green pepper in butter until tender. Set aside 1/2 cup broth. Add the tomatoes, sugar, pepper and remaining broth to pan; bring to a boil. Reduce heat; cover and simmer for 20 minutes.

Combine flour and reserved broth until smooth; gradually add to soup. Bring to a boil; cook and stir for 2 minutes or until thickened.

YIELD: 8 servings.

spill-the-beans minestrone

reuben tsujimura
WALLA WALLA, WASHINGTON

A meal in itself, here's a hearty soup that's chock-full of healthy veggies and vitamins. No one will miss the meat!

1 medium onion, chopped
1 tablespoon olive oil
2 garlic cloves, minced
2 cans (14-1/2 ounces *each*) reduced-sodium vegetable broth *or* chicken broth
1 can (16 ounces) kidney beans, rinsed and drained
1 can (15 ounces) garbanzo beans *or* chickpeas, rinsed and drained
1 can (14-1/2 ounces) stewed tomatoes, cut up
2 cups chopped fresh kale
1/2 cup water

1/2 cup uncooked small pasta shells
1 teaspoon Italian seasoning
1/4 teaspoon crushed red pepper flakes
6 teaspoons shredded Parmesan cheese

In a large saucepan, saute onion in oil until onion is tender. Add garlic; cook 1 minute longer. Add the broth, beans, tomatoes, kale, water, pasta, Italian seasoning and pepper flakes. Bring to a boil. Reduce heat; cover and simmer for 10-15 minutes or until pasta is tender. Sprinkle each serving with cheese.

YIELD: 6 servings.

cream of lentil soup

kim russell
NORTH WALES, PENNSYLVANIA

Lentil lovers will want a second bowl of this nourishing soup that features a subtle touch of curry. Fresh spinach adds an appealing pop of color.

6 cups reduced-sodium vegetable broth or chicken broth

2 cups dried lentils, rinsed

1 bay leaf

1 whole clove

1 medium red onion, chopped

2 celery ribs, chopped

2 tablespoons butter

2 medium carrots, chopped

1 teaspoon salt

1 teaspoon sugar

1/2 teaspoon curry powder

1/8 teaspoon pepper

2 garlic cloves, minced

3 cups coarsely chopped fresh spinach

1-1/2 cups heavy whipping cream

1 tablespoon lemon juice

1/3 cup minced fresh parsley

In a large saucepan, combine the broth, lentils, bay leaf and clove. Bring to a boil. Reduce heat; cover and simmer for 25-30 minutes or until the lentils are tender.

Meanwhile, in a Dutch oven, saute onion and celery in butter until crisp-tender. Add the carrots, salt, sugar, curry powder and pepper; saute for 2-3 minutes longer or until the vegetables are tender. Add garlic; cook for 1 minute.

Drain lentils; discard bay leaf and clove. Add to vegetable mixture. Stir in the spinach, cream, lemon juice and parsley; cook over low heat until heated through and spinach is wilted.

YIELD: 9 servings.

basil tomato soup

1 medium onion, chopped
1 medium carrot, shredded
1-1/2 teaspoons butter
4 medium tomatoes, peeled, seeded and quartered
1/4 teaspoon sugar
1/4 teaspoon salt
1/8 teaspoon coarsely ground pepper
1/4 cup loosely packed fresh basil leaves
1 cup reduced-sodium vegetable broth *or* chicken broth

In a small saucepan, saute onion and carrot in butter until tender. Stir in the tomatoes, sugar, salt and pepper. Reduce heat; cover and cook for 10 minutes or until tomatoes are softened. Cool slightly.

Transfer to a blender; add the basil. Cover and process until smooth. Return to the pan; stir in the broth and heat through.

YIELD: 2 servings.

sarah travis
EDINA, MINNESOTA

I've been making my aunt's from-scratch tomato soup for years. I love the addition of fresh basil, which perks up the flavor and can be used as a pretty garnish on top.

basil chiffonade

Basil is a lovely addition to recipes and can be used as a garnish, too. Basil chiffonade is a great way to quickly chop a lot of basil with attractive results. Stack basil leaves neatly in the same direction, then roll the stack lengthwise into a tight cigar shape. Slice across the rolled leaves for thin strips.

vegetable barley soup

1 large sweet potato, peeled and cubed
1-1/2 cups fresh baby carrots, halved
1-1/2 cups frozen cut green beans
1-1/2 cups frozen corn
3 celery ribs, thinly sliced
1 small onion, chopped
1/2 cup chopped green pepper
2 garlic cloves, minced
6 cups water
2 cans (14-1/2 ounces each) vegetable broth
1 cup medium pearl barley
1 bay leaf
1-3/4 teaspoons salt
1/2 teaspoon fennel seed, crushed
1/4 teaspoon pepper
1 can (14-1/2 ounces) Italian diced tomatoes, undrained

In a 5-qt. slow cooker, combine the first eight ingredients. Stir in the water, broth, barley, bay leaf and seasonings. Cover and cook on low for 8-9 hours or until barley and vegetables are tender.

Stir in tomatoes; cover and cook on high for 10-20 minutes or until heated through. Discard bay leaf.

YIELD: 12 servings.

mary tallman
ARBOR VITAE, WISCONSIN

Try my meatless soup brimming with vegetables and barley. You'll love its delicious flavor.

leah lyon

ADA, OKLAHOMA

Loaded with garden-fresh veggies, my ranchero soup goes with just about any grilled meat, fish or fowl. Carrots and fire-roasted tomatoes add great color, but the variations are endless. Just toss in whatever you have in the garden or fridge!

ranchero soup

1 large onion, quartered
3 celery ribs
1 medium zucchini, halved lengthwise
1 large sweet red pepper, quartered and seeded
1 poblano pepper, quartered and seeded
1 tablespoon olive oil
2 cans (14-1/2 ounces *each*) diced tomatoes, undrained
2 cans (14-1/2 ounces *each*) vegetable broth
1 cup frozen sliced carrots
1 cup cooked rice
1/2 teaspoon lemon-pepper seasoning

Brush the onion, celery, zucchini and peppers with oil. Using long-handled tongs, moisten a paper towel with cooking oil and lightly coat the grill rack. Grill vegetables, uncovered, over medium heat or broil

4 in. from the heat for 7-8 minutes on each side or until tender (pepper skins will char).

Immediately place peppers in a bowl; cover and let stand for 15-20 minutes. Peel off and discard charred skin. Coarsely chop grilled vegetables.

In a large saucepan, combine the tomatoes, broth and carrots. Bring to a boil. Reduce heat. Stir in grilled vegetables, rice and lemon-pepper; heat through.

YIELD: 8 servings.

EDITOR'S NOTE: We recommend wearing disposable gloves when cutting hot peppers. Avoid touching your face.

michele doucette

STEPHENVILLE, NEWFOUNDLAND AND LABRADOR

Even the pickiest pea soup eater will request this meatless version time and again. It's thick, well-seasoned and packs a nutritional punch.

vegetarian split pea soup

6 cups vegetable broth
2 cups dried green split peas, rinsed
1 medium onion, chopped
1 cup chopped carrots
2 celery ribs with leaves, chopped
2 garlic cloves, minced
1/2 teaspoon dried marjoram
1/2 teaspoon dried basil
1/4 teaspoon ground cumin
1/2 teaspoon salt
1/4 teaspoon pepper
5 tablespoons shredded carrots
2 green onions, sliced

In a large saucepan, combine the first nine ingredients; bring to a boil. Reduce heat; cover and simmer for 1 hour or until peas are tender, stirring occasionally.

Add salt and pepper; simmer 10 minutes longer. Cool slightly. In small batches, puree soup in a blender; return to the pan. Heat for 5 minutes. Garnish with shredded carrots and green onions.

YIELD: 7 servings.

sweet potato minestrone

4 cans (14-1/2 ounces *each*) reduced-sodium vegetable broth *or* beef broth

3 cups water

2 medium sweet potatoes, peeled and cubed

1 medium onion, chopped

4 garlic cloves, minced

2 teaspoons Italian seasoning

6 cups shredded cabbage

1 package (7 ounces) small pasta shells

2 cups frozen peas

In a soup kettle, combine the broth, water, sweet potatoes, onion, garlic and Italian seasoning; bring to a boil. Reduce heat; cover and simmer for 10 minutes.

Return to a boil. Add the cabbage, pasta and peas; cook for 8-10 minutes or until the pasta and vegetables are tender.

YIELD: 14 servings.

helen vail
GLENSIDE, PENNSYLVANIA

The pleasing taste of sweet potatoes is sure to make this recipe a keeper! My daughters love the flavor, and I love that it's high in beta-carotene and other nutrients.

joy maynard
ST. IGNATIUS, MONTANA

Here is one good-for-you dish that our kids really enjoy. Serve it as a hearty meatless entree or pair it with a favorite sandwich.

lentil vegetable soup

3 cans (14-1/2 ounces *each*) vegetable broth
1 medium onion, chopped
1/2 cup dried lentils, rinsed
1/2 cup uncooked long grain brown rice
1/2 cup tomato juice
1 can (5-1/2 ounces) spicy hot V8 juice
1 tablespoon reduced-sodium soy sauce
1 tablespoon canola oil
1 medium potato, peeled and cubed
1 medium tomato, cubed
1 medium carrot, sliced
1 celery rib, sliced

In a large saucepan, combine the first eight ingredients. Bring to a boil. Reduce heat; cover and simmer for 30 minutes.

Add the potato, tomato, carrot and celery; cover and simmer 30 minutes longer or until rice and vegetables are tender.

YIELD: 6 servings.

onion tomato soup

2 cups thinly sliced onions
4 teaspoons olive oil
2-2/3 cups tomato juice
2 cups water
2 tablespoons minced fresh basil
2 teaspoons minced fresh oregano
1 teaspoon sugar
1 teaspoon celery salt
2 cups diced seeded plum tomatoes

In a large saucepan, saute onion in oil until tender. Add the tomato juice, water, basil, oregano, sugar and celery salt. Bring to a boil. Reduce heat; simmer, uncovered, for 20 minutes, stirring occasionally. Add the tomatoes; cook 10 minutes longer.

YIELD: 6 servings.

lisa blackwell
HENDERSON, NORTH CAROLINA

Fresh herbs really pump up the flavor of my low-fat meatless soup. It tastes especially delicious on a cold day.

cheese-topped vegetable soup

1 can (28 ounces) Italian stewed tomatoes
1-1/2 cups water
1 can (8-3/4 ounces) whole kernel corn, drained
3/4 cup chopped sweet red pepper
2/3 cup chopped red onion
2/3 cup chopped green pepper
1/4 cup minced fresh basil
1 garlic clove, minced
1/2 teaspoon salt
1/4 teaspoon pepper
1/2 cup salad croutons
1/4 cup shredded part-skim mozzarella cheese

In a large saucepan, combine the first 10 ingredients. Bring to a boil. Reduce heat; simmer, uncovered, for 20-25 minutes or until heated through and vegetables are tender.

Ladle the soup into ovenproof bowls. Top each with croutons and cheese. Broil 6 in. from the heat until cheese is melted.

YIELD: 4 servings.

anna minegar
ZOLFO SPRINGS, FLORIDA

Just-picked garden flavor makes this vegetable soup a summer staple at our house. The cheese on top makes it extra indulgent.

cheesy floret soup

3 cups fresh broccoli florets
3 cups fresh cauliflowerets
3 celery ribs, sliced
1 small onion, chopped
2 cups water
1/2 teaspoon celery salt
3 tablespoons butter
3 tablespoons all-purpose flour
2-1/3 cups whole milk
1 pound process cheese (Velveeta), cubed

In a large saucepan, combine the first six ingredients. Bring to a boil. Reduce heat; cover and simmer for 12-15 minutes or until vegetables are tender.

Meanwhile, in a small saucepan, melt butter; stir in flour until smooth. Gradually stir in milk. Bring to a boil; cook and stir for 2 minutes or until thickened. Reduce heat; add cheese. Cook and stir until cheese is melted. Drain vegetables; add cheese sauce and heat through.

YIELD: 4-6 servings.

janice russell
KINGFISHER, OKLAHOMA

Talk about comfort food! My cheesy soup studded with cauliflower and broccoli warms the soul. It's especially good with crusty French bread.

process cheese

Process cheese is a blend of different cheeses and emulsifiers. It is stable at room temperature and stays smooth and creamy when it is heated. The most common brand name of process cheese is Velveeta.

nancy johnson
LAVERNE, OKLAHOMA

Vegetable flavors abound in every spoonful of my easy-to-make soup. The recipe makes enough for two, so you won't end up with lots of leftovers.

zucchini tomato soup

2 small zucchini, coarsely chopped

1/4 cup chopped red onion

1-1/2 teaspoons olive oil

1/8 teaspoon salt

1 cup spicy hot V8 juice

1 small tomato, cut into thin wedges

Dash *each* pepper and dried basil

2 tablespoons shredded cheddar cheese, optional

1 to 2 tablespoons crumbled cooked bacon, optional

In a large skillet, saute zucchini and onion in oil until crisp-tender. Sprinkle with salt. Add the V8 juice, tomato, pepper and basil; cook until heated through. Sprinkle with cheese and bacon if desired.

YIELD: 2 servings.

susan wright
YARMOUTH, MAINE

I downsized the yield but not the flavor of my favorite vegetarian chili. Use leftovers to spice up a taco or burrito.

chunky vegetarian chili

1 cup chopped onion

3/4 cup chopped green pepper

1 tablespoon canola oil

1 can (16 ounces) kidney beans, rinsed and drained

1 cup canned diced tomatoes

2/3 cup water

2 tablespoons tomato paste

1-1/2 teaspoons mustard seed

1-1/2 teaspoons chili powder

1/2 teaspoon cumin seeds

1/2 teaspoon baking cocoa

1/8 teaspoon ground cinnamon

ONION TOPPING:

1 cup water

2 teaspoons white vinegar, *divided*

1/2 large red onion, thinly sliced

1 teaspoon canola oil

1/4 teaspoon mustard seed

1/8 teaspoon ground cumin

Dash salt

In a large saucepan, saute onion and green pepper in oil for 5 minutes. Stir in the beans, tomatoes, water, tomato paste, mustard seed, chili powder, cumin seeds, cocoa and cinnamon. Bring to a boil. Reduce heat; simmer, uncovered, for 40 minutes or until heated through.

Meanwhile, in a small saucepan, bring water and 1 teaspoon vinegar to a boil. Add onion; cook, uncovered, over medium heat for 2 minutes. Drain and cool. In a bowl, combine the oil, mustard seed, cumin, salt and remaining vinegar; stir in onion. Serve over chili.

YIELD: 3 servings.

marjoram mushroom soup

1 large potato, peeled and diced

1 large leek (white portion only), chopped

1 medium onion, diced

2 tablespoons canola oil

1/2 pound sliced fresh mushrooms

4 cups vegetable broth *or* chicken broth

1 tablespoon minced fresh marjoram *or* 1 teaspoon dried marjoram, *divided*

1 cup (8 ounces) sour cream

2 tablespoons butter

Salt and pepper to taste

In a Dutch oven or soup kettle, saute the potato, leek and onion in oil for 4 minutes. Add mushrooms and cook for 2 minutes. Stir in broth and half of the marjoram. Cover and simmer for 10 minutes or until potato is tender. Cool slightly.

Puree in small batches in a blender; return all to pan. Whisk in sour cream and butter; season with salt and pepper. Heat through but do not boil. Just before serving, sprinkle soup with remaining marjoram.

YIELD: 6 servings.

michele odstrcilek
LEMONT, ILLINOIS

This hearty soup features fresh mushrooms and the pleasant addition of marjoram. You won't be able to get enough!

laura prokash
ALGOMA, WISCONSIN

Count on this pleasantly seasoned soup to satisfy the whole family. I love that I can make a big pot from a handy bean mix.

sixteen-bean soup

1 package (12 ounces) 16-bean soup mix
1 large onion, chopped
2 garlic cloves, minced
1 teaspoon salt
1 teaspoon chili powder
1/4 teaspoon pepper
1/8 teaspoon hot pepper sauce
1 bay leaf
8 cups water
1 can (14-1/2 ounces) stewed tomatoes
1 tablespoon lemon juice

Set aside seasoning packet from beans. Sort beans and rinse with cold water. Place beans in a Dutch oven; add water to cover by 2 in. Bring to a boil; boil for 2 minutes. Remove from the heat; cover and let stand for 1 to 4 hours or until beans are softened. Drain and rinse beans, discarding liquid.

Return beans to the pan. Add contents of bean seasoning packet, onion, garlic, salt, chili powder, pepper, pepper sauce, bay leaf and water. Bring to a boil.

Reduce heat; cover and simmer for 2-1/2 to 3 hours or until beans are tender. Add tomatoes and lemon juice. Simmer, uncovered, until heated through. Discard bay leaf.

YIELD: 10 servings.

hearty lentil soup

3 cups water
3 cups vegetable broth
3 medium carrots, sliced
1 medium onion, chopped
1 cup dried lentils, rinsed
2 celery ribs, sliced
1 small green pepper, chopped
1/4 cup uncooked brown rice
1 teaspoon dried basil
1 garlic clove, minced
1 bay leaf

3/4 cup tomato paste
1/2 cup frozen corn
1/2 cup frozen peas

In a large saucepan, combine the first 11 ingredients. Bring to a boil. Reduce heat; cover and simmer for 1 to 1-1/2 hours or until lentils and rice are tender.

Add the tomato paste, corn and peas; stir until blended. Cook, uncovered, for 15-20 minutes or until corn and peas are tender. Discard bay leaf.

YIELD: 6 servings.

joy maynard
ST. IGNATIUS, MONTANA

This simple-to-fix lentil soup packs 15 grams of fiber per serving! I often double the recipe and freeze half to enjoy later.

winter harvest vegetable soup

3 medium carrots, halved and thinly sliced
3/4 cup chopped celery
1 medium onion, chopped
2 green onions, thinly sliced
1 tablespoon butter
1 tablespoon olive oil
1 garlic clove, minced
7 cups reduced-sodium vegetable broth *or* chicken broth
3 cups cubed peeled potatoes
2 cups cubed peeled butternut squash
2 large tart apples, peeled and chopped
2 medium turnips, peeled and chopped
2 parsnips, peeled and sliced
1 bay leaf

1/2 teaspoon dried basil
1/4 teaspoon dried thyme
1/4 teaspoon pepper
Additional thinly sliced green onions, optional

In a Dutch oven over medium heat, cook and stir the carrots, celery and onions in butter and oil until tender. Add garlic; cook 1 minute longer.

Add the broth, potatoes, squash, apples, turnips, parsnips and bay leaf. Bring to a boil. Reduce heat; simmer, uncovered, for 20 minutes.

Stir in the basil, thyme and pepper; simmer 15 minutes longer or until vegetables are tender. Discard bay leaf before serving. Garnish with additional green onions if desired.

YIELD: 12 servings.

barbara marakowski
LOYSVILLE, PENNSYLVANIA

Rich, earthy root vegetables blend with savory spices and the tartness of apples in this low-fat soup. It's even better reheated!

tomato garlic soup

10 whole garlic bulbs
1/2 cup olive oil
4 cans (one 14-1/2 ounces, three 28 ounces) diced tomatoes, undrained
1 medium onion, diced
3 cans (14-1/2 ounces *each*) stewed tomatoes
2/3 cup heavy whipping cream
1 to 3 tablespoons chopped pickled jalapeno peppers
2 teaspoons garlic pepper blend
2 teaspoons sugar
1-1/2 teaspoons salt
Croutons and shredded Parmesan cheese, optional

Remove papery outer skin from garlic (do not peel or separate cloves). Cut top off of garlic bulb. Drizzle with oil. Wrap each bulb in heavy-duty foil. Bake at 425° for 30-35 minutes or until softened. Cool for 10-15 minutes. Squeeze softened garlic into a blender. Add the 14-1/2-oz. can of diced tomatoes; cover and process until smooth. Set aside.

Transfer 1/4 cup oil from the foil to a Dutch oven or soup kettle (discard the remaining oil). Saute onion in oil over medium heat until tender.

Stir in the stewed tomatoes, cream, jalapenos, garlic pepper, sugar, salt, pureed tomato mixture and remaining diced tomatoes. Bring to a boil. Reduce heat; cover and simmer for 1 hour. Garnish with croutons and cheese if desired.

YIELD: 18-20 servings.

lynn thompson
RESTON, VIRGINIA

Tomato soup is a great starter course for dinner parties. Guests have always given me rave reviews after sampling my garlic-infused creation.

jennifer shields
CHESNEE, SOUTH CAROLINA

I dress up canned minestrone to make a shortcut soup that's loaded with colorful veggies. Serve steaming bowls with a sandwich or salad for a satisfying yet fast meal.

fast vegetable soup

- 1 can (19 ounces) ready-to-serve minestrone soup
- 1 package (16 ounces) frozen mixed vegetables
- 1 can (14-3/4 ounces) whole kernel corn, drained
- 1 can (15 ounces) black beans, rinsed and drained
- 1 can (14-1/2 ounces) Italian diced tomatoes, undrained

In a 2-1/2 quart microwave-safe bowl, combine all the ingredients. Cover and microwave on high for 8-10 minutes, stirring twice.

YIELD: 9 servings.

EDITOR'S NOTE: This recipe was tested in a 1,100-watt microwave.

melissa mendez
GILBERT, MINNESOTA

Even my meat-loving family devours this robust meatless chili. It's more fun to eat with your hands, so we scoop it up with tortilla chips!

spicy three-bean chili

- 1 medium green pepper, chopped
- 1 medium sweet yellow pepper, chopped
- 1 jalapeno pepper, seeded and chopped
- 1 medium onion, chopped
- 1 tablespoon olive oil
- 3 garlic cloves, minced
- 2 cans (14-1/2 ounces each) diced tomatoes with mild green chilies, undrained
- 1 can (10 ounces) diced tomatoes and green chilies, undrained
- 1 can (16 ounces) kidney beans, rinsed and drained
- 1 can (15 ounces) black beans, rinsed and drained
- 1 cup vegetable broth
- 1 teaspoon chili powder
- 3/4 teaspoon ground cumin
- 1/2 teaspoon cayenne pepper
- 1 can (16 ounces) spicy fat-free refried beans
- 1/3 cup shredded reduced-fat cheddar cheese
- 1/3 cup thinly sliced green onions

In a Dutch oven coated with cooking spray, saute the peppers and onion in oil until tender. Add garlic; cook 1 minute longer. Stir in the tomatoes, kidney beans, black beans, broth, chili powder, cumin and cayenne. Bring to a boil. Reduce heat; simmer, uncovered for 10 minutes.

Stir in refried beans; simmer 10 minutes longer. Garnish each serving with 2 teaspoons each of cheese and green onions.

YIELD: 8 servings.

EDITOR'S NOTE: We recommend wearing disposable gloves when cutting hot peppers. Avoid touching your face.

spinach vegetable soup

1/2 cup chopped onion

1/2 cup chopped celery

1 tablespoon butter

2 cans (14-1/2 ounces *each*) reduced-sodium vegetable broth *or* chicken broth

1-1/2 cups diced peeled potatoes

1 small turnip, peeled and chopped

1 cup chopped carrot

1/2 cup chopped green pepper

1 teaspoon garlic powder

1 teaspoon *each* dried thyme, basil and rosemary, crushed

1 teaspoon rubbed sage

1/2 teaspoon salt

1/4 teaspoon pepper

Dash to 1/8 teaspoon cayenne pepper

2 packages (10 ounces *each*) frozen chopped spinach, thawed and well drained

1 can (14-3/4 ounces) cream-style corn

In a Dutch oven, saute onion and celery in butter until tender. Add the broth, potatoes, turnip, carrot, green pepper and seasonings. Bring to a boil. Reduce heat; cover and simmer for 15-20 minutes or until vegetables are tender.

Stir in spinach and corn; cool slightly. Puree half of the soup in a blender; return to the pan and heat through.

YIELD: 6 servings.

jennifer neilsen
WILLIAMSTON,
NORTH CAROLINA

Here's a thick, hearty soup that combines a bevy of fresh vegetables with fragrant herbs for an unbeatable flavor.

mushroom barley soup

darlene weise-appleby
CRESTON, OHIO

Looking for a filling, meatless meal in a bowl? Ladle up my delicious soup! It's a treasured favorite of my husband, five kids and grandkids.

1 medium leek (white portion only), halved and thinly sliced

1 cup chopped celery

2 teaspoons olive oil

4 garlic cloves, minced

3/4 pound sliced fresh mushrooms

1-1/2 cups chopped peeled turnips

1-1/2 cups chopped carrots

4 cans (14-1/2 ounces *each*) reduced-sodium vegetable broth *or* beef broth

1 can (14-1/2 ounces) diced tomatoes, undrained

1 bay leaf

1/2 teaspoon salt

1/2 teaspoon dried thyme

1/4 teaspoon pepper

1/4 teaspoon caraway seeds

1 cup quick-cooking barley

4 cups fresh baby spinach, cut into thin strips

In a large saucepan coated with cooking spray, cook leek and celery in oil for 2 minutes. Add garlic; cook 1 minute longer. Add the mushrooms, turnips and carrots; cook 4-5 minutes longer or until mushrooms are tender.

Stir in the broth, tomatoes and seasonings. Bring to a boil. Reduce heat; cover and simmer for 10-15 minutes or until turnips are tender. Add barley; simmer 10 minutes longer. Stir in spinach; cook 5 minutes more or until the spinach and barley are tender. Discard bay leaf.

YIELD: 10 servings.

spinach bean soup

1/2 cup chopped onion
1 tablespoon olive oil
3 garlic cloves, minced
2 cups water
1 can (15 ounces) tomato puree
1 can (14-1/2 ounces) reduced-sodium vegetable broth *or* chicken broth

1 teaspoon dried oregano
1/2 teaspoon sugar
1/2 teaspoon salt
1/4 teaspoon pepper
5 cups packed torn fresh spinach
1 can (16 ounces) navy beans, rinsed and drained
1-1/2 cups cooked small tube pasta *or* other small pasta
1/2 to 1 teaspoon hot pepper sauce
8 teaspoons shredded Parmesan cheese

In a large saucepan, saute onion in oil until tender. Add garlic; cook 1 minute longer. Stir in the water, tomato puree, broth, oregano, sugar, salt and pepper. Bring to a boil.

Reduce heat; cover and simmer for 20 minutes. Add the spinach, beans, cooked pasta and hot pepper sauce, heat through. Sprinkle with cheese.

YIELD: 5 servings.

melissa griffin
LANSING, MICHIGAN

This easy soup is so good, I try to share the recipe with as many people as possible. Swimming with pasta, beans and spinach, it makes a fresh-tasting and satisfying first course or a light meal in itself.

cream of potato soup

2 medium potatoes, peeled and diced
1 cup water
2 tablespoons chopped onion
2 tablespoons butter
2 tablespoons all-purpose flour
3 cups whole milk
1/2 teaspoon salt
1/8 teaspoon celery salt
Dash pepper
Paprika and minced fresh parsley

Place the potatoes and water in a saucepan; bring to a boil over medium-high heat. Cover and cook until tender; drain and set aside.

In the same pan, saute onion in butter until tender. Stir in flour until blended. Gradually stir in milk. Bring to a boil; cook and stir for 2 minutes or until thickened. Reduce heat; add the potatoes, salt, celery salt and pepper. Cook for 2-3 minutes or until heated through. Sprinkle with paprika and parsley.

YIELD: 2 servings.

ruth ann stelfox
RAYMOND, ALBERTA

I turn to hot potato soup when the temperatures take a plunge and I'm in need of a little pick-me-up. It's a simple supper that's short on prep time.

tomato basil soup

4 medium carrots, finely chopped
1 large onion, finely chopped
1/4 cup butter, cubed
1 can (49 ounces) reduced-sodium vegetable broth *or* 6 cups chicken broth, *divided*
1 can (29 ounces) tomato puree
5 teaspoons dried basil
1-1/2 teaspoons sugar
1/2 teaspoon salt
1/2 teaspoon white pepper
1 can (12 ounces) fat-free evaporated milk

In a Dutch oven, cook carrots and onion in butter over medium-low heat for 30 minutes or until vegetables are tender, stirring occasionally. Remove from the heat and cool slightly.

In a blender, place 1/2 broth and the cooled vegetables; cover and process until blended. Return to the Dutch oven. Stir in the tomato puree, basil, sugar, salt, pepper and remaining broth.

Bring to a boil. Reduce heat; simmer, uncovered, for 30 minutes. Reduce heat to low. Gradually stir in evaporated milk; heat through (do not boil).

YIELD: 6 servings.

chris baker
SOUTH LAKE TAHOE, CALIFORNIA

After one taste of this slightly sweet tomato and herb soup, my family vowed to never eat to the canned variety again! I adapted it from a recipe I found in an old cookbook.

cream soups

The ultimate comfort food in a bowl, cream soups promise unbridled mouthwatering bliss. You can expect your family and friends to come back for more when you prepare any one of these smooth soups made from vegetables, poultry or seafood mixed with just the right seasonings.

172   180   191

spinach cheese soup

maria regakis
SOMERVILLE, MASSACHUSETTS

Give yourself a delicious calcium boost with my cheesy soup. Add 2 cups cubed cooked chicken or turkey to pack in a little extra protein.

1 cup chicken broth

1 package (6 ounces) fresh baby spinach, chopped

1/2 teaspoon onion powder

1/8 teaspoon pepper

4 teaspoons all-purpose flour

1 can (5 ounces) evaporated milk

1 cup (4 ounces) shredded cheddar cheese

In a small saucepan, combine the broth, spinach, onion powder and pepper. Bring to a boil. Combine flour and milk until smooth; gradually add to the soup. Return to a boil. Reduce heat; cook and stir for 2 minutes or until thickened. Stir in the cheese until melted.

YIELD: 2 servings.

red potato soup

2-1/2 pounds unpeeled small red potatoes,
    cut into 1-inch cubes
    1 large onion, chopped
    3 celery ribs, chopped
    3 bacon strips, chopped
    8 cups milk
    4 cups water
    3 tablespoons chicken bouillon granules
    1 teaspoon salt
  1/2 teaspoon pepper
  3/4 cup butter, cubed
  3/4 cup all-purpose flour
    1 cup heavy whipping cream
  1/2 cup minced fresh parsley
Shredded cheddar cheese and chopped
    green onions

Place potatoes in a saucepan and cover with water. Bring to a boil. Reduce heat; cover and cook for 10-12 minutes or until tender. Drain and set aside.

In a Dutch oven or large soup kettle, saute the onion, celery and bacon until vegetables are tender; drain well. Add the milk, water, bouillon, salt and pepper; heat through (do not boil).

In a large saucepan, melt butter; stir in flour until smooth. Cook and stir over medium heat for 1 minute. Gradually add cream. Bring to a boil; cook and stir for 1-2 minutes or until thickened. Stir into soup. Add parsley and potatoes; heat through. Sprinkle with cheese and green onions.

YIELD: 18 servings.

bev bosveld
WAUPUN, WISCONSIN

This chunky potato soup is one of my go-to entertaining recipes. Onion, celery and bacon season the creamy broth.

red potatoes

Red potatoes are an excellent choice for soups because of their firmness and texture. These spuds are available year-round. Always select those that are firm, smooth-skinned and bright red in color. Store red potatoes in a cool (40 - 50° F), dry, well-ventilated, dark place to protect them from light exposure and to inhibit quick sprouts from growing.

pretty autumn soup

2-1/2 cups cubed peeled butternut squash
    1 large sweet potato, peeled and cubed
    3 medium carrots, sliced
  1/4 cup thawed orange juice concentrate
    3 cups fat-free milk
  1/4 teaspoon salt
  1/4 teaspoon pepper
    3 tablespoons reduced-fat sour cream
    2 tablespoons minced chives
    1 tablespoon sesame seeds, toasted

Place the squash, sweet potato and carrots in a steamer basket; place in a large saucepan over 1 in. of water. Bring to a boil; cover and steam for 12-16 minutes or until tender. Cool slightly. Transfer to a food processor; add juice concentrate. Cover and process until smooth.

Transfer to a large saucepan; stir in the milk, salt and pepper. Cook and stir over low heat until heated through (do not boil). Top each serving with 1-1/2 teaspoons sour cream, 1 teaspoon chives and 1/2 teaspoon sesame seeds.

YIELD: 6 servings.

gwen nelson
CASTRO VALLEY, CALIFORNIA

Carrots, squash and sweet potato combine to make this healthy, colorful soup.

stacy bockelman
CALIFORNIA, MISSOURI

I concocted this soup after I sampled something similar at a restaurant. Using chicken bouillon and frozen hash browns makes it easy to fix. It's especially delicious with sourdough bread.

cream cheese potato soup

6 cups water

7 teaspoons chicken bouillon granules

2 packages (8 ounces *each*) cream cheese, cubed

1 package (30 ounces) frozen cubed hash brown potatoes, thawed

1-1/2 cups cubed fully cooked ham

1/2 cup chopped onion

1 teaspoon garlic powder

1 teaspoon dill weed

In a Dutch oven, combine the water and bouillon. Add cream cheese; cook and stir until the cheese is melted. Stir in the remaining ingredients. Bring to a boil. Reduce heat; simmer, uncovered, for 18-20 minutes or until vegetables are tender.

YIELD: 12 servings.

laurel leslie
SONORA, CALIFORNIA

Everyone adores the lovely golden color and creamy consistency of my soup. A touch of ginger sparks the mild squash flavor.

ginger squash soup

3 cups chicken broth

2 packages (10 ounces *each*) frozen cooked winter squash, thawed

1 cup unsweetened applesauce

3 tablespoons sugar

1 teaspoon ground ginger

1/2 teaspoon salt

1/2 cup heavy whipping cream, whipped

In a large saucepan, simmer broth and squash. Add the applesauce, sugar, ginger and salt. Bring to a boil. Reduce heat to low; stir in cream. Cook for 30 minutes or until soup reaches desired consistency, stirring occasionally.

YIELD: 6 servings.

carol colvin
DERBY, NEW YORK

My husband is diabetic, and I'm watching my weight. Not only does this soup fit within our dietary requirements, it only takes 15 minutes to make!

makeover broccoli cheese soup

1 can (10-3/4 ounces) reduced-fat reduced-sodium condensed cream of celery soup, undiluted

1 can (10-3/4 ounces) reduced-fat reduced-sodium condensed cream of chicken soup, undiluted

3 cups fat-free milk

1 tablespoon dried minced onion

1 teaspoon dried parsley flakes

1/2 teaspoon garlic powder

1/4 teaspoon pepper

3 cups frozen chopped broccoli, thawed

1 can (14-1/2 ounces) sliced potatoes, drained

1/2 cup shredded reduced-fat cheddar cheese

In a large saucepan, combine the soups, milk, onion, parsley, garlic powder and pepper. Stir in broccoli and potatoes; heat through. Just before serving, sprinkle with cheese.

YIELD: 8 servings.

garlic fennel bisque

4 cups water

2-1/2 cups half-and-half cream

24 garlic cloves, peeled and halved

3 medium fennel bulbs, cut into 1/2-inch pieces

2 tablespoons chopped fennel fronds

1/2 teaspoon salt

1/8 teaspoon pepper

1/2 cup pine nuts, toasted

In a Dutch oven, bring the water, cream and garlic to a boil. Reduce heat; cover and simmer for 15 minutes or until garlic is very soft. Add fennel and fennel fronds; cover and simmer 15 minutes longer or until fennel is very soft.

Cool slightly. In a blender, process soup in batches until blended. Return all to the pan. Season with salt and pepper; heat through. Sprinkle each serving with pine nuts.

YIELD: 14 servings.

janet ondrich
THAMESVILLE, ONTARIO

Here's a wonderful, change-of-pace addition to any menu. The fennel in the bisque is so refreshing.

makeover cream of tomato soup

linda parkhurst
BROOKLYN, MICHIGAN

This makeover creation boasts the same creamy taste with half the fat and sodium of comparable tomato soup recipes.

1 can (14-1/2 ounces) stewed tomatoes

4 ounces reduced-fat cream cheese, cubed

1 medium onion, chopped

2 tablespoons butter

2 garlic cloves, minced

3 cans (10-3/4 ounces *each*) reduced-sodium condensed tomato soup, undiluted

4 cans (5-1/2 ounces *each*) reduced-sodium V8 juice

3 tablespoons tomato paste

1 cup fat-free half-and-half

1/2 teaspoon dried basil

SEASONED OYSTER CRACKERS:

3 cups oyster crackers

2 tablespoons canola oil

1 tablespoon ranch salad dressing mix

1/2 teaspoon garlic powder

1/2 teaspoon dill weed

9 tablespoons shredded part-skim mozzarella cheese

In a food processor, combine the stewed tomatoes and cream cheese; cover and process until smooth. Set aside.

In a large saucepan, saute onion in butter until crisp-tender; Add garlic; cook 1 minute longer. Whisk in tomato soup, V8 and tomato paste until blended. Gradually stir in cream cheese mixture, half-and-half and basil. Cook and stir until heated through (do not boil).

In a large bowl, combine the seasoned oyster crackers, oil, dressing mix, garlic powder and dill; toss to coat. Ladle soup into bowls; sprinkle with crackers and cheese.

YIELD: 9 servings (3 cups crackers).

golden squash soup

5 medium leeks (white portion only), sliced
2 tablespoons butter
1-1/2 pounds butternut squash, peeled, seeded and cubed (about 4 cups)
4 cups chicken broth
1/4 teaspoon dried thyme
1/4 teaspoon pepper
1-3/4 cups shredded cheddar cheese
1/4 cup sour cream
2 tablespoons thinly sliced green onion

In a large saucepan, saute leeks in butter until tender. Stir in the squash, broth, thyme and pepper. Bring to a boil. Reduce heat; cover and simmer for 10-15 minutes or until squash is tender. Cool slightly.

In a blender, cover and process squash mixture in small batches until smooth; return all to the pan. Bring to a boil. Reduce heat to low. Add cheese; stir until soup is heated through and cheese is melted. Garnish with sour cream and onion.

YIELD: 6 servings.

becky ruff
MCGREGOR, IOWA

The rich, golden color of my squash soup makes it perfect for the fall. Every spoonful is pure bliss.

cucumber soup

3 medium cucumbers
3 cups chicken broth
3 cups (24 ounces) sour cream
3 tablespoons cider vinegar
2 teaspoons salt, optional
1 garlic clove, minced
TOPPINGS:
2 medium tomatoes, chopped
3/4 cup sliced almonds, toasted
1/2 cup chopped green onions
1/2 cup minced fresh parsley

Peel cucumbers; halve lengthwise and remove seeds. Cut into chunks. In a blender, cover and puree cucumbers and broth in small batches.

Transfer to a large bowl; stir in the sour cream, vinegar, salt if desired and garlic until well blended. Cover and refrigerate for at least 4 hours. Stir before serving. Garnish with tomatoes, almonds, onions and parsley.

YIELD: 12 servings.

beverly sprague
BALTIMORE, MARYLAND

Dress up my smooth cucumber soup with a savory selection of garnishes. Toasted almonds on top add a pleasant crunch.

creamy asparagus soup

2 medium leeks (white portion only), sliced
12 green onions, chopped
2 tablespoons olive oil
1 tablespoon butter
2-1/2 pounds fresh asparagus, cut into 1-inch pieces
4 cups chicken broth
1 cup half-and-half cream
1/2 teaspoon salt
1/8 teaspoon pepper

In a large saucepan, saute leeks and onions in oil and butter until tender. Add the asparagus and broth. Bring to a boil. Reduce heat; simmer, uncovered, until vegetables are tender. Remove from the heat. Set aside 1 cup of asparagus pieces.

In a blender, process the remaining asparagus mixture in batches until smooth; return to the pan. Stir in the cream, salt and pepper. Cook over low heat until heated through. Garnish with reserved asparagus pieces.

YIELD: 6 servings.

pat stevens
GRANBURY, TEXAS

After trying several asparagus soup recipes, I combined the ingredients I liked best from each to create this version. It adds an elegant touch to any special-occasion meal.

suzanna snader

FREDERICKSBURG,
PENNSYLVANIA

*This thick and creamy
sensation is chock-full of
rich, cheesy flavor. I know
your family will enjoy it
as much as mine does.*

dash vs. pinch

Traditionally, a dash is a
very small amount of
seasoning added with a
quick downward stroke of the
hand. A pinch is the amount
of a dry ingredient that can be
held between your thumb
and forefinger. Both are
usually somewhere between
1/16 and a scant 1/8 teaspoon.

lois mcatee

OCEANSIDE, CALIFORNIA

*My kids wouldn't eat
asparagus when they
were little. But they all
asked for seconds after
trying this smooth soup.
Use frozen asparagus to
hurry along prep time.*

hearty cheese soup

1-1/2 cups cubed peeled potatoes
1/2 cup water
1/4 cup sliced celery
1/4 cup sliced fresh carrots
 2 tablespoons chopped onion
1/2 teaspoon chicken bouillon granules
1/2 teaspoon dried parsley flakes
1/4 teaspoon salt
Dash pepper
1-1/2 teaspoons all-purpose flour
3/4 cup milk
1/4 pound process cheese (Velveeta),
 cubed

In a small saucepan, combine the first nine
ingredients. Bring to a boil. Reduce the heat; cover
and simmer for 10-12 minutes or until the potatoes
are tender.

In a small bowl, combine flour and milk until
smooth. Stir into vegetable mixture. Bring to a boil;
cook and stir for 2 minutes or until thickened.
Reduce heat to low; stir in cheese until melted.

YIELD: 2 servings.

asparagus soup

1 package (10 ounces) frozen
 asparagus cuts
1 large onion, chopped
1 cup water
1 teaspoon salt
1 teaspoon chicken bouillon granules
1/2 teaspoon dried basil

1/8 teaspoon white pepper
1-1/2 cups milk
1/2 cup heavy whipping cream
Seasoned salad croutons

In a saucepan, combine asparagus, onion, water,
salt, bouillon, basil and pepper. Bring to a boil.
Reduce heat; cover and simmer for 10-12 minutes
or until vegetables are tender. Cool for 5 minutes;
stir in milk.

In a blender or food processor, process the
soup in batches until smooth; return to the pan. Stir
in cream; heat through. Garnish with croutons.

YIELD: 4-6 servings.

mexican shrimp bisque

1 small onion, chopped
1 tablespoon olive oil
2 garlic cloves, minced
1 tablespoon all-purpose flour
1 cup water
1/2 cup heavy whipping cream
1 tablespoon chili powder
2 teaspoons sodium-free chicken
   bouillon granules
1/2 teaspoon ground cumin
1/2 teaspoon ground coriander
1/2 pound uncooked medium shrimp,
   peeled and deveined
1/2 cup sour cream
Fresh cilantro and cubed avocado, optional

In a small saucepan, saute onion in oil until tender. Add garlic; cook 1 minute longer. Stir in flour until blended. Stir in the water, cream, chili powder, bouillon, cumin and coriander; bring to a boil. Reduce heat; cover and simmer for 5 minutes.

Cut shrimp into bite-size pieces; add to soup. Simmer 5 minutes longer or until shrimp turn pink. Gradually stir 1/2 cup hot soup into sour cream; return all to the pan, stirring constantly. Heat through (do not boil). Garnish with cilantro and avocado if desired.

YIELD: 3 servings.

karen harris
CASTLE ROCK, COLORADO

We live along the front range of the Rockies, and there's nothing that warms us up faster on a cold day than a steaming bowl of this succulent bisque. It features the perfect blend of seafood and Mexican flavors.

creamy carrot soup

bertha mcclung
SUMMERSVILLE, WEST VIRGINIA

My blended carrot soup is loaded with vegetables, so it's both delicious and good for you. The vibrant color adds a special touch to the table.

3 cups thinly sliced carrots
1 cup chopped onion
2/3 cup chopped celery
1-1/2 cups diced peeled potatoes
1 garlic clove, minced
1/2 teaspoon sugar
2 teaspoons canola oil
4 cups reduced-sodium chicken broth
Dash ground nutmeg
Pepper to taste

In a Dutch oven or soup kettle over medium-low heat, saute carrots, onion, celery, potatoes, garlic and sugar in oil for 5 minutes. Add broth, nutmeg and pepper; bring to a boil. Reduce heat; cover and simmer for 30-40 minutes or until vegetables are tender. Remove from the heat and cool to room temperature. Puree in batches in a blender or food processor. Return to the kettle and heat through.

YIELD: 4 servings.

garlic soup

6 garlic cloves, minced
1 tablespoon olive oil
8 cups chicken broth
1/2 teaspoon salt
1/8 teaspoon pepper
1/8 teaspoon dried thyme
1/8 teaspoon dried rosemary, crushed
3 egg yolks
1/2 cup half-and-half cream
8 slices frozen garlic bread, thawed and toasted
Grated Parmesan cheese

In a large saucepan, cook and stir the garlic in oil over low heat for 1 minute or until lightly browned. Stir in the broth, salt, pepper, thyme and rosemary; simmer, uncovered, for 1 hour.

Strain broth and return to the pan. In a small bowl, whisk egg yolks and cream. Stir in 1/2 cup hot broth. Return all to the pan, stirring constantly. Cook and stir over medium heat until soup reaches 160° (do not boil). Top each serving with a slice of garlic bread; sprinkle with cheese.

YIELD: 8 servings.

iola egle
BELLA VISTA, ARKANSAS

A wonderful garlicky aroma will fill your kitchen as this soup simmers! You will love the toasted bread floating on top of a rich and creamy bowlful.

minced garlic

Store-bought minced garlic, garlic that's been finely chopped by hand and garlic that's been put through a press can all be used interchangeably in recipes. Choose whichever is easiest and most convenient for you.

mushroom potato soup

2 medium leeks, sliced
2 large carrots, sliced
6 tablespoons butter, *divided*
6 cups chicken broth
5 cups diced peeled potatoes
1 tablespoon minced fresh dill
1 teaspoon salt
1/8 teaspoon pepper
1 bay leaf
1 pound sliced fresh mushrooms
1/4 cup all-purpose flour
1 cup heavy whipping cream

In a Dutch oven or soup kettle, saute leeks and carrots in 3 tablespoons butter for 5 minutes or until tender. Stir in the broth, potatoes, dill, salt, pepper and bay leaf. Bring to a boil. Reduce heat; cover and simmer for 15-20 minutes or until potatoes are tender.

Meanwhile, in a large skillet, saute mushrooms in the remaining butter for 4-6 minutes or until tender. Discard the bay leaf from the soup. Stir in the mushroom mixture.

In a small bowl, combine flour and cream until smooth; gradually stir into soup. Bring to a boil; cook and stir for 2 minutes or until thickened.

YIELD: 12 servings.

clare wallace
LYNCHBURG, VIRGINIA

A buttery mushroom flavor blends with leeks, potatoes and carrots in this filling soup. I use waxy red potatoes or all-purpose Yukon Golds because they hold together well in boiling water.

lori kimble

MCDONALD, PENNSYLVANIA

My rich and satisfying chowder took top honors at a local cooking competition. It's especially delicious served with sourdough bread.

creamy clam chowder

1 large onion, chopped

3 medium carrots, chopped

2 celery ribs, sliced

3/4 cup butter, cubed

2 cans (10-3/4 ounces *each*) condensed cream of potato soup, undiluted

3 cans (6-1/2 ounces *each*) minced clams

3 tablespoons cornstarch

1 quart half-and-half cream

In a large saucepan, saute the onion, carrots and celery in butter until tender. Stir in potato soup and two cans of undrained clams. Drain and discard juice from remaining can of clams; add the clams to the soup.

Combine cornstarch and a small amount of cream until smooth; stir into the soup. Add the remaining cream. Bring to a boil; cook and stir for 2 minutes or until thickened.

YIELD: 9 servings.

jean hall

RAPID CITY, SOUTH DAKOTA

A slow cooker makes easy work of my niece's classic soup. She simply tosses in all the ingredients except the cheese. When the veggies are tender, she adds the cubed cheese, and five minutes later, a nutritious meal is ready!

veggie cheese soup

1 medium onion, chopped

1 celery rib, chopped

2 small red potatoes, cut into 1/2-inch cubes

2-3/4 cups water

2 teaspoons reduced-sodium chicken bouillon granules

1 tablespoon cornstarch

1/4 cup cold water

1 can (10-3/4 ounces) reduced-fat reduced-sodium condensed cream of chicken soup, undiluted

3 cups frozen California-blend vegetables, thawed

1/2 cup chopped fully cooked lean ham

8 ounces reduced-fat process cheese (Velveeta), cubed

In a large nonstick saucepan coated with a cooking spray, cook onion and celery over medium heat until onion is tender. Stir in the potatoes, water and bouillon. Bring to a boil. Reduce heat; cover and simmer for 10 minutes.

Combine the cornstarch and cold water until smooth; gradually stir into soup. Return to a boil; cook and stir for 1-2 minutes or until slightly thickened. Stir in condensed soup until blended.

Reduce heat; add the vegetables and ham. Cook and stir until the vegetables are tender. Stir in the cheese until melted.

YIELD: 9 servings.

cream of mussel soup

3 pounds fresh mussels (about
   5 dozen), scrubbed and beards
   removed
2 medium onions, finely chopped
2 celery ribs, finely chopped
1 cup water
1 cup white wine *or* chicken broth
1 bottle (8 ounces) clam juice
1/4 cup minced fresh parsley
2 garlic cloves, minced
1/4 teaspoon salt
1/4 teaspoon pepper
1 cup half-and-half cream

Tap mussels; discard any that do not close. Set aside. In a stock pot, combine the onions, celery, water, wine or broth, clam juice, parsley, garlic, salt and pepper.

Bring to a boil. Reduce heat; add mussels. Cover and simmer for 5-6 minutes or until mussels have opened. Remove mussels with a slotted spoon, discarding any unopened mussels; set aside opened mussels and keep warm.

Cool cooking liquid slightly. In a blender, cover and process cooking liquid in batches until blended. Return all to pan. Add cream and reserved mussels; heat through (do not boil).

YIELD: 5 servings.

donna noel
GRAY, MAINE

Every New England cook has a personal version of mussel soup, depending on the favored regional herbs and cooking customs. Feel free to start with my recipe, and develop your own luscious variation.

cordon bleu potato soup

noelle myers
GRAND FORKS, NORTH DAKOTA

I came up with this recipe when I was looking for a way to use up some leftover ingredients. It's so yummy! It's also an easy way to simmer up some hearty comfort in a hurry.

2 cans (10-3/4 ounces *each*) condensed cream of potato soup, undiluted

1 can (14-1/2 ounces) chicken broth

1 cup (4 ounces) shredded Swiss cheese

1 cup diced fully cooked ham

1 cup 2% milk

1 can (5 ounces) chunk white chicken, drained

2 teaspoons Dijon mustard

In a 2-qt. microwave-safe dish, combine all the ingredients. Cover and microwave on high for 5-8 minutes or until heated through, stirring twice.

YIELD: 4 servings.

EDITOR'S NOTE: This recipe was tested in a 1,100-watt microwave.

apple pumpkin soup

- 2 cups finely chopped peeled tart apples
- 1/2 cup finely chopped onion
- 2 tablespoons butter
- 1 tablespoon all-purpose flour
- 4 cups chicken broth
- 3 cups canned pumpkin
- 1/4 cup packed brown sugar
- 1/2 teaspoon *each* ground cinnamon, nutmeg and ginger
- 1 cup unsweetened apple juice
- 1/2 cup half-and-half cream
- 1/4 teaspoon salt
- 1/4 teaspoon pepper

In a large saucepan, saute apples and onion in butter for 3-5 minutes or until tender. Stir in flour until blended. Gradually whisk in broth. Stir in the pumpkin, brown sugar, cinnamon, nutmeg and ginger. Bring to a boil. Reduce heat; cover and simmer for 25 minutes. Cool slightly.

In a blender, cover and process soup in batches until smooth. Pour into a bowl; cover and refrigerate for 8 hours or overnight.

Just before serving, transfer soup to a large saucepan. Cook over medium heat for 5-10 minutes. Stir in the apple juice, cream, salt and pepper; heat through.

YIELD: 12 servings.

pat habiger
SPEARVILLE, KANSAS

Relish autumn's color and flavors with this creamy, golden soup. For a creative Halloween treat, serve in hollow mini pumpkins.

easy substitute

If you don't have any half-and-half on hand, you can substitute 4-1/2 teaspoons melted butter plus enough whole milk to equal 1 cup to use in any dish that is cooked or baked. One cup of evaporated milk may also be substituted for each cup of half-and-half cream.

creamy turkey vegetable soup

- 1 cup chopped fresh carrots
- 1/2 cup chopped celery
- 1/3 cup chopped onion
- 2 tablespoons butter
- 2 cups diced cooked turkey
- 2 cups water
- 1-1/2 cups diced peeled potatoes
- 2 teaspoons chicken bouillon granules
- 1/2 teaspoon salt
- 1/2 teaspoon pepper
- 2-1/2 cups whole milk, *divided*
- 3 tablespoons all-purpose flour

In a large saucepan, saute the carrots, celery and onion in butter until tender. Stir in the turkey, water, potatoes, bouillon, salt and pepper. Bring to a boil. Reduce heat; cover and simmer for 10-12 minutes or until vegetables are tender.

Stir in 2 cups milk. Combine flour and remaining milk until smooth. Stir into soup. Bring to a boil; cook and stir for 2 minutes or until thickened.

YIELD: 4 servings.

stephanie moon
BOISE, IDAHO

Looking for a new way to use up leftover turkey? Give my comforting creation a try. It's melt-in-your-mouth delicious.

beth allard

BELMONT, NEW HAMPSHIRE

I started with a basic potato soup and added a few special touches to come up with my own recipe. I love the yummy combination of potatoes and Italian sausage.

hearty garlic potato soup

8 medium potatoes, peeled and cut into 1/2-inch cubes
1 large carrot, peeled and chopped
2 garlic cloves, peeled
1/2 pound bulk Italian sausage
1 small onion, chopped
1/4 cup butter, cubed
1/4 cup all-purpose flour
8 cups milk
2 teaspoons minced fresh parsley
1-1/2 teaspoons salt
1 teaspoon chicken bouillon granules
1/2 teaspoon seasoned salt
1/4 teaspoon pepper

Place potatoes, carrot and garlic in a Dutch oven and cover with water. Bring to a boil. Reduce heat; cover and simmer for 15-20 minutes or until tender. Drain. Place 3 cups potato mixture in a large bowl and mash. Set aside mashed potatoes and remaining potato mixture.

In a large skillet, cook sausage and onion over medium heat until meat is no longer pink; drain and set aside. In a Dutch oven, melt the butter. Stir in the flour until smooth; gradually add the milk. Bring to a boil; cook and stir for 2 minutes or until the soup is thickened.

Add the parsley, salt, bouillon, seasoned salt and pepper; mix well. Add mashed potato mixture; cook and stir until heated through. Add reserved potato and sausage mixtures. Heat through.

YIELD: 12 servings.

heidi wilcox

LAPEER, MICHIGAN

My delicate and lemony squash creation is perfect for a shower or luncheon. It features the best of late summer's produce in a hot, simmering soup.

summer squash soup

2 large sweet onions, chopped
1 medium leek (white portion only), chopped
2 tablespoons olive oil
6 garlic cloves, minced
6 medium yellow summer squash, seeded and cubed
4 cups reduced-sodium chicken broth
4 fresh thyme sprigs
1/4 teaspoon salt
2 tablespoons lemon juice
1/8 teaspoon hot pepper sauce
1 tablespoon shredded Parmesan cheese
2 teaspoons grated lemon peel

In a large saucepan, saute onions and leek in oil until tender. Add garlic; cook 1 minute longer. Add squash; saute 5 minutes. Stir in the broth, thyme and salt. Bring to a boil. Reduce heat; cover and simmer for 15-20 minutes or until squash is tender.

Discard thyme sprigs. Cool slightly. In a blender, process soup in batches until smooth. Return all to the pan. Stir in lemon juice and hot pepper sauce; heat through. Sprinkle each serving with cheese and lemon peel.

YIELD: 8 servings.

creamy chicken rice soup

1/2 cup chopped onion
1 medium carrot, chopped
1 celery rib, chopped
1 tablespoon canola oil
1/2 teaspoon minced garlic
2 cans (14-1/2 ounces) chicken broth
1/3 cup uncooked long grain rice
3/4 teaspoon dried basil
1/4 teaspoon pepper
3 tablespoons all-purpose flour
1 can (5 ounces) evaporated milk
1 package (9 ounces) frozen diced cooked chicken, thawed

In a large saucepan, saute the onion, carrot, celery in oil until tender. Add garlic; cook 1 minute longer. Stir in the broth, rice, basil and pepper. Bring to a boil. Reduce heat; cover and simmer for 15 minutes or until rice is tender.

In a small bowl, combine flour and milk until smooth; stir into soup. Bring to a boil; cook and stir for 2 minutes or until thickened. Stir in the chicken; heat through.

YIELD: 5 servings.

janice mitchell
AURORA, COLORADO

I came up with this thick, flavorful soup while making some adjustments to a favorite stovetop chicken casserole. We like this dish for lunch with a warm roll and fresh fruit.

classic broccoli cheese soup

jean parè
VERMILION, ALBERTA

Bright orange carrots contrast nicely with green broccoli in this colorful sensation. It makes use of the microwave, so it's a breeze to whip up!

1 cup thinly sliced carrots

2 tablespoons plus 1 cup water, *divided*

1 package (16 ounces) frozen broccoli florets, thawed

2-1/2 cups milk

1/4 cup all-purpose flour

2 teaspoons chicken bouillon granules

1/2 teaspoon salt

1/4 teaspoon pepper

1 cup (4 ounces) shredded cheddar cheese

In a 2-qt. microwave-safe dish, combine carrots and 2 tablespoons water. Cover and microwave on high for 2 minutes; stir. Cover and cook 2 minutes longer or until tender. Add broccoli. Cover and microwave for 2 minutes; stir. Cover and cook 1 to 1-1/2 minutes longer or until vegetables are tender. Stir in milk.

In a small bowl, combine the flour, bouillon, salt and pepper; stir in remaining water until smooth. Stir into broccoli mixture. Cover and microwave on high for 6-7 minutes or until mixture is boiling and thickened, stirring every minute. Stir in cheese until melted.

YIELD: 4-5 servings.

classic cream of mushroom soup

1/4 cup chopped onion
2 tablespoons butter
3 cups sliced fresh mushrooms
6 tablespoons all-purpose flour
2 cans (14-1/2 ounces *each*)
  chicken broth
1 cup half-and-half cream
1/2 teaspoon salt
1/8 teaspoon pepper

In a large saucepan, saute onion in butter until tender. Add mushrooms and saute until tender. Combine flour and broth until smooth; stir into the mushroom mixture. Bring to a boil; cook and stir for 2 minutes or until thickened. Reduce heat. Stir in the cream, salt and pepper. Simmer, uncovered, for 15 minutes, stirring often.

YIELD: 4-6 servings.

anne kulick
PHILLIPSBURG, NEW JERSEY

My daughter-in-law, a gourmet cook, served this classic soup as the first course for Thanksgiving dinner. It beats the canned variety any day.

cabbage sausage soup

4 cups chicken broth
1 small cabbage, chopped
  (about 10 cups)
1 medium onion, chopped
1/2 pound smoked sausage, halved
  lengthwise and sliced
1/2 cup all-purpose flour
1-1/2 teaspoons salt
1/4 teaspoon pepper
1 cup milk

In a Dutch oven, bring broth, cabbage and onion to a boil. Reduce heat; cover and simmer for 10-15 minutes or until cabbage is tender. Add sausage; heat through.

In a bowl, combine the flour, salt and pepper. Gradually add milk, stirring until smooth. Gradually stir into soup. Bring to a boil; cook and stir for 2 minutes or until thickened.

YIELD: 8 servings.

nancy allman
DERRY, PENNSYLVANIA

This hearty autumn soup featuring smoked sausage is perfect for time-pressed cooks. My mother often made it when we had a surplus of cabbage from our garden.

cheesy vegetable soup

1 large onion, chopped
5 tablespoons butter, *divided*
2 cups water
2 cups shredded cabbage
1-1/2 cups frozen lima beans, thawed
1 cup sliced carrots
1 cup diced peeled potatoes
1 tablespoon chicken bouillon granules
3 tablespoons all-purpose flour
1/4 teaspoon paprika
1/4 teaspoon pepper
2 cups milk
1 cup half-and-half cream
1-1/2 cups (6 ounces) shredded
  cheddar cheese
Minced fresh parsley

In a large saucepan, saute onion in 2 tablespoons butter until tender. Add the water, vegetables and bouillon. Bring to a boil. Reduce the heat; cover and simmer for 20 minutes or until the vegetables are tender.

Meanwhile, in a small saucepan, melt remaining butter. Stir in the flour, paprika and pepper until smooth. Gradually add milk and cream. Bring to a boil; cook and stir for 2 minutes or until thickened. Reduce heat; stir in cheese until melted. Add to soup; heat through. Sprinkle with parsley.

YIELD: 8 servings.

dana worley
LEBANON, TENNESSEE

Shredded cheddar cheese adds flavor to my smooth-as-silk soup that's loaded with good-for-you lima beans, cabbage, carrots and potatoes. It's always a crowd-pleaser!

lima beans

Sometimes called "butter beans" because of their starchy yet buttery texture, lima beans have a delicate flavor that complements a wide variety of dishes. Although fresh lima beans can be hard to find, they are worth looking for in summer and fall when they are in season. Dried, canned and frozen lima beans are available throughout the year.

phyllis clinehens
MAPLEWOOD, OHIO

I grew up on a farm, and we could eat soup every day of the week—as long as it didn't come from a can! A subtle hint of horseradish and ginger sparks every steaming spoonful of this rich, creamy concoction.

creamy carrot parsnip soup

8 cups chopped carrots
6 cups chopped peeled parsnips
4 cups chicken broth
3 cups water
2 teaspoons sugar
1 teaspoon salt
1 medium onion, chopped
4 garlic cloves, minced
1 teaspoon peeled grated horseradish
1 teaspoon minced fresh gingerroot
3 tablespoons butter
2 cups buttermilk
2 tablespoons sour cream
Fresh dill sprigs, optional

In a Dutch oven, combine the carrots, parsnips, broth, water, sugar and salt; bring to a boil. Reduce heat; cover and cook for 25-30 minutes or until vegetables are tender.

In a small skillet, saute the onion, garlic, horseradish and ginger in butter until tender. Add to the carrot mixture.

Transfer soup to a blender in batches; cover and process until smooth. Return to the pan. Stir in buttermilk; heat through (do not boil).

Garnish servings with sour cream and dill if desired.

YIELD: 12 servings.

carolyn zimmerman
FAIRBURY, ILLINOIS

An earthy mushroom flavor shines in my hearty soup. It will have your clan arguing over who gets the last drop!

cream of mushroom soup

1 teaspoon beef bouillon granules
1/4 cup boiling water
3 cups sliced fresh mushrooms
1/4 cup chopped onion
2 tablespoons butter
2 tablespoons all-purpose flour
1 cup 2% milk
6 ounces cream cheese, cubed

In a small bowl, dissolve bouillon in water; set aside. In a small saucepan, saute mushrooms and onion in butter until tender. Stir in flour.

Gradually add milk and reserved broth. Bring to a boil over medium heat, stirring constantly; cook for 1-2 minutes or until thickened. Reduce heat; stir in cream cheese until melted and soup is heated through.

YIELD: 3 servings.

linda manuszak
CLINTON TOWNSHIP, MICHIGAN

I created this soup while trying to duplicate one I enjoyed at a restaurant in Philadelphia. My husband and I savor it alongside grilled cheese sandwiches.

creamy tomato basil soup

2 tablespoons chopped green onion
2 garlic cloves, minced
1-1/2 teaspoons olive oil
1 can (28 ounces) crushed tomatoes
1 can (10-1/2 ounces) condensed chicken broth, undiluted
1-1/3 cups water
1/4 teaspoon pepper
3/4 cup heavy whipping cream
2 tablespoons sherry *or* additional chicken broth
2 tablespoons minced fresh basil
2 teaspoons sugar

In a large saucepan, saute the onion and garlic in oil until tender. Add the tomatoes, broth, water and pepper. Bring to a boil. Reduce the heat; simmer for 10 minutes.

Stir in the cream, sherry or additional broth, basil and sugar. Cook for 1 minute or until heated through (do not boil).

YIELD: 6 servings.

beer cheese soup

- 2 tablespoons finely chopped onion
- 1/2 teaspoon butter
- 2 cans (10-3/4 ounces *each*) condensed cream of celery soup, undiluted
- 1 cup beer *or* nonalcoholic beer
- 1 cup whole milk
- 1 teaspoon Worcestershire sauce
- 1/2 teaspoon dried parsley flakes
- 1/4 teaspoon paprika
- 3/4 pound process cheese (Velveeta), cubed

In a large saucepan, saute onion in butter. Stir in the soup, beer, milk, Worcestershire sauce, parsley and paprika. Reduce heat to medium-low; stir in cheese until melted. Heat through (do not boil).

YIELD: 6 servings.

sharon lock
FORMAN, NORTH DAKOTA

A family friend used to invite us over for Sunday dinner and got us hooked on this classic beer cheese soup. Onion, paprika and beer perfectly unite for a smooth, rich flavor.

creamy reuben soup

jay davis
KNOXVILLE, TENNESSEE

I had a college professor who had a penchant for Reubens. When I heard he was down with the flu, I whipped up this creamy wonder that features all the classic sandwich flavors. He loved it!

1/2 cup chopped onion
1/4 cup chopped celery
1/4 cup chopped green pepper
1/4 cup butter, cubed
2 tablespoons all-purpose flour
1 cup beef broth
2 cups half-and-half cream
1/4 pound sliced deli corned beef, coarsely chopped
3/4 cup sauerkraut, rinsed and well drained
1/4 teaspoon salt
1/4 teaspoon pepper
1 cup (4 ounces) shredded Swiss cheese

In a large saucepan, saute the onion, celery and green pepper in butter until tender. Stir in flour until blended; gradually add broth. Bring to a boil; cook and stir for 2 minutes or until thickened.

Reduce heat to low. Add the cream, corned beef, sauerkraut, salt and pepper; heat through (do not boil). Stir in cheese until melted.

YIELD: 5 servings.

cream of broccoli soup

2 cups water
4 teaspoons chicken bouillon granules
6 cups frozen chopped broccoli
2 tablespoons finely chopped onion
2 cans (10-3/4 ounces *each*) condensed cream of chicken soup, undiluted
2 cups evaporated milk
2 cups (16 ounces) sour cream
1 teaspoon dried parsley flakes
1/4 teaspoon pepper

In a large saucepan, combine the water and bouillon. Add the broccoli and onion. Bring to a boil; reduce heat. Simmer for 10 minutes or until the broccoli is crisp-tender.

In a large bowl, combine the soup, milk, sour cream, parsley and pepper; add to the broccoli mixture. Cook and stir for 3-5 minutes or until heated through.

YIELD: 6-8 servings.

gaylene anderson
SANDY, UTAH

This soup is a great meal starter, but I also serve it as the main course when I'm in need of something quick and nourishing.

cheesy ham 'n' rice soup

4 celery ribs, chopped
1 large onion, chopped
1/4 cup butter, cubed
4 medium carrots, shredded
1/3 cup all-purpose flour
1 teaspoon salt
1/2 teaspoon pepper
2 cups half-and-half cream
8 ounces process cheese (Velveeta), cubed
4 cups cooked wild rice
3 cups cubed fully cooked ham
2-2/3 cups cooked brown rice
3 tablespoons chicken bouillon granules

8 cups water
Slivered almonds, optional

In a large saucepan, saute the celery and onion in butter until tender. Add the carrots; cook and stir for 1-2 minutes. In a large kettle or Dutch oven, combine the flour, salt and pepper. Gradually stir in the cream. Bring to a boil; cook and stir for 2 minutes or until thickened.

Remove from the heat; stir in the cheese until melted. Stir in the wild rice, ham, brown rice, bouillon, celery mixture and water. Return to a boil. Sprinkle with almonds if desired.

YIELD: 12 servings.

nicole weir
HAGER CITY, WISCONSIN

Here's a real gem! I tasted a similar soup at a local restaurant in the Twin Cities and decided to come up with my own version. Slivered almonds on top yield a fun crunch.

asparagus cheese soup

1/4 cup butter
1/4 cup all-purpose flour
2 teaspoons salt
1/8 teaspoon pepper
6 cups milk
4 cups cut fresh asparagus (1-inch pieces), cooked and drained *or* 2 packages (10 ounces *each*) frozen cut asparagus, thawed
3 cups (12 ounces) shredded cheddar cheese
4 teaspoons minced fresh thyme *or* 1-1/2 teaspoons dried thyme
1/8 teaspoon ground nutmeg
Croutons and additional shredded cheddar cheese, optional

In a large saucepan, melt butter. Stir in the flour, salt and pepper until smooth. Gradually add milk; bring

to a boil. Cook and stir for 2 minutes. Add asparagus and heat through. Add the cheese, thyme and nutmeg. Cook until the cheese is melted, stirring frequently (do not boil). Garnish with croutons and additional cheese if desired.

YIELD: 6-8 servings.

elizabeth montgomery
ALLSTON, MASSACHUSETTS

Looking for a something different to include on an Easter or spring menu? You'll love my cheesy soup pleasantly flavored with thyme and nutmeg.

revive limp asparagus

To give new life to limp asparagus, cut 1/4 inch from the bottom of each spear. Place spears in a glass of ice water; cover with a plastic bag and refrigerate for 2 hours—the asparagus will crisp right up.

joanne eickhoff
PEQUOT LAKES, MINNESOTA

This is a quick way to add a homemade touch to canned soup. It's thick and creamy with added texture from crunchy wild rice and a subtle smoky bacon flavor.

wild rice soup

1/2 cup water
4-1/2 teaspoons dried minced onion
2/3 cup condensed cream of potato soup, undiluted
1/2 cup shredded Swiss cheese
1/2 cup cooked wild rice
1/2 cup half-and-half cream
2 bacon strips, cooked and crumbled

In a small saucepan, bring water and onion to a boil. Reduce heat. Stir in the potato soup, cheese, rice and cream; heat through (do not boil). Garnish with bacon.

YIELD: 2 servings.

patterson watkins
PHILADELPHIA, PENNSYLVANIA

Get your next dinner party off to an impressive start with this savory cream soup. Guests will love the roasted tomato flavor and crispy bread slices. If you prefer, you may also grill the tomatoes.

yellow tomato soup
with goat cheese croutons

3 pounds yellow tomatoes, halved (about 9 medium)
2 tablespoons olive oil, *divided*
4 garlic cloves, minced, *divided*
1 teaspoon salt
1 teaspoon pepper
1 teaspoon minced fresh rosemary
1 teaspoon minced fresh thyme
1 large onion, chopped
1 cup vegetable broth
1/2 cup milk
1/2 cup heavy whipping cream

CROUTONS:
12 slices French bread baguette (1/2 inch thick)
1 tablespoon olive oil
2 tablespoons prepared pesto
1/2 cup crumbled goat cheese
1 teaspoon pepper

Place tomatoes, cut side down, in a greased 15-in. x 10-in. x 1-in. baking pan; brush with 1 tablespoon oil. Sprinkle with 2 teaspoons garlic and the salt, pepper, rosemary and thyme.

Bake at 400° for 25-30 minutes or until tomatoes are tender and skins are charred. Cool slightly. Discard tomato skins. In a blender, process tomatoes until blended.

In a large saucepan, saute onion in remaining oil until tender. Add remaining garlic; saute 1 minute longer. Add broth and milk; bring to a boil. Carefully stir in tomato puree. Simmer, uncovered, for 15 minutes to allow flavors to blend. Stir in cream; heat through (do not boil).

Meanwhile, for croutons, place bread on a baking sheet and brush with oil. Bake for 5-6 minutes or until golden brown. Spread with pesto and sprinkle with goat cheese and pepper. Bake 2 minutes longer. Ladle soup into bowls and top with croutons.

YIELD: 6 servings.

enchilada chicken soup

- 1 can (11 ounces) condensed fiesta nacho cheese soup, undiluted
- 1 can (10-3/4 ounces) condensed cream of chicken soup, undiluted
- 2-2/3 cups whole milk
- 1 can (10 ounces) chunk white chicken, drained
- 1 can (10 ounces) enchilada sauce
- 1 can (4 ounces) chopped green chilies

Sour cream

In a large saucepan, combine the soups, milk, chicken, enchilada sauce and chilies. Cook until heated through. Serve with sour cream.

YIELD: 7 servings.

cristin fischer
BELLEVUE, NEBRASKA

Canned soups, bottled enchilada sauce and a few other convenience items make this recipe one of my fast-to-fix favorites. Use mild green chilies if they suit your tastes, or try a spicier variety to give the soup more kick.

roasted garlic potato soup

misty brown
GLENDALE HEIGHTS, ILLINOIS

Slow roasting mellows and sweetens the blend of veggies in my flavorful soup. It's perfect for a cozy night indoors.

🥄 roasted garlic

Garlic turns golden and buttery when it is roasted. Its flavor mellows and becomes slightly sweet and nutty. Roasted garlic is terrific in a variety of dishes or spread on bread and grilled meats. You can roast garlic and refrigerate it in an airtight container for up to 1 week.

1 whole garlic bulb
1-1/2 teaspoons plus 2 tablespoons butter, *divided*
2 pounds potatoes (about 6 medium), peeled and cubed
2 medium onions, quartered
2 tablespoons olive oil
1/2 teaspoon salt
1/4 teaspoon pepper
6 cups vegetable broth, *divided*
4-1/2 teaspoons all-purpose flour
1/2 cup milk

Remove papery outer skin from garlic (do not peel or separate cloves); cut top off bulb. Melt 1-1/2 teaspoons butter; drizzle over garlic. Wrap in heavy-duty foil. Place in a 9-in. round baking pan; set aside.

Place the potatoes and onions in a single layer in an ungreased 15-in. x 10-in. x 1-in. baking pan. Drizzle with the oil; sprinkle with the salt and pepper. Toss to coat.

Bake garlic and potato mixture at 400° for 35-40 minutes or until tender, stirring vegetables once. Cool slightly.

In a blender, combine 2 cups broth and half of the vegetable mixture; cover and process until blended. Repeat with 2 cups broth and remaining vegetable mixture; set aside.

In a large saucepan, melt remaining butter. Stir in flour until smooth; gradually add remaining broth. Bring to a boil; cook and stir for 2 minutes or until thickened. Squeeze softened garlic into pan. Stir in milk and pureed vegetables; heat through.

YIELD: 8 servings.

creamy corn crab soup

1 medium onion, chopped
2 tablespoons butter
3 cups chicken broth
3 cups frozen corn
3 medium potatoes, peeled and diced
1 can (6 ounces) crabmeat, drained, flaked and cartilage removed *or* 1 cup flaked imitation crabmeat
1 cup milk
1/2 teaspoon salt
1/4 teaspoon pepper

In a large saucepan, saute onion in butter until tender. Add the broth, corn and potatoes; bring to a boil. Reduce the heat; cover and simmer for 15 minutes. Remove from the heat; cool slightly.

In a blender, puree half of the corn mixture. Return to the pan. Stir in the crab, milk, salt and pepper; cook mixture over low heat until heated through (do not boil).

YIELD: 7 servings.

carol ropchan
WILLINGDON, ALBERTA

My creamy soup is fast, easy and delicious. Corn is the star ingredient, and crabmeat adds a special touch. It's guaranteed to earn you compliments.

imitation crabmeat

Imitation crabmeat, also called surimi, is fish that is shaped, flavored and colored to resemble crab. It is typically made from Alaskan pollock, a lean, firm fish with a delicate flavor. Both natural and artificial flavors are used as well as artificial coloring.

savory cheese soup

3 cans (14-1/2 ounces *each*) chicken broth
1 small onion, chopped
1 large carrot, chopped
1 celery rib, chopped
1/4 cup chopped sweet red pepper
2 tablespoons butter
1 teaspoon salt
1/2 teaspoon pepper
1/3 cup all-purpose flour
1/3 cup cold water
1 package (8 ounces) cream cheese, cubed and softened
2 cups (8 ounces) shredded cheddar cheese
1 can (12 ounces) beer, optional
Optional toppings: croutons, popcorn, crumbled cooked bacon, sliced green onions

In a 3-qt. slow cooker, combine the first eight ingredients. Cover and cook on low for 7-8 hours.

Combine flour and water until smooth; stir into soup. Cover and cook on high 30 minutes longer or until soup is thickened.

Stir in the cream cheese and cheddar cheese until blended. Stir in the beer if desired. Cover and cook on low until heated through. Serve soup with desired toppings.

YIELD: 6-8 servings.

ann huseby
LAKEVILLE, MINNESOTA

Here's a cheesy soup that's great for parties. Guests can serve themselves, choosing fun garnishes such as popcorn, croutons, green onions or bacon bits.

slow cooker tips

Choose the correct size slow cooker for your soup. A slow cooker should be from half to two-thirds full. Unless the recipe instructs you to stir or add ingredients, refrain from lifting the lid while cooking. Every time you lift the lid, steam is lost and you add 15 to 30 minutes of cooking time. Remove soup from the slow cooker within 1 hour after cooking is complete. Promptly refrigerate leftovers.

**taste of home
test kitchen**

GREENDALE, WISCONSIN

*Coupled with a salad and
breadsticks, this thick dish
makes a warming, filling
meal. Chicken and cheese
are a classic duo everyone
will enjoy.*

chicken cheese soup

1 medium onion, chopped

2 to 3 garlic cloves, minced

1 tablespoon canola oil

1 tablespoon butter

2 tablespoons all-purpose flour

2 cups chicken broth

1 can (14-1/2 ounces) diced tomatoes, drained

1 cup frozen corn

1 can (4 ounces) chopped green chilies

2 cups chopped cooked chicken

1 can (12 ounces) evaporated milk

8 ounces process cheese (Velveeta), cubed

1/2 to 1 teaspoon ground cumin

In a large saucepan, saute onion and garlic in oil and butter until tender. Stir in the flour until blended. Gradually add broth. Bring to a boil; cook and stir for 2 minutes or until thickened.

Stir in the tomatoes, corn and chilies; bring to a boil. Add chicken. Reduce heat; simmer, uncovered, for 15 minutes. Add the milk, cheese and cumin. Cook and stir until cheese is melted (do not boil).

YIELD: 6 servings.

marilyn shaw

MIDDLETOWN, DELAWARE

*A friend passed along her
famous crab soup recipe.
It's tasty, and I love the
ease of preparation.*

cream of crab soup

1 large onion, finely chopped

1 medium green pepper, finely chopped

2 tablespoons butter

2 garlic cloves, minced

3 pints half-and-half cream

2 cups frozen shredded hash brown potatoes, thawed

1 can (10-3/4 ounces) condensed cream of mushroom soup, undiluted

1 can (10-3/4 ounces) condensed cream of asparagus soup, undiluted

2 cans (6 ounces *each*) lump crabmeat, drained

1 package (8 ounces) imitation crabmeat, chopped

1-1/2 cups frozen corn, thawed

1 tablespoon dried parsley flakes

1-1/2 teaspoons dill weed

1-1/2 teaspoons seafood seasoning

1 teaspoon pepper

In a Dutch oven, saute onion and green pepper in butter until tender. Add garlic; saute 1 minute longer. Stir in the remaining ingredients. Cook and stir over medium-low heat until heated through (do not boil).

YIELD: 14 servings.

white bean bisque

1/4 cup shredded Parmesan cheese
Cayenne pepper
1/4 pound Italian turkey sausage links
2 tablespoons chopped onion
1 teaspoon olive oil
1 garlic clove, minced
1 can (15 ounces) white kidney or
  cannellini beans, rinsed and drained
1 cup reduced-sodium chicken broth
1/4 cup heavy whipping cream
2 teaspoons sherry, optional
1 teaspoon minced fresh parsley
1/8 teaspoon salt
1/8 teaspoon dried thyme

Spoon cheese into six mounds 3 in. apart on a parchment paper-lined baking sheet. Spread into 1-1/2-in. circles. Sprinkle with a dash of cayenne. Bake at 400° for 5-6 minutes or until light golden brown. Cool.

In a large saucepan, cook sausage and onion in oil over medium heat until meat is no longer pink; drain. Remove and keep warm.

In the same pan, saute garlic for 1 minute or until tender. Stir in beans, broth, cream, sherry if desired, parsley, salt, thyme and a dash of cayenne. Bring to a boil. Reduce heat; simmer, uncovered, for 12-15 minutes or until heated through. Cool slightly.

Transfer to a blender; cover and process on high until almost blended. Pour into soup bowls; sprinkle with sausage mixture and Parmesan crisps.

YIELD: 2 servings.

linda miranda
WAKEFIELD, RHODE ISLAND

My bean soup packs a nutritional punch with protein-rich beans. The lean turkey sausage and reduced-sodium broth make this a great choice for health-conscious cooks.

turkey sausage

Turkey sausage has fewer calories and grams of fat per serving than beef or pork sausage, making it a healthier choice for those watching what they eat. It's a tasty addition to soups, stews, casseroles, pasta and breakfast dishes.

chowders
& bisques

Soothe and satisfy your family with a thick and chunky chowder or bisque. It can be the perfect everyday lunch or prelude to a special meal—the choice is yours. With a variety of options, from ham and rice to seafood and potatoes, you'll find empty bowls on your table soon after you serve any of these home-style classics.

195

203

220

corney welsh
BATON ROUGE, LOUISIANA

I decided to try my hand at making a light seafood soup after tasting one while dining out. I came up with this low-fat bisque and everyone loved it. It was even featured on a local TV show recently!

evelyn southwell
ETTERS, PENNSLYVANIA

Cayenne pepper gives a little kick to bowls of this pretty golden soup, a first course that everyone seems to love. It can be made several days in advance to fit a busy schedule then heated up when needed.

karen davies
WANIPIGOW, MANITOBA

I invented this recipe by accident. It came about when I was a novice cook and didn't know that a chowder was a kind of soup. Now I make it all the time!

crab bisque

2 cups chopped onions
1 cup chopped celery
1 cup chopped green pepper
4 garlic cloves, minced
1/4 cup reduced-fat margarine
4 cups diced peeled potatoes
2 cups fat-free milk
4 cups fat-free half-and-half
10 ounces reduced-fat process cheese (Velveeta), cut into 1-inch cubes
1 can (1 pound) crabmeat, drained, flaked and cartilage removed
3/4 teaspoon salt
1/4 teaspoon white pepper

In a soup kettle or Dutch oven, saute the onions, celery, green pepper and garlic in margarine until

tender. Reduce heat to medium; add the potatoes and milk. Cook, uncovered, for 20 minutes or until potatoes are just tender, stirring occasionally.

Remove 1-1/2 cups of the potato mixture; mash and return to the pan. Reduce heat to low. Stir in half-and-half and process cheese. Cook and stir until cheese is melted. Add the crab, salt and pepper. Cook 10 minutes longer or until heated through.

YIELD: 12 servings.

curried squash soup

1 butternut squash (about 1-3/4 pounds)
1 large onion, chopped
2 garlic cloves, minced
2 tablespoons canola oil
1 tablespoon all-purpose flour
1 teaspoon salt
1 teaspoon curry powder
1/8 teaspoon cayenne pepper
5 cups chicken broth
1 bay leaf

CILANTO CREAM TOPPING:

1/2 cup sour cream
1/4 cup heavy whipping cream
1/4 cup minced fresh cilantro

Cut squash in half lengthwise; discard seeds. Place squash cut side down in a greased or foil-lined baking pan. Bake, uncovered, at 400° for 40-50 minutes or until tender. When cool enough to handle, scoop out pulp; set aside.

In a large saucepan, saute onion and garlic in oil until tender. Add the flour, salt, curry powder and cayenne until blended. Stir in broth. Add bay leaf. Bring to a boil; cook and stir for 2 minutes or until thickened. Reduce heat; simmer, uncovered, for 20 minutes. Discard bay leaf. Cool to room temperature.

In a blender, combine half of the broth mixture and squash; cover and process until smooth. Repeat with remaining broth mixture and squash. Return to the saucepan; heat through. Combine the topping ingredients; place a dollop on each serving.

YIELD: 6 servings.

cheeseburger broccoli chowder

1/2 pound lean ground beef (90% lean)
1/2 cup chopped onion
1/4 cup chopped green pepper
1 can (10-3/4 ounces) condensed cheddar cheese soup, undiluted
3/4 cup whole milk
1 teaspoon Worcestershire sauce
1 cup chopped broccoli
1 to 2 potatoes, peeled and diced

In a large saucepan, cook beef with onion and green pepper until the beef is no longer pink; drain. Stir in soup, milk and Worcestershire sauce. Add broccoli and potatoes. Bring to a boil, reduce heat and simmer, covered, about 30 minutes or until potatoes are tender.

YIELD: 4 servings.

veggie salmon chowder

1 medium sweet potato, peeled and
    cut into 1/2-inch cubes
1 cup chicken broth
1/2 cup fresh *or* frozen corn
1/2 small onion, chopped
2 garlic cloves, minced
1-1/2 cups fresh spinach, torn
1/2 cup flaked smoked salmon fillet
1 teaspoon pickled jalapeno slices,
    chopped
1 tablespoon cornstarch
1/2 cup 2% milk
1 tablespoon minced fresh cilantro
Dash pepper

In a large saucepan, combine the potato, broth,
corn, onion and garlic. Bring to a boil. Reduce heat;
cover and simmer for 8-10 minutes or until potato
is tender.

Add the spinach, salmon and jalapeno; cook for
1-2 minutes or until spinach is wilted. Combine
cornstarch and milk until smooth. Stir into chowder.
Bring to a boil; cook and stir for 2 minutes or until
thickened. Stir in cilantro and pepper.

YIELD: 2 servings.

liv vors
PETERBOROUGH, ONTARIO

*I created this recipe as a
way to use up odds and
ends in my fridge. It may
have started as a fun
experiment, but it ended
up as mainstay in our
house. I know your family
will enjoy it, too.*

fish chowder

margaret jean
AYER, MASSACHUSETTS

Living in New England, we love any dish that features fish as its star ingredient. We especially enjoy it when there's a chill in the air.

  1 bacon strip, diced
  2 tablespoons chopped onion
  2 tablespoons chopped celery
2/3 cup condensed cream of potato soup, undiluted
  1/2 cup water
  1/8 teaspoon pepper
Dash salt
  1/2 pound haddock fillets, cut into 1-inch pieces
  1/2 cup whole milk
1-1/2 teaspoons butter
Oyster crackers, optional

In a small saucepan, saute the bacon, onion and celery until vegetables are tender. Add the soup, water, pepper and salt. Bring to a boil; reduce heat. Add haddock; cover and simmer for 8-12 minutes or until fish flakes easily with a fork. Stir in milk and butter; heat through. Serve with oyster crackers if desired.

YIELD: 2 servings.

bacon tomato chowder

3 bacon strips, diced
1/4 cup butter, cubed
1/4 cup all-purpose flour
Dash ground nutmeg
1 can (14-1/2 ounces) chicken broth
3/4 cup canned diced tomatoes, undrained
2/3 cup half-and-half cream

In a large saucepan, cook bacon over medium heat until crisp. Using a slotted spoon, remove to paper towels to drain. Discard drippings.

In the same pan, melt butter. Stir in flour and nutmeg until smooth. Gradually whisk in broth. Bring to a boil; cook and stir for 2 minutes or until thickened. Stir in tomatoes. Reduce heat; stir in cream. Heat through (do not boil). Add bacon.

YIELD: 2 servings.

heidi sollinger
BECHTELSVILLE, PENNSYLVANIA

My tomato chowder suits any occasion. But it's so warm and comforting that I often make it just for my husband and me.

tomato bisque

2 garlic cloves, minced
2 tablespoons butter
2 tablespoons all-purpose flour
4 cups chicken broth
1 can (6 ounces) tomato paste
1/8 to 1/4 teaspoon cayenne pepper
1 cup half-and-half cream
Chopped fresh tomatoes, optional

In a medium saucepan, saute garlic in butter for 1 minute. Stir in flour until blended; gradually add chicken broth. Stir in tomato paste and cayenne until well blended.

Bring to a boil; cook and stir for 2 minutes or until thickened. Reduce heat; gradually stir in cream. (Do not boil.) Garnish with chopped tomatoes if desired.

YIELD: 6 servings.

taste of home test kitchen
GREENDALE, WISCONSIN

A bowl brimming with this fresh, creamy soup is sure to impress. With its outstanding flavor, guests will think you fussed for hours!

asparagus leek chowder

1 pound fresh asparagus, trimmed and cut into 1-inch pieces
3 cups sliced fresh mushrooms
3 large leeks (white portion only), sliced
6 tablespoons butter
1/4 cup all-purpose flour
1/2 teaspoon salt
Dash pepper
2 cups chicken broth
2 cups half-and-half cream
1 can (11 ounces) whole kernel corn, drained
1 tablespoon chopped pimientos

In a large saucepan, saute the asparagus, mushrooms and leeks in butter for 10 minutes or until tender. Stir in the flour, salt and pepper until blended.

Gradually stir in the broth and cream. Bring to a boil. Reduce the heat; cook and stir for 2 minutes or until thickened. Stir in the corn and pimientos; heat through.

YIELD: 7 servings.

elisabeth harders
WEST ALLIS, WISCONSIN

To us, asparagus is the taste of spring, so we enjoy it in as many meals as we can. When this chunky chowder is on the table, we know the balmy season has finally arrived.

lois hofmeyer
SUGAR GROVE, ILLINOIS

My sisters and I made this soup with our mom when we were young. Now it's the traditional holiday-leftover soup for our own families.

traditional turkey vegetable soup

1 large onion, finely chopped
2 tablespoons butter
3 cups diced small red potatoes
2 cans (14-1/2 ounces *each*) chicken broth
2 cups cooked cubed turkey breast
2 cups frozen mixed vegetables, thawed
1/2 teaspoon salt
1/2 teaspoon white pepper
1/2 teaspoon poultry seasoning
2 cups heavy whipping cream

In a large saucepan, saute onion in butter until tender. Add potatoes and broth. Bring to a boil. Reduce heat; cover and simmer for 20 minutes. Stir in the turkey, vegetables, salt, pepper and poultry seasoning. Cook 10-12 minutes longer or until the vegetables are tender. Stir in cream; heat through (do not boil).

YIELD: 8 servings.

darlene brenden
SALEM, OREGON

My chowder is ready in 15 minutes but tastes as if it simmered for hours. The original recipe I came across was a little bland, so I jazzed it up with extra corn and bacon bits.

ramen corn chowder

2 cups water
1 package (3 ounces) chicken ramen noodles
1 can (15-1/4 ounces) whole kernel corn, drained
1 can (14-3/4 ounces) cream-style corn
1 cup 2% milk
1 teaspoon dried minced onion
1/4 teaspoon curry powder
3/4 cup shredded cheddar cheese
1 tablespoon crumbled cooked bacon
1 tablespoon minced fresh parsley

In a small saucepan, bring water to a boil. Break noodles into large pieces. Add noodles and contents of seasoning packet to water. Reduce heat to medium. Cook, uncovered, for 2-3 minutes or until noodles are tender.

Stir in the corn, cream-style corn, milk, onion and curry; heat through. Stir in the cheese, bacon and parsley until blended.

YIELD: 4 servings.

curry powder

Curry powder is a blend of many different individual ground spices used in the cuisines of India and Asia. It imparts a distinctive flavor and a rich golden color and can be found in both mild and hot versions. Most cooks season dishes lightly with curry powder and add more as desired to reach an acceptable spice level.

wild rice and ham chowder

1/2 cup chopped onion

1/4 cup butter, cubed

2 garlic cloves, minced

6 tablespoons all-purpose flour

1/2 teaspoon salt

1/4 teaspoon pepper

4 cups chicken broth

1-1/2 cups cubed peeled potatoes

1/2 cup chopped carrot

1 bay leaf

1/2 teaspoon dried thyme

1/4 teaspoon ground nutmeg

3 cups cooked wild rice

2-1/2 cups cubed fully cooked ham

2 cups half-and-half cream

1 can (15-1/4 ounces) whole kernel corn, drained

Minced fresh parsley

In a Dutch oven, over medium heat, saute onion in butter until tender. Add garlic; cook 1 minute longer. Stir in the flour, salt and pepper until blended. Gradually add broth. Bring to a boil. Cook and stir for 2 minutes or until thickened and bubbly.

Add the potatoes, carrot, bay leaf, thyme and nutmeg; return to a boil. Reduce heat; cover and simmer for 30 minutes or until vegetables are tender. Stir in the rice, ham, cream and corn; heat through (do not boil). Discard bay leaf. Garnish with the parsley.

YIELD: 8-10 servings.

elma friesen
WINNIPEG, MANITOBA

A few years ago, my sister graciously passed along her famous wild rice and ham chowder recipe. Everyone loves its rich, comforting taste.

chowder defined

A chowder is a thick, chunky soup frequently made with seafood or vegetables, but it can also contain other meats such as ham or chicken. Chowders have a milk or cream base and can be thickened with flour.

chunky salmon chowder

cindy st. martin
PORTLAND, OREGON

After my husband and I caught four large salmon one summer, my mother-in-law combined several recipes to create this yummy chowder. It has become one of our household favorites.

2 pounds red potatoes, peeled and cubed

1 large onion, chopped

1 can (49-1/2 ounces) chicken broth

1 pound salmon fillets, cut into 1-inch pieces

1/2 pound sliced bacon, cooked and crumbled

2 cups whole milk

1 cup half-and-half cream

1 tablespoon butter

1/2 teaspoon salt

Pepper to taste

In a Dutch oven, combine the potatoes, onion and broth. Bring to a boil. Reduce heat; cover and cook for 10-15 minutes or until potatoes are tender. Add salmon and bacon; cook over medium heat until fish flakes easily with a fork.

Reduce heat; stir in the milk, cream, butter, salt and pepper; heat through (do not boil). Thicken if desired.

YIELD: 14 servings.

country potato chowder

6 bacon strips, diced
1 medium onion, chopped
3 celery ribs, chopped
1/4 cup all-purpose flour
4 cups half-and-half cream
4 medium potatoes, peeled and
   cut into 1/2-inch cubes

2 cans (10-3/4 ounces *each*) condensed
   cream of celery soup, undiluted
2 tablespoons dried parsley flakes
1 tablespoon Worcestershire sauce
1 teaspoon seasoned salt
1/2 teaspoon pepper
1 cup sliced carrots
1 cup fresh *or* frozen green beans,
   cut into 2-inch pieces
1 can (14-3/4 ounces) cream-style corn

In a Dutch oven, cook bacon over medium heat until crisp; remove with a slotted spoon to paper towels. Drain, reserving 2 tablespoons drippings. In the drippings, saute onion and celery until tender. Sprinkle with flour and stir until blended. Gradually add cream. Stir in the potatoes, soup, parsley, Worcestershire sauce, seasoned salt and pepper. Bring to a boil; cook and stir for 1 minute. Reduce heat; cover and simmer for 25 minutes, stirring occasionally.

Add carrots and beans. Cover and simmer 15 minutes longer or until vegetables are tender. Stir in corn and reserved bacon; heat through.

YIELD: 12 servings.

sara phillips
TOPEKA, KANSAS

This comforting dish is brimming with carrots, potatoes, green beans and corn. Leftovers, if there are any, taste just as delicious the next day.

potato chowder

A tasty potato chowder recipe can be very versatile. You can use potato chowder as a hearty base when making similar recipes, such as clam chowder or corn chowder.

ham cheddar chowder

3 cups water
3 cups cubed peeled potatoes
1 cup chopped carrots
1 cup chopped celery
1 medium onion, chopped
2 teaspoons salt
1/2 teaspoon pepper
6 tablespoons butter
6 tablespoons all-purpose flour
4 cups whole milk
3 cups (12 ounces) shredded
   cheddar cheese
1 cup cubed fully cooked ham

In a large saucepan, bring water to a boil. Add the potatoes, carrots, celery, onion, salt and pepper. Reduce heat. Cover and simmer for 20 minutes or until vegetables are tender; drain and set vegetables aside.

In same pan, melt the butter. Stir in flour until smooth. Gradually add milk. Bring to a boil; cook and stir for 2 minutes or until thickened. Remove from the heat; stir in cheese until melted. Add ham and reserved vegetables. Cook on low until heated through. Do not boil.

YIELD: 8 servings.

ruth protz
OSHKOSH, WISCONSIN

I'm a proud Wisconsinite, so I like to make dishes that feature cheese. This chowder is one of my all-time favorites. It makes a great meal served with a salad and rye rolls.

cheddar cheese

Select sharp cheddar when using packaged shredded cheese for recipes that you'd like to have a bolder flavor. If you will be shredding cheese at home from bulk cheddar, you can choose from mild, medium, sharp and extra sharp.

della clarke
VISTA, CALIFORNIA

With its pleasant garlic flavor and golden orange color, my rich and creamy soup is sure to be a hit whether you serve it for an everyday meal or a holiday dinner.

garlic butternut bisque

2 whole garlic bulbs
1 teaspoon olive oil
3 large onions, chopped
3/4 cup chopped carrots
1/2 cup chopped celery
3/4 cup butter, *divided*
4 pounds butternut squash, peeled, seeded and cubed (about 8 cups)
6 cups chicken broth
3 tablespoons chopped fresh sage, *divided*
1/2 cup plus 1 tablespoon heavy whipping cream, *divided*
1-1/2 teaspoons salt
1/4 teaspoon pepper

Remove papery outer skin from garlic (do not peel or separate cloves). Cut tops off bulbs; brush with oil. Wrap each in heavy-duty foil. Bake at 425° for 30-35 minutes or until softened. Cool 10-15 minutes.

Meanwhile, in a Dutch oven, saute the onions, carrots and celery in 1/2 cup butter until tender. Add the squash, broth and 2 tablespoons sage. Bring to a boil. Reduce heat; simmer, uncovered, for 25-30 minutes or until squash is tender.

Squeeze softened garlic into a small bowl; mash with a fork. Stir into squash mixture. Cool slightly. Puree squash mixture in batches in a blender; return to pan. Stir in 1/2 cup cream, salt and pepper and remaining butter; heat through. Garnish with remaining cream and sage.

YIELD: 9 servings.

belinda desselle
WESTLAKE, LOUISIANA

I turn to this classic every fall, but I love it so much I whip it up throughout the year, too. Cayenne pepper, sausage and ham lend a fabulous Cajun flavor.

autumn sausage corn soup

3/4 pound fully cooked smoked sausage, sliced
1/4 cup all-purpose flour
1/4 cup canola oil
1/2 cup chopped onion
1/2 cup chopped green pepper
3 green onions, chopped
3-1/2 cups water
1 package (16 ounces) frozen corn
1-1/2 cups cubed fully cooked ham
1 can (14-1/2 ounces) diced tomatoes, undrained
1 cup chopped fresh tomatoes
1 can (6 ounces) tomato paste
1/4 teaspoon salt, optional
1/8 teaspoon cayenne pepper
Hot pepper sauce to taste

In a large skillet, cook and stir sausage over medium-high heat until browned; drain well and set aside.

In a Dutch oven or soup kettle, cook and stir the flour in oil over medium heat for 5 minutes or until golden brown. Add the onion, green pepper and green onions; saute until tender.

Stir in the water, corn, ham, tomatoes, tomato paste, salt, if desired, cayenne, hot pepper sauce and sausage. Bring to a boil. Reduce heat; cover and simmer for 1 hour, stirring occasionally.

YIELD: 11 servings.

parmesan potato soup

mary shivers
ADA, OKLAHOMA

8 medium potatoes, peeled and
    cut into 1/2-inch cubes

6 cups chicken broth

1 large onion, chopped

1 jar (7 ounces) roasted sweet red
    peppers, drained and chopped

1 small celery rib, chopped

1/2 teaspoon garlic powder

1/2 teaspoon seasoned salt

1/2 teaspoon pepper

1/8 teaspoon rubbed sage

1/3 cup all-purpose flour

2 cups heavy whipping cream, *divided*

1 cup grated Parmesan cheese, *divided*

8 bacon strips, cooked and crumbled

2 tablespoons minced fresh cilantro

In a 5- or 6-qt. slow cooker, combine the first nine ingredients. Cover and cook on low for 5-6 hours or until vegetables are tender.

In a small bowl, combine flour and 1/2 cup cream until smooth; add to slow cooker. Stir in 3/4 cup cheese, bacon, cilantro and remaining cream. Cover and cook for 30 minutes or until slightly thickened. Ladle into bowls; sprinkle with remaining cheese.

YIELD: 12 servings.

I decided to add some character to a basic potato chowder by tossing in roasted red peppers. The extra punch of flavor adds a deliciously unique twist to what might otherwise be an ordinary bowl of soup.

vicki kerr

PORTLAND, MAINE

My brothy chowder showcases potatoes, carrots and corn for a delightful entree. Since it's not too heavy, I also enjoy it alongside my favorite grilled sandwich.

veggie chowder

2 cups reduced-sodium chicken broth

2 cups cubed peeled potatoes

1 cup chopped carrots

1/2 cup chopped onion

1 can (14-3/4 ounces) cream-style corn

1 can (12 ounces) fat-free evaporated milk

3/4 cup shredded reduced-fat cheddar cheese

1/2 cup sliced fresh mushrooms

1/4 teaspoon pepper

2 tablespoons real bacon bits

In a large saucepan, combine the broth, potatoes, carrots and onion. Bring to a boil. Reduce heat; simmer, uncovered, for 10-15 minutes or until vegetables are tender.

Add the corn, milk, cheese, mushrooms and pepper. Cook and stir 4-6 minutes longer or until heated through. Sprinkle with bacon.

YIELD: 7 servings.

butternut bisque

3-1/2 pounds butternut squash, peeled, seeded and cubed
1 cup sliced carrots
1 medium tart apple, peeled and chopped
1/2 cup chopped shallots
2 tablespoons olive oil
3 large tomatoes, seeded and chopped
4 cups chicken broth
1-1/4 cups half-and-half cream
1-1/2 teaspoons salt
1/4 teaspoon cayenne pepper
3/4 cup frozen corn, thawed
2 tablespoons minced chives
Sour cream and additional chives, optional

In a large bowl, toss the squash, carrots, apple, shallots and oil. Transfer to a large roasting pan.

Bake, uncovered, at 400° for 1 hour or until browned and tender, stirring twice. Cool slightly. Place in a food processor; cover and process until almost smooth.

In a Dutch oven or soup kettle, cook tomatoes over medium heat for 5 minutes. Add the pureed vegetables, broth, cream, salt and cayenne; heat through (do not boil). Stir in the corn and chives. Garnish servings with the sour cream and chives if desired.

YIELD: 10 servings.

kristin arnett
ELKHORN, WISCONSIN

I've served butternut bisque for both weeknight dinners and special occasions to rave reviews each time. It's especially delightful on a cool, crisp fall day.

bisque defined

A bisque is a thick, rich soup that usually consists of pureed seafood and cream. Poultry, vegetables or rice are sometimes substituted. Bisque is quicker to serve than a traditional soup because it doesn't have to simmer for hours.

tomato clam chowder

5 to 6 medium potatoes, peeled and diced
6 bacon strips, diced
1 small onion, finely chopped
2 celery ribs, chopped
1 garlic clove, minced
2 cans (6 ounces *each*) minced clams
2 cups water
1 can (15 ounces) tomato sauce
1 can (14-1/2 ounces) diced tomatoes, undrained
1/2 to 1 teaspoon pepper
1/4 teaspoon salt
2 teaspoons minced fresh parsley

Place the potatoes in a soup kettle or Dutch oven and cover with water. Bring to a boil. Reduce heat; cover and cook for 10-15 minutes or until tender.

Meanwhile, in a large skillet, cook bacon over medium heat until crisp. Using a slotted spoon, remove bacon to paper towels; drain, reserving 2 tablespoons drippings. In the drippings, saute the onion, celery and garlic until tender.

Drain clams, reserving liquid; set clams aside. Drain potatoes and return to the pan. Add onion mixture, bacon and reserved clam liquid. Stir in the water, tomato sauce, tomatoes, pepper and salt. Bring to a boil. Reduce heat; simmer, uncovered, for 30-35 minutes or until heated through. Add clams and parsley; simmer 5 minutes longer.

YIELD: 11 servings.

weda mosellie
PHILLIPSBURG, NEW JERSEY

Steaming bowls of this Manhattan-style clam chowder are guaranteed to be gobbled up in a hurry.

phyllis watson

HAVELOCK, NORTH CAROLINA

Both my grandmother and mother made this dish for their families, and now I'm proud to make it for mine. We can't get enough of the home-style flavor.

classic corn chowder

6 potatoes, peeled and diced
Water
   1 can (16 ounces) whole kernel corn, drained
   4 cups whole milk
   1 large onion, diced
   4 bacon strips, cooked and crumbled
   1 teaspoon salt
1/4 teaspoon pepper
1/4 teaspoon dried thyme

Place potatoes in a Dutch oven and cover with water. Bring to a boil. Reduce heat; cover and cook for 10-15 minutes or until tender. Drain. Add remaining ingredients; bring to a boil. Reduce heat and simmer for 15 minutes or until onion is soft.

YIELD: 4-6 servings.

kendra doss

KANSAS CITY, MISSOURI

This recipe is close to one my mom used to make for us when the weather turned cold. Mom's called for heavy cream, but my slimmer version still boasts a flavor that is pretty true to the original!

curried chicken corn chowder

2 medium onions, chopped
2 celery ribs, chopped
1 tablespoon butter
3 cans (14-1/2 ounces *each*) reduced-sodium chicken broth
5 cups frozen corn
2 teaspoons curry powder
1/4 teaspoon salt
1/4 teaspoon pepper
Dash cayenne pepper
1/2 cup all-purpose flour
1/2 cup 2% milk
  3 cups cubed cooked chicken breast
1/3 cup minced fresh cilantro

In a Dutch oven, saute onions and celery in butter until tender. Stir in the broth, corn, curry, salt, pepper and cayenne. Bring to a boil. Reduce heat; cover and simmer for 15 minutes.

In a small bowl, whisk flour and milk until smooth. Whisk into the pan. Bring to a boil; cook and stir for 2 minutes or until thickened. Add chicken and cilantro; heat through.

YIELD: 9 servings.

easy seafood bisque

1/2 cup chopped onion

1 tablespoon butter

2-1/4 cups milk

1 can (10-3/4 ounces) condensed cream of celery soup, undiluted

1 can (10-3/4 ounces) condensed cream of shrimp soup, undiluted

1 package (8 ounces) imitation crabmeat, chopped

1 teaspoon chicken bouillon granules

1/2 teaspoon dried parsley flakes

1/4 teaspoon garlic powder

1/4 teaspoon dried marjoram

1/4 teaspoon pepper

In a 3-qt. saucepan, saute onion in butter until tender. Stir in remaining ingredients. Cover and cook over medium-low heat for 20 minutes or until heated through, stirring occasionally.

YIELD: 4-5 servings.

cindy rogowski

LANCASTER, NEW YORK

I've always enjoyed seafood bisque whenever I've tried it at restaurants. One day I decided to create my own special recipe. Everyone says this is one of the best versions they've ever tasted.

clam chowder

rosemary peterson
ARCHIE, MISSOURI

This satisfying, classic chowder is quick to prepare and so comforting on a cold day.

2 cans (6-1/2 ounces *each*) minced clams

6 medium potatoes, peeled and diced

6 medium carrots, diced

1/2 cup chopped onion

1/2 cup butter, cubed

1-1/2 cups water

2 cans (12 ounces *each*) evaporated milk

2 cans (10-3/4 ounces *each*) condensed cream of mushroom soup, undiluted

1 teaspoon salt

1/2 teaspoon pepper

Drain clams, reserving liquid; set the clams aside.

In a large kettle, combine the potatoes, carrots, onion, butter, water and reserved clam juice. Cook over medium heat for 15 minutes or until the vegetables are tender. Stir in the milk, soup, salt and pepper. Simmer, uncovered, until heated through. Stir in clams.

YIELD: 12 servings.

winter chowder

3 medium potatoes, peeled and cut into 1/4-inch pieces
1/2 cup chopped onion
1 cup water
3/4 teaspoon onion salt *or* onion powder
1/2 teaspoon pepper
1/8 teaspoon salt
2 drops Louisiana-style hot sauce
1/2 cup cubed fully cooked ham (1/4-inch pieces)
1 cup fresh *or* frozen brussels sprouts, quartered
1-1/2 cups milk
3/4 cup shredded Colby-Monterey Jack cheese, *divided*

In a large saucepan, bring the potatoes, onion and water to a boil. Reduce heat; cover and cook for 10-12 minutes or until tender. Do not drain. Mash potatoes (mixture will not be smooth). Stir in the onion salt, pepper, salt and hot sauce; set aside.

In a large nonstick skillet coated with cooking spray, saute ham and brussels sprouts for 5-6 minutes or until sprouts are tender. Stir into the potato mixture. Add milk. Bring to a boil. Reduce heat; simmer, uncovered, for 5-6 minutes or until heated through, stirring occasionally.

Gradually stir in 1/2 cup cheese; cook for 2-3 minutes or until cheese is melted. Garnish with remaining cheese.

YIELD: 5 servings.

brenda turner
SCHERERVILLE, INDIANA

As a mother of three, my time is short but precious. So I look for recipes that are short on prep and high in nutrition! This chunky chowder is a standby.

brussels sprouts

To prepare brussels sprouts for cooking, remove any loose or yellowed outer leaves; trim stem end. Rinse the sprouts. When cooking whole, cut an X in the core end with a sharp knife.

chicken tortilla chowder

1 can (14-1/2 ounces) chicken broth
1 can (10-3/4 ounces) condensed cream of chicken soup, undiluted
1 can (10-3/4 ounces) condensed cream of potato soup, undiluted
1-1/2 cups milk
2 cups cubed cooked chicken
1 can (11 ounces) Mexicorn
1 jar (4-1/2 ounces) sliced mushrooms, drained
1 can (4 ounces) chopped green chilies
1/4 cup thinly sliced green onions
4 flour tortillas (6 to 7 inches), cut into 1/2-inch strips
1-1/2 cups (6 ounces) shredded cheddar cheese

In a Dutch oven, combine the broth, soups and milk. Stir in the chicken, corn, mushrooms, chilies and onions. Bring to a boil. Add the tortilla strips. Reduce heat; simmer, uncovered, for 8-10 minutes or until heated through. Add cheese; stir just until melted. Serve immediately.

YIELD: 8-10 servings.

jennifer gouge
LUBBOCK, TEXAS

This recipe is great for time-pressed cooks. My husband loves it with tortilla strips that puff up like homemade noodles.

hazel fritchie
PALESTINE, ILLINOIS

I like to serve this cheesy chowder whenever guests drop in. The mild flavor, tender chicken and fresh vegetables even appeal to kids and picky eaters.

cheesy chicken chowder

3 cups chicken broth
2 cups diced peeled potatoes
1 cup diced carrots
1 cup diced celery
1/2 cup diced onion
1-1/2 teaspoons salt
1/4 teaspoon pepper
1/4 cup butter, cubed
1/3 cup all-purpose flour
2 cups milk
2 cups (about 8 ounces) shredded cheddar cheese
2 cups diced cooked chicken

In a 4-quart saucepan, bring chicken broth to a boil. Reduce heat; add the potatoes, carrots, celery, onion, salt and pepper. Cover and simmer for 12-15 minutes or until vegetables are tender.

Meanwhile, melt butter in a medium saucepan; stir in flour until smooth. Gradually stir in milk. Bring to a boil over medium heat; cook and stir for 2 minutes or until thickened. Reduce heat; add cheese, stirring until melted; add to broth along with chicken. Cook and stir until heated through.

YIELD: 6-8 servings.

germaine stank
POUND, WISCONSIN

Looking for a different way to serve a bounty of zucchini? Try my bisque! A food processor eases preparation of the full-flavored blend accented by just a hint of nutmeg.

zucchini bisque

4 medium zucchini, shredded
1 medium onion, chopped
1/2 cup butter, cubed
2-1/2 cups chicken broth
1 cup heavy whipping cream
3/4 teaspoon salt
1/2 teaspoon minced fresh basil
1/2 teaspoon pepper
1/4 teaspoon ground nutmeg
Sour cream and additional nutmeg, optional

In a large saucepan, saute zucchini and onion in butter for 5-6 minutes or until tender. Stir in broth. Bring to a boil. Reduce heat; cover and simmer for 12-15 minutes. Cool slightly.

Transfer to a food processor; cover and process on low until smooth. Return to the pan. Stir in the cream, salt, basil, pepper and nutmeg. Bring to a boil. Reduce the heat; simmer, uncovered, for 1-2 minutes or until heated through. Garnish with sour cream and additional nutmeg if desired.

YIELD: 6 servings.

corn chowder

1 medium onion, chopped
6 cups fresh *or* frozen corn, *divided*
3 cups reduced-sodium chicken broth, *divided*
1/2 cup chopped sweet red pepper
1/2 teaspoon dried rosemary, crushed
1/2 teaspoon dried thyme
1/8 teaspoon pepper
Dash cayenne pepper

Coat a large saucepan with cooking spray. Add onion; cook and stir over medium heat for 4 minutes or until tender. Add 4 cups corn; cook and stir until corn is softened, about 5 minutes. Add 2 cups broth; bring to a boil. Reduce heat; cover and simmer for 10 minutes or until corn is tender. Cool slightly.

In a blender, process the soup in batches until smooth; return all to the pan. Add the red pepper, rosemary, thyme, pepper, cayenne and remaining corn and broth; cook and stir for 10 minutes or until the corn is tender.

YIELD: 6 servings.

nancy johnson
CONNERSVILLE, INDIANA

My thick, creamy chowder always hits the spot. I like to serve it with cornbread for a simple supper.

vicki thompson

BRISTOL, NEW BRUNSWICK

This light chowder delivers many levels of flavor and is sure to add a little coziness to cold winter nights.

salmon

Salmon can be purchased fresh, frozen, smoked or canned. Wild salmon can be eaten without fear of excess contaminants or mercury, and it is very high in nutrition. It contains protein, vitamin D and omega-3 fatty acids.

salmon chowder

1 small onion, chopped

1 garlic clove, minced

1/4 teaspoon dried thyme

1/4 teaspoon dried basil

1 tablespoon butter

2 cups 1% milk

1 can (10-1/2 ounces) condensed chicken broth, undiluted

1/2 cup frozen corn

1/2 cup chopped carrot

1 medium red potato, cut into 1/2-inch cubes

3 tablespoons all-purpose flour

1/4 cup cold water

1/2 pound salmon fillet, cut into 1-inch pieces

1/2 cup chopped zucchini

1/2 teaspoon salt

1/4 teaspoon pepper

1/2 cup shredded reduced-fat cheddar cheese

In a large saucepan over medium heat, cook and stir the onion, garlic, thyme and basil in butter until onion is tender. Stir in the milk, broth, corn, carrot and potato. Bring to a boil. Reduce the heat; cover and simmer for 6-8 minutes or until the vegetables are tender.

Combine flour and water until smooth; stir into onion mixture. Bring to a boil; cook and stir for 2 minutes or until thickened. Reduce heat; add salmon and zucchini. Simmer, uncovered, for 3-5 minutes or until fish flakes easily with a fork. Stir in salt and pepper. Sprinkle with cheese before serving.

YIELD: 6 servings.

zesty tomato soup

2 cans (10-3/4 ounces each) condensed tomato soup, undiluted

2-2/3 cups water

2 teaspoons chili powder

Oyster crackers or shredded Monterey Jack cheese, optional

In a large saucepan, combine the soup, water and chili powder; heat through. Garnish with crackers or cheese if desired.

YIELD: 4-5 servings.

joann gunio
FRANKLIN, NORTH CAROLINA

When friends stop by unexpectedly, my husband quickly concocts his famous tomato soup that tastes homemade. Two basic ingredients give canned soup just the right amount of zip.

garden chowder

1/2 cup chopped green pepper

1/2 cup chopped onion

1/4 cup butter

1 cup each diced potato, celery, cauliflower, carrot and broccoli

3 cups water

3 chicken bouillon cubes

1 teaspoon salt

1/4 teaspoon pepper

1/2 cup all-purpose flour

2 cups whole milk

1 tablespoon minced fresh parsley

3 cups (12 ounces) shredded cheddar cheese

In a Dutch oven, saute green pepper and onion in butter until tender. Add the vegetables, water, bouillon, salt and pepper; bring to a boil. Reduce heat; cover and simmer for 20 minutes or until the vegetables are tender.

Combine flour and milk until smooth; stir into pan. Bring to a boil; cook and stir for 2 minutes. Add the parsley. Just before serving, stir in the cheese until melted.

YIELD: 6-8 servings.

darlene brenden
SALEM, OREGON

If you have a green thumb or simply enjoy visiting your local farmers market, then this is the chowder for you. It's full of fresh garden flavor.

snowflake tomato soup

2 cans (28 ounces each) crushed tomatoes

1 can (14-1/2 ounces) chicken broth

2 tablespoons minced fresh oregano or 2 teaspoons dried oregano

1 to 2 tablespoons sugar

1 cup heavy whipping cream

1/3 cup sour cream

In a blender, process tomatoes, one can at a time, until smooth. Transfer to a large saucepan. Stir in the broth; bring to a boil. Reduce heat; cover and simmer for 10 minutes. Stir in the oregano and sugar. Add a small amount of hot tomato mixture to whipping cream; return all to the saucepan. Cook until slightly thickened (do not boil).

Cut a small hole in the corner of a pastry or plastic bag; fill with sour cream. Pipe a snowflake on each bowl of soup.

YIELD: 8-10 servings.

taste of home test kitchen
GREENDALE, WISCONSIN

Your family is bound to dig into our delectable soup! It packs lots of pleasing ingredients and is extra fun to eat with a piped snowflake on top.

tonya michelle burkhard
ENGLEWOOD, FLORIDA

My Southwestern chowder comes together in no time. Its sweet corn, pearl onions, smoky bacon, hash brown spuds and menagerie of spices work together perfectly.

south-of-the-border chowder

1/2 cup chopped onion
4 bacon strips, diced
2 tablespoons all-purpose flour
1/2 teaspoon ground cumin
1/2 teaspoon chili powder
1/8 teaspoon garlic powder
1 package (32 ounces) frozen cubed hash brown potatoes
2 cans (14-1/2 ounces each) chicken broth
1 can (14-3/4 ounces) cream-style corn
1 can (11 ounces) Mexicorn, drained
1 can (4 ounces) chopped green chilies
1/4 cup pearl onions
Sour cream and minced fresh cilantro, optional

In a Dutch oven, saute onion and bacon until onion is tender and bacon is crisp. Stir in the flour, cumin, chili powder and garlic powder. Bring to a boil; cook and stir for 1 minute or until thickened.

Stir in the hash browns, broth, cream corn, Mexicorn, chilies and pearl onions. Bring to a boil. Reduce heat; simmer, uncovered, for 10 minutes or until heated through. Garnish with sour cream and cilantro if desired.

YIELD: 10 servings.

dulyse molnar
OSWEGO, NEW YORK

Nothing beats a bowl of hot soup, especially when this is the delicious result! Winter days seem a little bit warmer when I prepare my gram's thick, savory chowder.

grandmother's chowder

1 pound lean ground beef (90% lean)
1 medium onion, chopped
12 medium potatoes, peeled and cubed
3 cups water
Salt and pepper to taste
2 cups whole milk
1 can (15-1/4 ounces) whole kernel corn, drained
2 teaspoons dried parsley flakes
1 cup (8 ounces) sour cream

In a Dutch oven, cook beef and onion over medium heat until meat is no longer pink; drain. Add the potatoes, water, salt and pepper; bring to a boil. Reduce heat; cover and simmer for 15-20 minutes or until potatoes are tender.

Stir in the milk, corn and parsley; cook for 5 minutes or until heated through. Add a small amount of hot soup to sour cream. Gradually return all to pan, stirring constantly. Heat through but do not boil.

YIELD: 14 servings.

black bean corn chowder

1/2 cup half-and-half cream

1 can (15 ounces) black beans, rinsed and drained, *divided*

1/2 cup chopped onion

1 teaspoon olive oil

2 garlic cloves, minced

1/2 cup salsa

1/3 cup fresh *or* frozen corn

1 tablespoon lime juice

3/4 teaspoon ground cumin

1/2 medium ripe avocado, peeled and chopped

Sour cream and shredded cheddar cheese, optional

In a blender, combine the cream and 3/4 cup black beans; cover and process until smooth. Set aside.

In a small saucepan, saute onion in oil until tender. Add garlic; cook 1 minute longer. Stir in the salsa, corn, lime juice, cumin and remaining beans.

Reduce the heat; stir in cream mixture. Cook, uncovered, for 2-3 minutes or until heated through. Stir in avocado. Serve with sour cream and cheese if desired.

YIELD: 2 servings.

shelly platten
AMHERST, WISCONSIN

This thick, Southwestern-style chowder is seasoned with salsa, lime juice and cumin for a little kick. We enjoy it with gourmet-style tortilla chips.

wild rice chowder

amy chop

OAK GROVE, LOUISIANA

I found this recipe years ago, and it has become a family favorite. Add cooked chicken or smoked sausage to make it heartier. There are endless possibilities for new and exciting variations.

 8 bacon strips, diced
1/3 cup chopped onion
1/3 cup all-purpose flour
1/2 to 1 teaspoon salt
 4 cups water
 1 can (14-1/2 ounces) chicken broth
1-1/2 cups cooked wild rice
 1 can (12 ounces) evaporated milk
 2 cups (8 ounces) cubed process American cheese (Velveeta)
 2 tablespoons minced fresh parsley

In a large saucepan, cook bacon until crisp. Remove with a slotted spoon to paper towels. Drain, reserving 1 tablespoon drippings. Saute onion in drippings until tender. Stir in flour and salt. Gradually stir in water and broth. Bring to a boil; cook and stir for 2 minutes or until slightly thickened.

Stir in the wild rice. Reduce heat; cover and simmer for 5 minutes. Add the milk, cheese, parsley and bacon; cook and stir until heated through and cheese is melted.

YIELD: 6-8 servings.

winter squash soup

2 celery ribs, chopped
1 medium onion, chopped
1 garlic clove, minced
3 tablespoons butter
3 tablespoons all-purpose flour
3 cups chicken broth
2 cups mashed cooked butternut, acorn *or* Hubbard squash
2 tablespoons minced fresh parsley
1/2 teaspoon salt
1/4 teaspoon dried savory
1/4 teaspoon dried rosemary, crushed
1/8 to 1/4 teaspoon ground nutmeg
1/8 teaspoon pepper
1 cup half-and-half cream

In a large saucepan, saute the celery, onion and garlic in butter until tender. Stir in the flour until blended. Gradually add the broth. Bring to a boil; cook and stir for 2 minutes or until thickened. Reduce heat; stir in the squash, parsley, salt, savory, rosemary, nutmeg and pepper. Simmer, uncovered, for 10 minutes or until heated through. Cool slightly.

In a blender, process the soup in batches until smooth. Return soup to the pan and heat through. Gradually stir in the cream. Cook 5 minutes longer, stirring occasionally.

YIELD: 6 servings.

angela liette
SIDNEY, OHIO

I enjoy trying new dishes and adding different seasonings to enhance the flavor. This is a tasty way to serve squash.

new england seafood chowder

4 pounds haddock fillets, cut into 3/4-inch pieces
1/4 pound uncooked medium shrimp, peeled and deveined
1/4 pound bay scallops
4 bacon strips, diced
3 medium onions, quartered and thinly sliced
2 tablespoons all-purpose flour
2 cups diced peeled potatoes
4 cups milk
2 tablespoons butter
1 tablespoon minced fresh parsley
2 teaspoons salt
1/2 teaspoon lemon-pepper seasoning
1/4 teaspoon pepper

Place haddock in a Dutch oven; cover with water. Bring to a boil over medium heat. Reduce heat; simmer, uncovered, for 20 minutes. Add the shrimp and scallops; simmer 10 minutes longer. Drain, reserving 2 cups cooking liquid; set liquid and seafood aside.

In a soup kettle, cook bacon over medium heat until crisp; drain on paper towels. In the drippings, saute onions until tender. Stir in flour until blended. Gradually stir in reserved cooking liquid. Bring to a boil; cook and stir for 2 minutes or until thickened. Reduce heat. Add potatoes; cover and cook for 15-20 minutes or until potatoes are tender.

Add the milk, seafood, butter, parsley, salt, lemon-pepper and pepper; heat through. Sprinkle with bacon.

YIELD: 15 servings.

kristine lowel
SOUTHBOROUGH, MASSACHUSETTS

We have an abundance of fresh seafood in our area, so I like to find delicious recipes to make use of it. This classic chowder features a combination of haddock, shrimp and scallops.

scallops

A member of the bivalve mollusk family, scallops are commonly divided into two groups: the sea scallop, yielding 10-20 per pound, and the much smaller bay scallop, yielding 60-90 per pound. Sold fresh or frozen, scallops are usually available shucked and range in color from pale beige to creamy pink. They can be broiled, grilled, pan-fried or deep-fried.

mrs. h.l. sosnowski

GRAND ISLAND, NEW YORK

Give my autumn soup a try after an outing to a pumpkin patch or haunted house. The combination of squash, applesauce and spices lends an appealing flavor everyone will love.

harvest squash soup

1-1/2 cups chopped onions
1 tablespoon canola oil
4 cups mashed cooked butternut squash
3 cups chicken broth
2 cups unsweetened applesauce
1-1/2 cups milk
1 bay leaf
1 tablespoon sugar
1 tablespoon lime juice
1 teaspoon curry powder
1/2 teaspoon salt, optional
1/2 teaspoon ground cinnamon
1/4 teaspoon ground nutmeg
1/4 teaspoon pepper

In a Dutch oven, saute onions in oil until tender. Add the remaining ingredients. Bring to a boil. Reduce heat; simmer, uncovered, for 30 minutes. Discard bay leaf before serving.

YIELD: 10 servings.

dorothy faulkner

BENTON, ARKANSAS

My friends and family always dig in when I serve this speedy delight. It pairs well with a salad or sandwich.

quick corn chowder

1/4 cup chopped green pepper
2 tablespoons chopped onion
2 garlic cloves, minced
2 tablespoons butter
2 cans (10-3/4 ounces *each*) condensed cream of potato soup, undiluted
1 can (14-3/4 ounces) cream-style corn
2 cups milk
1 package (3 ounces) cream cheese, cubed
Pepper to taste

In a large saucepan, saute the green pepper, onion and garlic in butter until tender. Stir in the soup, corn, milk, cream cheese and pepper. Bring to a boil, stirring frequently. Reduce heat; simmer, uncovered, for 5 minutes or until cream cheese is melted.

YIELD: 4-6 servings.

will zunio

GRETNA, LOUISIANA

Rely on the convenience of your slow cooker to simmer up my rich and creamy creation. The chowder is ready in less than 4 hours, so it can be prepared in the afternoon and served that night.

shrimp chowder

1/2 cup chopped onion
2 teaspoons butter
2 cans (12 ounces *each*) evaporated milk
2 cans (10-3/4 ounces *each*) condensed cream of potato soup, undiluted
2 cans (10-3/4 ounces *each*) condensed cream of chicken soup, undiluted
1 can (7 ounces) white *or* shoepeg corn, drained
1 teaspoon Creole seasoning
1/2 teaspoon garlic powder
2 pounds cooked small shrimp, peeled and deveined
1 package (3 ounces) cream cheese, cubed

In a small skillet, saute onion in butter until tender. In a 5-qt. slow cooker, combine the onion mixture, milk, soups, corn, Creole seasoning and garlic powder.

Cover and cook on low for 3 hours. Stir in shrimp and cream cheese. Cook 30 minutes longer or until shrimp are heated through and cheese is melted. Stir to blend.

YIELD: 12 servings.

EDITOR'S NOTE: The following spices may be substituted for 1 teaspoon of Creole seasoning: 1/4 teaspoon *each* of dried thyme, ground cumin and cayenne pepper.

north pacific chowder

8 bacon strips

1 small onion, chopped

1 celery rib, chopped

1 carton (32 ounces) chicken broth

4 medium red potatoes, cubed

2 tablespoons all-purpose flour

1 pint half-and-half cream

1 pound halibut fillets, cubed

1 tablespoon minced fresh tarragon
  or 1 teaspoon dried tarragon

1/2 teaspoon salt

1/4 teaspoon pepper

Tarragon sprigs, optional

In a large saucepan over medium heat, cook bacon until crisp. Drain, reserving 1 teaspoon drippings. Crumble bacon and set aside. Saute the onion and celery in the drippings. Add broth and potatoes. Bring to a boil. Reduce heat; cover and cook for 15-20 minutes or until potatoes are tender.

Combine flour and cream until smooth; gradually stir into soup. Bring to a boil; cook and stir for 2 minutes. Stir in the halibut, tarragon, salt, pepper and reserved bacon. Reduce the heat; simmer, uncovered, for 5-10 minutes or until fish flakes easily with a fork. Garnish with tarragon sprigs if desired.

YIELD: 9 servings.

pam woolgar
QUALICUM BEACH,
BRITISH COLUMBIA

You'll love my yummy, fresh chowder! Tender vegetables and tarragon add fantastic flavor to this smooth fish soup.

broccoli and crab bisque

dorothy child
MALONE, NEW YORK

Our son supplies us with a huge stock of the broccoli he grows, so I'm always on the lookout for recipes that call for the cruciferous vegetable. This chunky bisque creates an easy, delicious supper that's full of nutrition.

1 cup sliced leeks (white part only)
1 cup sliced fresh mushrooms
1 cup fresh broccoli florets
1 garlic clove, minced
1/4 cup butter, cubed
1/4 cup all-purpose flour
1/4 teaspoon dried thyme, crushed
1/8 teaspoon pepper
1 bay leaf
2 cans (10-1/2 ounces each) condensed chicken broth, undiluted
1 cup half-and-half cream
3/4 cup shredded Swiss cheese
1 package (6 ounces) frozen crabmeat, thawed, drained and flaked

In a large saucepan, cook the leeks, mushrooms, broccoli and garlic in butter until broccoli is crisp-tender. Stir in flour and seasonings until blended. Gradually add broth and cream.

Bring to a boil. Cook and stir for 1-2 minutes or until thickened. Add cheese; stir until melted. Add crab; heat through but do not boil. Discard bay leaf before serving.

YIELD: 5 servings.

oyster corn chowder

2 cans (8 ounces each) whole oysters, undrained
1 can (14-3/4 ounces) cream-style corn
1 cup half-and-half cream
2 cans (4 ounces each) mushroom stems and pieces, drained
2 tablespoons butter
1/4 teaspoon Worcestershire sauce
1/8 teaspoon pepper

In a large saucepan, combine all ingredients. Cook, uncovered, over medium-low heat until heated through (do not boil), stirring occasionally.

YIELD: 4 servings.

lewy olfson
MADISON, WISCONSIN

Chock-full of mushrooms, corn and oysters, this robust soup comes together easily with a can of cream-style corn and a little half-and-half cream.

new england clam chowder

4 center-cut bacon strips
2 celery ribs, chopped
1 large onion, chopped
1 garlic clove, minced
3 small potatoes, peeled and cubed
1 cup water
1 bottle (8 ounces) clam juice
3 teaspoons reduced-sodium chicken bouillon granules
1/4 teaspoon white pepper
1/4 teaspoon dried thyme
1/3 cup all-purpose flour
2 cups fat-free half-and-half cream, *divided*
2 cans (6-1/2 ounces each) chopped clams, undrained

In a Dutch oven, cook the bacon over medium heat until crisp. Remove to paper towels to drain; set aside. Saute celery and onion in the drippings until tender. Add garlic; cook 1 minute longer. Stir in the potatoes, water, clam juice, bouillon, pepper and thyme. Bring to a boil. Reduce the heat; simmer, uncovered, for 15-20 minutes or until the potatoes are tender.

In a small bowl, combine the flour and 1 cup half-and-half until smooth. Gradually stir into the soup. Bring to a boil; cook and stir for 1-2 minutes or until thickened.

Stir in clams and remaining half-and-half; heat through (do not boil). Crumble the reserved bacon; sprinkle over each serving.

YIELD: 5 servings.

sandy larson
PORT ANGELES, WASHINGTON

In the Pacific Northwest, we dig our own razor clams, and I grind them for recipes like this one. If fresh clams aren't readily available, canned works just as well.

CHAPTER eight

chilled soups

When we hear the term soup, cold concoctions don't usually come to mind. But a cool fruit or veggie soup is not only a great refresher—it can be nutritious, too! Give one of these soups a try as a starter for a special meal or as a cooler on a sultry summer day. Fruit-based soups also make great desserts!

224   228   232

cool tomato soup

wendy nickel
KIESTER, MINNESOTA

The fresh flavors of summer star in this delightful chilled soup.

🥄 seeding tomatoes

To seed a tomato, cut in half horizontally and remove the stem. Holding a tomato half over a bowl or sink, scrape out seeds with a small spoon, or squeeze the tomato to force out the seeds. Then slice or dice as directed in the recipe.

4 cups tomato juice, *divided*
5 medium tomatoes, peeled, seeded and chopped
2 medium cucumbers, peeled, seeded and cut into chunks
1 medium green pepper, quartered
1 medium sweet red pepper, quartered
1 medium onion, peeled and quartered
2 garlic cloves, peeled
1 tablespoon minced fresh thyme
1/4 cup white balsamic vinegar
4 cups cubed bread, crusts removed
2 tablespoons olive oil
1/4 teaspoon pepper
Fat-free sour cream, fat-free croutons and parsley, optional

In a blender, cover and process 1 cup tomato juice and half of the tomatoes, cucumbers, peppers, onion, garlic and thyme until chopped. Transfer to a large bowl. Repeat.

Place vinegar and remaining tomato juice in the blender. Add the bread; cover and process until smooth. Add to vegetable mixture; stir in oil and pepper.

Cover and refrigerate for 1-2 hours before serving. Garnish with sour cream, croutons and parsley if desired.

YIELD: 9 servings.

summer soup

- 1 bottle (46 ounces) reduced-sodium V8 juice
- 2 cans (14-1/2 ounces *each*) Italian diced tomatoes, undrained
- 2 cans (5-1/2 ounces *each*) spicy hot V8 juice
- 1 medium green pepper, chopped
- 1 cup shredded carrots
- 1/2 cup chopped green onions
- 1/2 cup reduced-fat zesty Italian salad dressing
- 2 tablespoons lemon juice
- 1 tablespoon sugar
- 2 teaspoons Worcestershire sauce
- 1 garlic clove, minced
- 3/4 teaspoon celery salt
- 1/2 teaspoon salt

In a large bowl, combine all of the ingredients. Cover and refrigerate for at least 2 hours before serving.
YIELD: 12 servings.

liz fick
LITCHVILLE, NORTH DAKOTA

Unlike many chilled soups, this one isn't pureed, so you'll find plenty of chunky vegetable bits in each savory spoonful.

peppers and onions

A medium green pepper, chopped, will yield about 1 cup. A large green pepper, chopped, will yield about 1-1/3 to 1-1/2 cups. A medium onion, chopped, will equal about 1/2 cup; a large onion will yield about 1 cup. Green peppers can be frozen for up to 6 months. Onions can be frozen for up to 1 year.

shrimp gazpacho

- 6 cups spicy hot V8 juice
- 2 cups cold water
- 1 pound cooked medium shrimp, peeled and deveined
- 2 medium tomatoes, seeded and diced
- 1 medium cucumber, seeded and diced
- 2 medium ripe avocados, diced
- 1/2 cup lime juice
- 1/2 cup minced fresh cilantro
- 1/2 teaspoon salt
- 1/4 to 1/2 teaspoon hot pepper sauce

In a large bowl, combine all ingredients. Cover and refrigerate for 1 hour. Serve cold.

YIELD: 12 servings.

EDITOR'S NOTE: This recipe is best served the same day it's made.

taste of home test kitchen
GREENDALE, WISCONSIN

This refreshing tomato-based soup features shrimp, cucumber and avocados. Serve a batch as an appetizer or a light meal on its own.

gazpacho defined

Gazpacho is an uncooked cold soup. The most common version calls for tomatoes, cucumbers, sweet peppers, onion and garlic.

sherri cyr
CANTON, MAINE

Chill out with this fun, fruity soup. Its smooth, velvety texture and sweet-tart taste are sure to please.

🥄 orange spirals

Orange spirals make an attractive garnish. To make them, use a citrus stripper to remove the peel of an orange in one continuous motion, working from end to end. Tightly wind the strips around straws; trim and secure ends with tape. Let wrapped straws stand for at least 20 minutes.

strawberry orange soup

- 1 cup orange juice
- 2 cups fresh strawberries, hulled
- 2 teaspoons cornstarch
- 3/4 cup white grape juice
- 2 tablespoons seedless strawberry jam
- 2 teaspoons honey

Whipped topping and orange peel strips, optional

In a blender, combine orange juice and strawberries; cover and process until blended. Press mixture through a fine meshed sieve; discard seeds.

In a large saucepan; combine cornstarch and grape juice until smooth. Stir in strawberry puree and jam. Bring to a boil over medium heat; cook and stir for 2 minutes or until thickened. Reduce heat; add honey. Simmer, uncovered, for 10 minutes.

Transfer to a bowl; cover and refrigerate until chilled. Garnish with whipped topping and orange peel if desired.

YIELD: 2-3 servings.

dave schmitt
HARTLAND, WISCONSIN

There's a bounty of goodness in this tantalizing chilled soup. Its refreshing flavor makes it an ideal addition to summer luncheons or light suppers.

spanish gazpacho

- 5 pounds tomatoes, peeled and quartered
- 3 medium carrots, quartered
- 1 large cucumber, peeled and quartered
- 1 large sweet red pepper, quartered
- 1 large green pepper, quartered
- 1 sweet onion, quartered
- 2 garlic cloves, minced
- 1/3 cup olive oil
- 3 tablespoons balsamic vinegar
- 1-1/2 teaspoons salt
- 1/2 teaspoon pepper

In batches, place the ingredients in a blender; cover and process until soup reaches desired texture. Pour into a large bowl. Cover and refrigerate for 1-2 hours before serving.

YIELD: 12 servings.

shrimp blitz

- 1 bottle (8 ounces) clam juice
- 1 package (8 ounces) cream cheese, softened
- 1 bottle (32 ounces) tomato juice
- 1 package (5 ounces) frozen cooked salad shrimp, thawed
- 1 medium ripe avocado, peeled and diced
- 1/2 cup chopped cucumber
- 1/3 cup chopped green onions
- 2 tablespoons red wine vinegar
- 2 teaspoons sugar
- 1 teaspoon dill weed
- 1 garlic clove, minced
- 1/2 teaspoon salt
- 1/4 teaspoon hot pepper sauce
- 1/8 teaspoon pepper

In a blender, combine clam juice and cream cheese; cover and process until smooth. Pour into a large serving bowl. Stir in the remaining ingredients. Cover and chill for at least 4 hours.

YIELD: 8 servings.

jeannette aiello
PLACERVILLE, CALIFORNIA

This refreshing soup hits the spot on hot summer days. I've made it for special-occasion lunches as well as casual dinners with friends.

nicole deelah
NASHVILLE, TENNESSEE

I promise you'll love my delightfully simple watermelon gazpacho. Serve as a refreshing side dish or with pita bread and hummus for a snack.

watermelon gazpacho

4 cups cubed watermelon, seeded, *divided*

2 tablespoons lime juice

1 tablespoon grated lime peel

1 teaspoon minced fresh gingerroot

1 teaspoon salt

1 cup chopped tomato

1/2 cup chopped cucumber

1/2 cup chopped green pepper

1/4 cup minced fresh cilantro

2 tablespoons chopped green onion

1 tablespoon finely chopped seeded jalapeno pepper

Puree 3 cups watermelon in a blender. Cut remaining watermelon into 1/2-inch pieces; set aside.

In a large bowl, combine the watermelon puree, lime juice, lime peel, ginger and salt. Stir in the tomato, cucumber, green pepper, cilantro, onion, jalapeno and cubed watermelon. Chill until serving.

YIELD: 4 servings.

EDITOR'S NOTE: We recommend wearing disposable gloves when cutting hot peppers. Avoid touching your face.

garbanzo gazpacho

1 can (15 ounces) garbanzo beans *or* chickpeas, rinsed and drained
1 can (14-1/2 ounces) Italian diced tomatoes, undrained
1-1/4 cups V8 juice
1 cup beef broth
1 cup quartered cherry tomatoes
1/2 cup chopped seeded cucumber
1/4 cup chopped red onion
1/4 cup minced fresh cilantro
3 tablespoons lime juice
1 garlic clove, minced
1/2 teaspoon salt
1/4 teaspoon hot pepper sauce

In a large bowl, combine all the ingredients; cover and refrigerate until serving.

YIELD: 6 servings.

mary ann gomez
LOMBARD, ILLINOIS

This chunky, chilled soup is terrific in warm weather, but our family loves it so much I often prepare it in winter, too. I made some slight changes to suit our tastes, and the fresh, flavorful combination has been a favorite ever since.

chilled peach soup

1-1/2 cups chopped peeled fresh peaches
1/2 cup plain yogurt
1/2 teaspoon lemon juice
1/8 teaspoon almond extract
2 tablespoons sliced almonds, toasted

In a blender, combine the peaches, yogurt, lemon juice and extract; cover and process until smooth. Refrigerate until chilled. Sprinkle with almonds just before serving.

YIELD: 2 servings.

lane mcloud
SILOAM SPRINGS, ARKANSAS

Welcome summer with the creamy taste of chilled peach soup. Toasted almonds lend a pleasant crunch on top.

peach pointers

Purchase fresh peaches that have an intense fragrance and that give slightly to palm pressure. Avoid those that are hard or have soft spots. A half pound of whole peaches will yield about 1 cup chopped.

beulah goodenough
BELLEVILLE, NEW JERSEY

On a sultry summer day, nothing can top the flavor of the season's finest fruits combined in one sensational soup.

honey

If honey crystallizes, place the jar or bottle in warm water and stir until the crystals dissolve. Or pour honey into a microwave-safe container and heat on high, stirring every 30 seconds, until the crystals dissolve.

fresh fruit soup

2 cups water
2 tablespoons quick-cooking tapioca
1 can (6 ounces) frozen orange juice concentrate, thawed
1 to 2 tablespoons sugar
1 tablespoon honey
1/8 teaspoon almond extract
Pinch salt
2-1/2 cups fresh fruit of your choice

In a large saucepan, combine water and tapioca; let stand for 10 minutes. Bring to a boil; cook and stir for 2 minutes or until thickened. Remove from the heat; stir in orange juice concentrate, sugar, honey, extract and salt. Chill until cold. Add fruit; refrigerate until ready to serve.

YIELD: 4 servings.

chris brooks
PRESCOTT, ARIZONA

"Simple as can be" best describes this cold soup. You just chop and combine the ingredients, then chill for a few hours. It tastes great with crunchy croutons or breadsticks.

easy gazpacho

1 can (46 ounces) vegetable juice
1 can (10-1/2 ounces) condensed beef consomme, undiluted
2 cups chopped cucumber
2 cups chopped tomatoes
1 cup chopped green pepper
1/2 cup chopped onion
1/2 cup chopped celery

1/3 cup red wine vinegar
2 tablespoons lemon juice
2 garlic cloves, minced
3 to 4 drops hot pepper sauce

In a large bowl, combine all ingredients. Cover and chill for 2-3 hours before serving. Serve cold.

YIELD: 12 servings.

icy olive soup

- 2 cups (16 ounces) plain yogurt
- 2 cans (10-1/2 ounces *each*) condensed chicken broth, undiluted
- 2 cans (2-1/4 ounces *each*) sliced ripe olives, drained
- 1 cup coarsely chopped cucumber
- 1/2 cup chopped green onions
- 1/2 cup chopped green pepper
- 1/2 cup sliced pimiento-stuffed olives
- 1/8 teaspoon white pepper

Seasoned croutons, optional

In a large bowl, stir yogurt until smooth. Whisk in broth. Add the next six ingredients; mix well. Cover and chill for 4 hours. Stir before serving. Garnish with croutons if desired.

YIELD: 6 servings.

theresa goble
MUSCATINE, IOWA

When summer turns up the heat, I reach for this cool, refreshing soup. The color of the olives contrasts nicely with the creamy yogurt base.

summer strawberry soup

verna bollin
POWELL, TENNESSEE

You'll be amazed that just five ingredients can create something so spectacular! This fruity chilled soup is certain to become a new summertime favorite.

2 cups vanilla yogurt
1/2 cup orange juice
2 pounds fresh strawberries, halved (8 cups)
1/2 cup sugar
Additional vanilla yogurt and fresh mint leaves, optional

In a blender, combine the yogurt, orange juice, strawberries and sugar in batches; cover and process until blended. Refrigerate for at least 2 hours. Garnish with additional yogurt and mint leaves if desired.

YIELD: 6 servings.

chilled mixed berry soup

- 1 cup sliced fresh strawberries
- 1/2 cup fresh raspberries
- 1/2 cup fresh blackberries
- 1 cup unsweetened apple juice
- 1/2 cup water
- 1/4 cup sugar
- 2 tablespoons lemon juice
- Dash ground nutmeg
- 1-1/2 cups (12 ounces) raspberry yogurt

In a heavy saucepan, combine the berries, apple juice, water, sugar, lemon juice and nutmeg. Cook, uncovered, over low heat for 20 minutes or until berries are softened. Strain, reserving juice. Press berry mixture through a fine meshed sieve; discard seeds. Add pulp to the reserved juice; cover and refrigerate until chilled.

Place the berry mixture in a food processor or blender; add the yogurt. Cover and process until smooth. Pour into bowls.

YIELD: 4 servings.

taste of home test kitchen
GREENDALE, WISCONSIN

Looking for a lovely addition to a spring or summer menu? Give our cool, berry-liscious soup a try.

brambles

Blackberries and raspberries are often referred to as brambles. All bramble fruits are aggregate fruits, which means they're formed by the aggregation of several smaller fruits called drupelets. Brambles are often used in preserves, baked goods, ice cream, yogurt and smoothies.

cool raspberry soup

- 1 package (20 ounces) frozen unsweetened raspberries, thawed
- 1-1/4 cups water
- 1/4 cup white wine, optional
- 1 cup cran-raspberry juice
- 1/2 cup sugar
- 1-1/2 teaspoons ground cinnamon
- 3 whole cloves
- 1 tablespoon lemon juice
- 1 cup (8 ounces) raspberry yogurt
- 1/2 cup sour cream

In a blender, puree raspberries, water and wine if desired. Transfer to a large saucepan; add the cran-raspberry juice, sugar, cinnamon and cloves. Bring just to a boil over medium heat. Remove from the heat; strain and allow to cool.

Whisk in lemon juice and yogurt. Refrigerate. To serve, pour into small bowls and top with a dollop of sour cream.

YIELD: 4-6 servings.

janice mooberry
PEORIA, ILLINOIS

An exquisite combination of spices and a rich flavor make this ruby-red soup so refreshing. It's the perfect treat for a shower or special ladies' luncheon.

raspberries

Purchase brightly colored raspberries without the hulls attached. One-half pint equals about 1 cup. Discard any raspberries that are soft, shriveled or moldy. Rinse remaining berries in water, then place in a single layer in a paper towel-lined bowl. They'll stay fresh in the refrigerator for up to 3 days.

neva arthur
NEW BERLIN, WISCONSIN

I spice up my sweet-tart soup with a hint of cinnamon. Serve it as a light first course or for dessert topped with a dollop of nonfat yogurt or whipped topping.

tart cherry soup

2 cans (14-1/2 ounces *each*) water-packed pitted tart cherries
1/2 cup orange juice
1/2 cup sugar
2 tablespoons lime juice
1 teaspoon grated lime peel
1/2 teaspoon ground cinnamon
4 lime slices

Place the cherries in a blender or food processor; cover and process until finely chopped. Transfer to a saucepan; add the orange juice, sugar, lime juice, peel and cinnamon. Bring to a boil. Reduce heat; cover and simmer for 10 minutes. Refrigerate until chilled. Garnish with lime slices.

YIELD: 4 servings.

phyllis hammes
ROCHESTER, MINNESOTA

I enjoyed a cool berry soup at a restaurant several years ago. The manager gave me some of the ingredients but none of the amounts, so I tinkered until I concocted this refreshing rendition.

strawberry soup

1 pound fresh strawberries
1-1/4 cups vanilla yogurt, *divided*
3 tablespoons confectioners' sugar
2 tablespoons orange juice concentrate
1/8 teaspoon almond extract *or*
1/2 teaspoon lemon juice

In a food processor, combine the strawberries, 1 cup yogurt, confectioners' sugar, orange juice concentrate and extract; cover and process until blended. Garnish each serving with a dollop of remaining yogurt.

YIELD: 3 servings.

strawberries

Purchase strawberries that are shiny, firm and fragrant. A strawberry should be almost completely red, though some whiteness near the leafy cap is acceptable.

chilled avocado soup

1 medium ripe avocado, peeled, halved and pitted

1 can (14-1/2 ounces) reduced-sodium chicken broth

1/2 cup reduced-fat sour cream

1 green onion, chopped

1-1/2 teaspoons minced fresh cilantro

1/8 teaspoon salt

1/8 teaspoon ground cumin

Dash cayenne pepper

Dash pepper

Place avocado in a blender, cover and process until smooth. While processing, gradually add broth; process until smooth. Add the remaining ingredients; cover and process until blended. Refrigerate for 1 hour or until chilled.

YIELD: 3 servings.

edith herring
GRAND CANE, LOUISIANA

No cooking is necessary for this rich and creamy soup with a kick! I like to line the bowl with crumbled corn chips and pour the soup on top.

smooth strawberry soup

janice mitchell
AURORA, COLORADO

Every summer, we wait impatiently for the strawberry crop to peak so we can make this luscious soup. The berry flavor is complemented by a sprinkling of sweetly spiced croutons.

1 quart strawberries, halved
2 cups apple juice
1 cup (8 ounces) sour cream
1/2 cup packed brown sugar
1/2 cup honey
2 tablespoons lemon juice
1-1/2 cups half-and-half cream
3 tablespoons orange juice, optional

CINNAMON-SUGAR CROUTONS:

3 slices white bread, crusts removed and cubed
2 tablespoons butter
1 teaspoon cinnamon-sugar

In a large bowl, combine the first six ingredients. Place half of the mixture in a blender; cover and process until pureed. Transfer to a large bowl. Repeat with the remaining strawberry mixture.

Stir in cream and orange juice if desired. Cover and refrigerate for 2 hours.

Meanwhile, in a small skillet over medium heat, saute bread cubes in butter until golden brown. Remove from the heat. Sprinkle with cinnamon-sugar; toss to coat. Cool. Stir soup before serving; garnish with croutons.

YIELD: 6 servings.

raspberry-cranberry soup for two

1 cup fresh *or* frozen cranberries
1 cup unsweetened apple juice
1/2 cup fresh *or* frozen raspberries, thawed
1/4 to 1/2 cup sugar
1-1/2 teaspoons lemon juice
1/8 teaspoon ground cinnamon
1 cup half-and-half cream, *divided*
1-1/2 teaspoons cornstarch
Whipped cream and additional raspberries, optional

In a large saucepan, bring cranberries and apple juice to a boil. Reduce heat and simmer, uncovered, for 10 minutes. Press through a sieve; return to the pan. Press the raspberries through the sieve; discard skins and seeds. Add to cranberry mixture; bring to a boil. Stir in the sugar, lemon juice and cinnamon; remove from heat.

Cool for 4 minutes. Stir 1/2 cup soup into 3/4 cup cream. Return all to pan; bring to a gentle boil. Mix cornstarch with remaining cream until smooth; gradually stir into soup. Cook and stir for 2 minutes or until thickened. Serve hot or chilled. Serve with whipped cream and additional raspberries if desired.

YIELD: 2 servings.

susan stull
CHILLICOTHE, MISSOURI

Looking for a delicious recipe for two? You'll love the sweet flavor of my chilled berry soup.

frozen berries

Many berries can be kept frozen for up to 1 year without sacrificing flavor. Before adding to a recipe, allow them to thaw slowly in the refrigerator.

gazpacho

6 medium tomatoes, seeded and chopped
1 medium green pepper, chopped
1 cup chopped peeled cucumber
1 cup chopped red onion
4 cups tomato juice
1 teaspoon dried oregano
1 teaspoon dried basil
1/2 teaspoon salt
1/2 teaspoon minced garlic
1/4 teaspoon pepper
Dash hot pepper sauce
3 tablespoons minced chives
Chopped sweet yellow pepper, optional

In a large bowl, combine the tomatoes, green pepper, cucumber and onion. In another large bowl, combine the tomato juice, oregano, basil, salt, garlic, pepper and hot pepper sauce; pour over vegetables. Cover and refrigerate for at least 4 hours or overnight. Sprinkle with chives and yellow pepper if desired.

YIELD: 6 servings.

taste of home test kitchen
GREENDALE, WISCONSIN

Healthy vegetables are the basis of this soup. Use a spicy tomato juice if you like a little more bite.

renee parker
CHESTER, SOUTH CAROLINA

This pretty soup is perfect for spring or summer. My whole family loves the fresh flavor of rhubarb, so it's always a hit!

🥄 rhubarb

Look for rhubarb stalks that are crisp and brightly colored. Tightly wrap in a plastic bag and store in the refrigerator for up to 3 days. Wash the stalks and remove the poisonous leaves before using. One pound of rhubarb yields about 3 cups chopped.

spiced rhubarb soup

8 cups diced fresh *or* frozen rhubarb, thawed

3-1/2 cups water, *divided*

1 cup sugar

4 cinnamon sticks (3 inches)

1/4 teaspoon salt

3 tablespoons plus 1-1/2 teaspoons cornstarch

1 lemon slice

4 tablespoons reduced-fat sour cream

In a large saucepan, bring rhubarb, 3-1/4 cups water, sugar, cinnamon sticks and salt to a boil. Reduce heat; simmer, uncovered, for 20 minutes or until rhubarb is tender. Discard cinnamon sticks. Strain rhubarb mixture; discard pulp. Return liquid to the pan; bring to a boil.

Combine cornstarch and remaining water until smooth; stir into saucepan. Cook and stir for 2 minutes or until thickened. Remove from the heat; add lemon slice. Cover and refrigerate until chilled. Discard lemon slice. Ladle soup into bowls. Garnish each serving with 1 tablespoon sour cream.

YIELD: 4 servings.

sharon delaney-chronis
SOUTH MILWAUKEE, WISCONSIN

My husband prefers this sweet soup warm, while I like it chilled. We drizzle leftovers over ice cream or frozen custard for a fresh, fruity topping.

strawberry dessert soup

1 cup water, *divided*

1 cup unsweetened apple juice

2/3 cup sugar

1/2 teaspoon ground cinnamon

1/8 teaspoon ground cloves

2 cups fresh strawberries, hulled

2 cups strawberry yogurt

2 to 3 drops red food coloring, optional

1/4 cup sour cream

2 tablespoons whole milk

In a large saucepan, combine 3/4 cup water, apple juice, sugar, cinnamon and cloves. Bring to a boil, stirring occasionally. Remove from the heat.

Place strawberries and remaining water in a blender; cover and process until smooth. Pour into apple juice mixture. Stir in yogurt and food coloring if desired. Cover and refrigerate for at least 2 hours or until chilled.

Ladle soup into bowls. Combine sour cream and milk; spoon about 2-1/2 teaspoons into the center of each bowl. Using a toothpick, pull mixture out, forming a flower or design of your choice.

YIELD: 7 servings.

chilled blueberry soup

1/2 cup sugar

2 tablespoons cornstarch

2-3/4 cups water

2 cups fresh *or* frozen blueberries

1 cinnamon stick (3 inches)

1 can (6 ounces) frozen orange juice concentrate

Sour cream, optional

In a large saucepan, combine sugar and cornstarch. Gradually stir in water until smooth. Bring to a boil over medium heat; cook and stir for 2 minutes or until thickened.

Add blueberries and cinnamon stick; return to a boil. Remove from the heat. Stir in the orange juice concentrate until thawed. Cover and refrigerate for at least 1 hour. Discard cinnamon stick. Garnish with sour cream if desired.

YIELD: 4 servings.

edith richardson
JASPER, ALABAMA

With 100 blueberry bushes in my garden, I'm always looking for recipes calling for this sweet-tart fruit. I was delighted when my granddaughter shared this one with me.

chilled melon soup

mary lou timpson
COLORADO CITY, ARIZONA

Looking for something to put a little pizazz in a summer luncheon? Give my refreshing melon soup a try. A bit of cayenne pepper will get the conversation going.

3/4 cup orange juice
1 cup (8 ounces) plain yogurt
1 medium cantaloupe, peeled, seeded and cubed
1 tablespoon honey
1/4 teaspoon salt
1/4 teaspoon ground nutmeg
1/8 teaspoon cayenne pepper
6 mint sprigs

Place the orange juice, yogurt and cantaloupe in a blender; cover and process until pureed. Add the honey, salt, nutmeg and cayenne; cover and process until smooth. Refrigerate for at least 1 hour before serving. Garnish with mint sprigs.

YIELD: 6 servings.

herbed gazpacho

1 can (46 ounces) V8 juice, chilled
1 can (14-1/2 ounces) Italian stewed tomatoes
3 medium tomatoes, chopped
1 medium green pepper, chopped
1 medium cucumber, chopped
1/2 cup Italian salad dressing
1/4 cup minced fresh parsley
4 to 6 garlic cloves, minced
1 teaspoon Italian seasoning
1 teaspoon salt
1/4 teaspoon pepper
Cooked chopped shrimp, optional

In a large bowl, combine the first 11 ingredients. Cover and refrigerate for at least 1 hour. Garnish with shrimp if desired.

YIELD: 10-12 servings.

carole benson
CABAZON, CALIFORNIA

Chilled tomato juice is the base for my gazpacho that's full of chunks of chopped tomatoes, green pepper and cucumber. Garnish each bowl with shrimp for a fancy finish.

black bean gazpacho

3 cans (11-1/2 ounces *each*) spicy hot V8 juice
4 medium tomatoes, seeded and chopped
1 can (15 ounces) black beans, rinsed and drained
1 cup cubed fully cooked ham
1/2 cup *each* chopped green, sweet yellow and red pepper
1/2 cup chopped cucumber
1/2 cup chopped zucchini
1/4 cup finely chopped green onions
2 tablespoons Italian salad dressing
3/4 teaspoon salt
1/8 to 1/4 teaspoon hot pepper sauce

Combine all of the ingredients in a large bowl. Cover and refrigerate for at least 2 hours.

YIELD: 10 servings.

EDITOR'S NOTE: Two 14-1/2-ounce cans of diced tomatoes, drained, can be substituted for the fresh tomatoes.

shelley graff
PHILO, ILLINOIS

I first tried this cool, colorful soup at my best friend's house during one of the hottest summers I can remember. Its garden-fresh flavor really hit the spot!

black beans

Also commonly known as Spanish beans or turtle beans, black beans are thought to have originated in southern Mexico and Central America over 7,000 years ago. They are a popular ingredient in Mexican and Southwestern dishes, particularly in soups, stews and sauces.

chili

You can't go wrong when you serve crowd-pleasing chili. Whether it's your daily dinnertime crowd or a party of friends or relatives, you'll win raves if you serve one of these recipes. The variety found here will please all palates. So if you crave a spicy dish, we have it—but if mild is your taste, you're all set, too.

246   262   269

sherry hulva
DECATUR, ILLINOIS

Potatoes add a unique layer to ordinary chili. My husband loves spicy foods, so I sprinkle extra chili powder on top to please his palate.

spuds

You can also use cubed potatoes in place of the scalloped in this chili recipe. Another fun variation is to put a dollop of mashed potatoes in soup bowls, spoon chili on top and sprinkle with your favorite shredded cheese.

scalloped potato chili

1-1/2 pounds lean ground beef (90% lean)
3/4 cup chopped onion
1/2 cup chopped green pepper
2 cans (16 ounces *each*) kidney beans, rinsed and drained
2 cans (14-1/2 ounces *each*) stewed tomatoes
1 package (5-1/4 ounces) scalloped potatoes
1 can (8 ounces) sliced mushrooms, drained
1 cup water
1 teaspoon salt
3/4 teaspoon chili powder
Shredded Parmesan cheese

In a large saucepan, cook the beef, onion and green pepper over medium heat until meat is no longer pink; drain. Stir in the beans, tomatoes, contents of potato package, mushrooms, water, salt and chili powder; bring to a boil. Reduce the heat; cover and simmer for 40-45 minutes or until potatoes are tender. Sprinkle with cheese.

YIELD: 10 servings.

EDITOR'S NOTE: If you're making Scalloped Potato Chili for a potluck, prepare it at home on the stove, then take it to the gathering in a slow cooker.

elizabeth hunt
KIRBYVILLE, TEXAS

It's not spicy, but this chili is sure to warm you up during those cold winter evenings. The recipe calls for precooked shrimp and canned goods, so preparation is a cinch.

shrimp 'n' black bean chili

1/2 cup chopped onion
1/2 cup chopped green pepper
1 tablespoon canola oil
1 can (15 ounces) black beans, rinsed and drained
1 can (14-1/2 ounces) diced tomatoes, undrained
1 cup chicken broth
1/3 cup picante sauce
1 teaspoon ground cumin
1/2 teaspoon dried basil
1 pound cooked medium shrimp, peeled and deveined
Hot cooked rice, optional

In a large saucepan, saute onion and green pepper in oil for 4-5 minutes or until crisp-tender. Stir in the beans, tomatoes, broth, picante sauce, cumin and basil. Reduce heat; simmer, uncovered, for 10-15 minutes or until heated through.

Add shrimp; simmer 3-4 minutes longer or until heated through. Serve with rice if desired.

YIELD: 6 servings.

spiced chili

1-1/2 pounds lean ground beef (90% lean)
1/2 cup chopped onion
4 garlic cloves, minced
2 cans (16 ounces *each*) kidney beans, rinsed and drained
2 cans (15 ounces *each*) tomato sauce
2 cans (14-1/2 ounces *each*) stewed tomatoes, cut up
1 cup water
2 bay leaves
1/4 cup chili powder
1 tablespoon salt
1 tablespoon brown sugar
1 tablespoon dried basil
1 tablespoon Italian seasoning
1 tablespoon dried thyme
1 tablespoon pepper
1 teaspoon dried oregano
1 teaspoon dried marjoram
Shredded cheddar cheese, optional

In a large skillet, cook beef and onion over medium heat until meat is no longer pink. Add garlic; cook 1 minute longer. Drain.

Transfer to a 5-qt. slow cooker. Stir in the beans, tomato sauce, tomatoes, water and seasonings. Cover and cook on low for 4-5 hours. Discard bay leaves. Garnish with cheese if desired.

YIELD: 12 servings.

julie brendt
GOLD RIVER, CALIFORNIA

My father was a cook in the Army. His chili recipe is one I'm proud to make for my own family.

speedy on the stovetop

You can also make this chili on the stovetop. Use a Dutch oven instead of a skillet to cook the beef, onion and garlic. Add the ingredients to the Dutch oven instead of the slow cooker. Bring to a boil. Reduce heat; cover and simmer for 45 minutes. Discard bay leaves.

**taste of home
cooking school**

GREENDALE, WISCONSIN

Folks will enjoy a departure from the usual when they taste this flavorful blend of white beans and tender chunks of chicken.

white chicken chili

1 medium onion, chopped

1 tablespoon olive oil

2 cloves garlic, minced

4 boneless skinless chicken breast halves (4 ounces *each*), chopped

2 cans (14 ounces *each*) chicken broth

1 can (4 ounces) chopped green chilies

2 teaspoons ground cumin

2 teaspoons dried oregano

1-1/2 teaspoons cayenne pepper

3 cans (14-1/2 ounces *each*) great northern beans, drained, *divided*

1 cup (4 ounces) shredded Monterey Jack cheese

Chopped jalapeno pepper, optional

In a large saucepan over medium heat, cook onion in oil for 10 minutes or until tender. Add garlic; cook 1 minute longer. Add the chicken, chicken broth, green chilies, cumin, oregano and cayenne pepper; bring to a boil.

Reduce heat to low. With a potato masher, mash one can of beans until smooth. Add to saucepan. Add remaining beans to saucepan. Simmer for 20-30 minutes or until heated through.

Top each serving with cheese and jalapeno pepper if desired.

YIELD: 10 servings.

jalapeno pepper chili

1/2 pound lean ground beef (90% lean)

1/2 pound ground pork

2 cans (16 ounces *each*) kidney beans, rinsed and drained

2 cans (14-1/2 ounces *each*) diced tomatoes with garlic and onion, undrained

1 can (14-1/2 ounces) beef broth

1 can (8 ounces) tomato sauce

2 tablespoons chili powder

1 jalapeno pepper, seeded and chopped

12 hard rolls (about 4-1/2 inches), optional

Shredded cheddar cheese, sliced green onions and sour cream, optional

In a large saucepan, cook beef and pork over medium heat until no longer pink; drain. Stir in the beans, tomatoes, broth, tomato sauce, chili powder and jalapeno. Bring to a boil. Reduce heat; cover and simmer for 20 minutes.

Serve in soup bowls or, if desired, cut the top fourth off of each roll; carefully hollow out bottom, leaving a 1/2-in. shell. Cube removed bread. Spoon chili into bread bowls. Serve with cubed bread, shredded cheddar cheese, sliced green onions and sour cream if desired.

YIELD: 12 servings.

EDITOR'S NOTE: We recommend wearing disposable gloves when cutting hot peppers. Avoid touching your face.

tonya michelle burkhard
ENGLEWOOD, FLORIDA

I like meals that are simple to prepare yet offer maximum taste. My hearty chili offers extra zip with two kinds of meat, beans and jalapeno pepper.

firehouse chili

4 pounds lean ground beef (90% lean)

2 medium onions, chopped

1 medium green pepper, chopped

3 cans (14-1/2 ounces *each*) stewed tomatoes, cut up

4 cans (16 ounces *each*) kidney beans, rinsed and drained

1 can (14-1/2 ounces) beef broth

3 tablespoons chili powder

2 tablespoons ground coriander

2 tablespoons ground cumin

4 garlic cloves, minced

1 teaspoon dried oregano

In a Dutch oven, cook the beef, onions and green pepper over medium heat until meat is no longer pink; drain.

Stir in the remaining ingredients. Bring to a boil. Reduce heat; cover and simmer for 1-1/2 hours or until flavors are blended.

YIELD: 11 servings.

richard clements
SAN DIMAS, CALIFORNIA

I'm one of the cooks at our local firehouse. This chili is among the favorites of the members of my unit.

slow-cooked chili

2 pounds lean ground beef (90% lean)

1/2 cup chopped onion

2 garlic cloves, minced

2 cans (16 ounces *each*) dark red kidney beans, rinsed and drained

2 cans (16 ounces *each*) light red kidney beans, rinsed and drained

2 cans (14-1/2 ounces *each*) stewed tomatoes, cut up

1 can (15 ounces) pizza sauce

1 can (4 ounces) chopped green chilies

4 teaspoons chili powder

1 teaspoon dried basil

1/2 teaspoon salt

1/8 teaspoon pepper

In a Dutch oven, cook beef, onion and garlic over medium heat until meat is no longer pink; drain. Transfer to a 5-qt. slow cooker; stir in the remaining ingredients. Cover and cook on low for 6 hours.

YIELD: 14 servings.

sandra mckenzie
BRAHAM, MINNESOTA

My savory slow-cooked wonder is hearty and filling. It will warm both body and soul.

elaine peters
OSLER, SASKATCHEWAN

I came across this chunky chili recipe while planning my holiday menu a few years ago. I decided to give it a whirl, and it has been a much-requested dish ever since.

chuck wagon chili

1-1/2 pounds lean ground beef (90% lean)
1 can (16 ounces) kidney beans, undrained
1 can (10-3/4 ounces) condensed tomato soup, undiluted
1 can (8 ounces) sliced mushrooms, undrained
6 hot dogs, halved and cut into bite-size pieces
2 medium carrots, sliced
1 medium onion, chopped
1 teaspoon salt
1 teaspoon chili powder
1/4 teaspoon pepper

In a large saucepan, cook the beef over medium heat until no longer pink; drain. Add the remaining

ingredients and bring to a boil. Reduce heat; cover and simmer for 1 hour or until thick and bubbly.

YIELD: 6-8 servings.

taste of home test kitchen
GREENDALE, WISCONSIN

You will love the zesty flavor of this hefty stew. Serve it over rice, noodles or mashed potatoes.

green chili stew

1/4 cup all-purpose flour
1/2 teaspoon salt
1/4 teaspoon pepper
2 pounds boneless pork, cut into 1-1/2-inch cubes
2 tablespoons canola oil
1 large onion, chopped
2 garlic cloves, minced
1 can (14-1/2 ounces) diced tomatoes, undrained
1 cup water
2 cans (4 ounces *each*) chopped green chilies
Minced fresh cilantro, optional

In a large resealable plastic bag, combine the flour, salt and pepper. Add pork, a few pieces at a time, and shake to coat.

In a pressure cooker over medium heat, brown pork in oil. Add onion and garlic; cook and stir for 3 minutes. Add the tomatoes, water and chilies.

Close cover securely; place pressure regulator on vent pipe. Bring cooker to full pressure over high heat. Reduce heat to medium-high and cook for 8 minutes. (Pressure regulator should maintain a slow steady rocking motion; adjust the heat if necessary.)

Remove from the heat. Immediately cool according to manufacturer's directions until pressure is completely reduced. Sprinkle with cilantro if desired.

YIELD: 6 servings.

spicy two-bean chili

2 pounds lean ground beef (90% lean)

3 large onions, chopped

6 garlic cloves, minced

2 cans (16 ounces *each*) kidney beans, rinsed and drained

2 cans (15 ounces *each*) black beans, rinsed and drained

2 cans (10 ounces *each*) diced tomatoes and green chilies, undrained

1 can (14-1/2 ounces) chicken broth

1/2 cup lime juice

6 tablespoons cornmeal

1/4 cup chili powder

4 teaspoons dried oregano

3 teaspoons ground cumin

2 teaspoons salt

2 teaspoons rubbed sage

1/2 teaspoon white pepper

1/2 teaspoon paprika

1/2 teaspoon pepper

Hot cooked rice

Shredded cheddar cheese

In a Dutch oven, cook beef and onions over medium heat until meat is no longer pink. Add garlic; cook 1 minute longer. Drain.

Transfer mixture to a 5-qt. slow cooker. Stir in the beans, tomatoes, broth, lime juice, cornmeal and seasonings.

Cover and cook on low for 8 hours or until heated through. Serve chili with hot rice; sprinkle with cheese.

YIELD: 11 servings.

lesley pew

LYNN, MASSACHUSETTS

Chili fans will get a kick out of this untraditional recipe. Tomatoes with green chilies, lime juice and kidney and black beans give it an original twist. It's wonderful ladled over steaming rice.

slow 'n' easy chili

ginny puckett
LUTZ, FLORIDA

The best feature about this slow cooker chili is that you can add any extras, such as chopped bell peppers or sliced fresh mushrooms, to make your own specialty.

1/2 pound lean ground beef (90% lean), cooked and drained

1/2 pound bulk pork sausage, cooked and drained

1 can (28 ounces) crushed tomatoes

1 can (16 ounces) chili beans, undrained

1 can (10-3/4 ounces) condensed tomato soup, undiluted

1 large onion, chopped

2 envelopes chili seasoning

Shredded cheddar cheese, optional

In a 3-qt. slow cooker, combine the first seven ingredients. Cover and cook on low for 6-8 hours or until thickened and heated through, stirring occasionally. Garnish with cheese if desired.

YIELD: 6-8 servings.

turkey chili

1 pound lean ground turkey
3/4 cup *each* chopped onion, celery and green pepper
1 can (28 ounces) diced tomatoes, undrained
1 jar (26 ounces) meatless spaghetti sauce
1 can (16 ounces) hot chili beans, undrained
1-1/2 cups water
1/2 cup frozen corn
2 tablespoons chili powder
1 teaspoon ground cumin
1/4 teaspoon pepper
1/8 to 1/4 teaspoon cayenne pepper
1 can (16 ounces) kidney beans, rinsed and drained
1 can (15 ounces) pinto beans, rinsed and drained
Sour cream, optional

In a large nonstick skillet, cook turkey, onion, celery and green pepper over medium heat until meat is no longer pink and vegetables are tender; drain.

Transfer to a 5-qt. slow cooker. Add tomatoes, spaghetti sauce, chili beans, water, corn and seasonings. Cover and cook on high for 1 hour.

Reduce heat to low; cook for 5-6 hours. Add kidney and pinto beans; cook 30 minutes longer. Garnish with sour cream if desired.

YIELD: 13 servings.

celesta zanger
BLOOMFIELD HILLS, MICHIGAN

I took my mother's mild chili recipe and punched up the flavor to make it more robust. We enjoy it most in winter and fall.

elk meat chili

2 pounds ground elk *or* buffalo meat
1/2 cup chopped onion
3 garlic cloves, minced
2 cans (14-1/2 ounces *each*) diced tomatoes, undrained
1 can (28 ounces) pork and beans, undrained
3 tablespoons salsa
1 tablespoon brown sugar
1 tablespoon chili powder
1/2 teaspoon garlic salt
1/2 teaspoon pepper

In a Dutch oven, cook elk and onion over medium heat until meat is no longer pink. Add garlic; cook 1 minute longer. Drain. Stir in the remaining ingredients; bring to a boil. Reduce heat; cover and simmer for 2 hours.

YIELD: 6-8 servings.

jo maasberg
FARSON, WYOMING

The longer this Western specialty simmers, the better it tastes! It's a cold-weather favorite at our ranch in Wyoming.

mushroom salsa chili

1 pound lean ground beef (90% lean)
1 pound bulk pork sausage
2 cans (16 ounces each) kidney beans, rinsed and drained
1 jar (24 ounces) chunky salsa
1 can (14-1/2 ounces) diced tomatoes, undrained
1 large onion, chopped
1 can (8 ounces) tomato sauce
1 can (4 ounces) mushroom stems and pieces, drained
1/2 cup *each* chopped green pepper, sweet red and yellow pepper
1/2 teaspoon dried oregano
1/4 teaspoon garlic powder
1/8 teaspoon dried thyme
1/8 teaspoon dried marjoram
Shredded cheddar cheese, sour cream and thinly sliced green onions, optional

In a large skillet, cook beef and sausage over medium heat until meat is no longer pink; drain. Transfer to a 5-qt. slow cooker.

Stir in the beans, salsa, tomatoes, onion, tomato sauce, mushrooms, peppers and seasonings. Cover and cook on low for 8-10 hours or until flavors are blended. Garnish with cheese, sour cream and green onions if desired.

YIELD: 8 servings.

richard rundels
WAVERLY, OHIO

Peppers give my hearty chili a splash of color. I use mild salsa to keep it on the tame side, but you can use a hotter variety if you prefer.

denise habib
POOLESVILLE, MARYLAND

Looking for a thick, chunky chili with an extra-special kick? I've made this version for many occasions, and the gang always enjoys it.

chili pie

When preparing chili, make extra to use in a main-dish pie the next day. Simply warm about 4 cups of chili and pour into a deep-dish pie pan. Prepare a small box of corn bread mix according to package directions and drop batter over chili. Bake at 375° for 30 minutes or until the corn bread is done. Sprinkle with shredded cheddar cheese.

barb schlafer
APPLETON, WISCONSIN

My chili was the star of our family's annual pumpkin patch party. The hungry crowd enthusiastically ladled it up. Even the kids loved it!

brown sugar

There's no need to run to the store if you're out of brown sugar. You can simply substitute 1 tablespoon of granulated sugar or 2 tablespoons of sifted confectioners' sugar for every tablespoon of brown sugar.

zippy steak chili

- 1 pound beef top sirloin steak, cut into 1/2-inch cubes
- 1/2 cup chopped onion
- 2 tablespoons canola oil
- 2 tablespoons chili powder
- 1 teaspoon garlic powder
- 1 teaspoon ground cumin
- 1 teaspoon dried oregano
- 1 teaspoon pepper
- 2 cans (10 ounces *each*) diced tomatoes and green chilies, undrained
- 1 can (15-1/2 ounces) chili starter
- Shredded cheddar cheese, chopped onion and sour cream, optional

In a large skillet, cook steak and onion in oil over medium heat until meat is no longer pink. Sprinkle with seasonings.

In a 5-qt. slow cooker, combine tomatoes and chili starter. Stir in beef mixture. Cover and cook on low for 6-8 hours or until meat is tender. Serve with cheese, onion and sour cream if desired.

YIELD: 5 servings.

scarecrow chili

- 1-1/2 pounds lean ground beef (90% lean)
- 2 celery ribs, chopped
- 1 medium onion, chopped
- 1 can (46 ounces) tomato juice
- 1 can (28 ounces) diced tomatoes, undrained
- 1 can (16 ounces) kidney beans, rinsed and drained
- 1 can (10-3/4 ounces) condensed tomato soup, undiluted
- 1/2 cup water
- 2 tablespoons chili powder
- 1 to 2 tablespoons brown sugar
- 3 bay leaves
- Salt and pepper to taste
- 2 cups elbow macaroni, cooked and drained

In a Dutch oven, cook the beef, celery and onion over medium heat until meat is no longer pink; drain. Add the tomato juice, tomatoes, beans, soup, water, chili powder, brown sugar, bay leaves, salt and pepper. Bring to a boil. Reduce heat; cover and simmer for 30 minutes.

Stir in macaroni. Cook, uncovered, 5 minutes longer or until heated through. Discard bay leaves before serving.

YIELD: 16 servings.

black bean 'n' pumpkin chili

1 medium onion, chopped

1 medium sweet yellow pepper, chopped

2 tablespoons olive oil

3 garlic cloves, minced

3 cups chicken broth

2 cans (15 ounces *each*) black beans, rinsed and drained

2-1/2 cups cubed cooked turkey

1 can (15 ounces) solid-pack pumpkin

1 can (14-1/2 ounces) diced tomatoes, undrained

2 teaspoons dried parsley flakes

2 teaspoons chili powder

1-1/2 teaspoons dried oregano

1-1/2 teaspoons ground cumin

1/2 teaspoon salt

In a large skillet, saute the onion and yellow pepper in oil until tender. Add garlic; cook 1 minute longer. Transfer to a 5-qt. slow cooker; stir in the remaining ingredients. Cover and cook on low for 4-5 hours or until heated through.

YIELD: 10 servings.

deborah vliet

HOLLAND, MICHIGAN

My family loves this slow-cooked recipe, especially on cold days. It's a wonderful variation on standard chili that freezes well and tastes even better as leftovers.

chili with barley

shirley mcclanahan
FALMOUTH, KENTUCKY

Looking for a quick one-dish wonder? My chili is perfect for a weeknight supper or as a special dish to bring to a potluck. Even our minister raved about it at a church supper!

1 pound lean ground beef (90% lean)
1 medium onion, chopped
2 garlic cloves, minced
4 cups water
1 cup quick-cooking barley
1 can (16 ounces) chili beans, undrained
1 can (14-1/2 ounces) diced tomatoes, undrained
1 can (6 ounces) tomato paste
1 envelope chili seasoning

In a large saucepan, cook beef and onion over medium heat until meat is no longer pink. Add garlic; cook 1 minute longer. Drain. Add water; bring to a boil.

Stir in barley. Reduce heat; cover and simmer for 10 minutes or until barley is tender. Stir in the beans, tomatoes, tomato paste and chili seasoning; heat through.

YIELD: 6-8 servings.

30-minute chili

1 pound bulk pork sausage
1 large onion, chopped
1 can (28 ounces) crushed tomatoes
2 cans (16 ounces *each*) chili beans, undrained
3 cups water
1 can (4 ounces) chopped green chilies
1 envelope chili seasoning mix
2 tablespoons sugar

In a Dutch oven, cook sausage and onion over medium heat until meat is no longer pink; drain. Add remaining ingredients; cover and simmer for 20 minutes, stirring often.

YIELD: 12 servings.

janice westmoreland
BROOKSVILLE, FLORIDA

A neighbor gave me a pot of this delicious chili, and I had to ask for the recipe. The pork sausage is a nice change of pace from the usual ground beef.

spicy pork chili

1-1/2 pounds pork tenderloin, cubed
2 large onions, diced
4 celery ribs, diced
2 tablespoons butter
6 cans (15-1/2 ounces *each*) great northern beans, rinsed and drained
4 cans (14-1/2 ounces *each*) chicken broth
2 cups water
2 jalapeno peppers, seeded and chopped
2 teaspoons chili powder
1/2 teaspoon *each* white pepper, cayenne pepper, ground cumin and pepper
2 garlic cloves, minced
1/2 teaspoon salt
1/4 teaspoon dried parsley flakes
1/4 teaspoon hot pepper sauce, optional
1 cup (4 ounces) shredded Monterey Jack cheese

In a Dutch oven, cook the pork, onions and celery in butter over medium heat until meat is no longer pink. Stir in the beans, broth, water, jalapenos, spices, garlic, salt, parsley and hot pepper sauce if desired. Bring to a boil. Reduce heat; cover and simmer for 1-1/2 hours.

Uncover; simmer 30-40 minutes longer or until chili reaches desired consistency. Sprinkle with cheese.

YIELD: 15 servings.

EDITOR'S NOTE: We recommend wearing disposable gloves when cutting hot peppers. Avoid touching your face.

larry laatsch
SAGINAW, MICHIGAN

My chili, loaded with white beans and pork, has plenty of bite. But if it's not spicy enough for you, top it with shredded jalapeno jack cheese and finely diced onions.

nancy zimmerman
CAPE MAY COURT HOUSE, NEW JERSEY

My veggie-packed chili makes a healthy meal. It's great with oat bran bread.

taste of home test kitchen
GREENDALE, WISCONSIN

Try our stick-to-your-ribs chicken specialty for a tasty change of pace.

so many possibilites

The variations on chili are endless. Most are made with tomatoes and chili powder, while others are white. A chili can be mild or hot, it can have ground beef, stew meat, sausage or poultry or it can be meatless. Some recipes call for macaroni or spaghetti or no pasta at all.

spicy vegetable chili

1 medium onion, chopped
1 medium carrot, thinly sliced
1 medium green pepper, chopped
1/2 pound sliced fresh mushrooms
1 small zucchini, sliced
1 tablespoon olive oil
4 garlic cloves, minced
1 can (28 ounces) diced tomatoes, undrained
2 cans (16 ounces *each*) kidney beans, rinsed and drained
2 cans (8 ounces *each*) no-salt-added tomato sauce
1 can (4 ounces) chopped green chilies
3 tablespoons chili powder
3 teaspoons dried oregano
2 teaspoons ground cumin
2 teaspoons paprika
1/4 teaspoon crushed red pepper flakes
1 tablespoon white wine vinegar
Minced fresh cilantro and fat-free sour cream, optional

In a Dutch oven, saute the onion, carrot, pepper, mushrooms and zucchini in oil until tender. Add garlic; cook 1 minute longer. Add the tomatoes, beans, tomato sauce, green chilies and seasonings. Bring to a boil. Reduce heat; simmer, uncovered, for 35 minutes, stirring occasionally.

Stir in vinegar. Serve in soup bowls; garnish each with cilantro and sour cream if desired.

YIELD: 8 servings.

chicken chili

1-1/2 pounds boneless skinless chicken breasts, cut into 1/2-inch cubes
1 cup chopped onion
3 tablespoons canola oil
1 can (15 ounces) white kidney *or* cannellini beans, rinsed and drained
1 can (14-1/2 ounces) diced tomatoes, undrained
1 can (14-1/2 ounces) diced tomatoes with mild green chilies, undrained
1 cup frozen corn
1 teaspoon salt
1 teaspoon ground cumin
1 teaspoon minced garlic
1/2 teaspoon celery salt
1/2 teaspoon ground coriander
1/2 teaspoon pepper
Sour cream and shredded cheddar cheese, optional

In a large skillet, saute chicken and onion in oil for 5 minutes or until chicken is browned.

Transfer to a 5-qt. slow cooker. Stir in the beans, tomatoes, corn and seasonings. Cover and cook on low for 5 hours or until chicken is no longer pink. Garnish with sour cream and cheese if desired.

YIELD: 6 servings.

cincinnati chili

3 pounds lean ground beef (90% lean)
1-1/2 cups chopped onions
1-1/2 teaspoons minced garlic
2 cans (16 ounces *each*) kidney beans, rinsed and drained
2 cans (15 ounces *each*) tomato sauce
2 cups beef broth
1/4 cup chili powder
1/4 cup red wine vinegar
1/4 cup Worcestershire sauce
1 ounce unsweetened chocolate, coarsely chopped
1-1/2 teaspoons ground cinnamon
1-1/2 teaspoons ground cumin
1 teaspoon salt
1 teaspoon dried oregano
1/2 teaspoon pepper
1/8 teaspoon ground cloves
Hot cooked spaghetti
Shredded cheddar cheese and sliced green onions, optional

In a Dutch oven, cook the beef and onions over medium heat until meat is no longer pink. Add garlic; cook 1 minute longer. Drain.

In a 5-qt. slow cooker, combine the beans, tomato sauce, broth, chili powder, vinegar, Worcestershire sauce, chocolate, cinnamon, cumin, salt, oregano, pepper and cloves. Stir in beef mixture. Cover and cook on low for 5-1/2 to 6 hours or until heated through.

Serve with spaghetti. Garnish with cheese and green onions if desired.

YIELD: 10 servings.

joyce alm
THORP, WASHINGTON

The addition of chocolate and cinnamon may seem odd at first. But after one taste, you'll never go back to regular chili again! Add a heaping mound of shredded cheese on top to make it truly authentic.

no-bean chili

molly butt
GRANVILLE, OHIO

I combine the ingredients for this zesty chili the night before I plan to serve it. In the morning, I load up the slow cooker and let it do its magic!

1-1/2 pounds lean ground beef (90% lean)
  1 can (14-1/2 ounces) stewed tomatoes, undrained
  1 can (8 ounces) tomato sauce
  1 small onion, chopped
  1 small green pepper, chopped
  1 can (4 ounces) chopped green chilies
1/2 cup minced fresh parsley
  1 tablespoon chili powder
  1 garlic clove, minced
1-1/4 teaspoons salt
1/2 teaspoon paprika
1/4 teaspoon pepper

Hot cooked rice *or* pasta
Optional toppings: Shredded cheddar cheese, sour cream and sliced green onions

Crumble beef into a 3-qt. slow cooker. Add the next 11 ingredients and mix well. Cover and cook on high for 4-6 hours or until heated through. Serve with rice or pasta with toppings of your choice.
YIELD: 6 servings.

chili con carne

1/2 pound lean ground beef (90% lean)
1/2 cup chopped onion
1 garlic clove, minced
1 can (10 ounces) diced tomatoes and green chilies
1 can (8 ounces) tomato sauce
3/4 cup canned pinto beans, rinsed and drained
2-1/2 teaspoons chili powder
1/2 teaspoon dried oregano
1/4 teaspoon salt, optional
1/4 teaspoon ground cumin
1/4 teaspoon pepper

In a large saucepan, cook the beef and onion over medium heat until the meat is no longer pink. Add the garlic; cook 1 minute longer; drain. Stir in the tomatoes, tomato sauce, beans, chili powder, oregano, salt if desired, cumin and pepper. Bring to a boil. Reduce heat; cover and simmer for 1 hour.

YIELD: 2 servings.

karleen warkentin
MCALLEN, TEXAS

We're always on the go, so to say I'm a time-pressed cook is an understatement. This is a fantastic recipe when you're in need of a speedy weeknight meal.

chili muffins

The next time you bake a batch of corn muffins, don't fill the muffin cups full. Instead, put a heaping spoonful of leftover chili in the center of each, and bake. The batter will rise up around the chili. These delicious muffins go well with any Mexican-style meal.

spicy slow-cooked chili

2 pounds lean ground beef (90% lean)
2 to 3 hot chili peppers of your choice
3 cans (16 ounces *each*) kidney beans, rinsed and drained
1 can (6 ounces) tomato paste
1 medium onion, chopped
1 medium green pepper, seeded and chopped
2 teaspoons chili powder
2 teaspoons cider vinegar
1 teaspoon garlic powder
1 teaspoon dried oregano
1/4 to 1/2 teaspoon ground cinnamon
1/4 teaspoon pepper
2 to 4 cups tomato juice

In a large skillet, cook the beef over medium heat until no longer pink; drain. Transfer to a 5-qt. slow cooker. Remove the seeds from the chili peppers if desired; chop the peppers. Add to the slow cooker. Stir in the beans, tomato paste, onion, green pepper, seasonings and 2 cups tomato juice.

Cover and cook on low for 4-6 hours or until heated through, adding more tomato juice if needed to achieve desired thickness.

YIELD: 8 servings.

EDITOR'S NOTE: We recommend wearing disposable gloves when cutting hot peppers. Avoid touching your face.

sabrina corrigan
WILLIAMSBURG, PENNSYLVANIA

If you like your chili thick and hearty, you'll love my version. The use of a slow cooker keeps things easy.

laura manning
LILBURN, GEORGIA

This Southwestern classic is perfect for any holiday or family get-together.

🥄 shoepeg corn

The term "shoepeg corn" dates back to before the American Civil War. The corn was named for its peg-like shape. Shoepeg has smaller kernels and is sweeter than yellow corn. If you can't find it at your local grocery store, you can substitute either white or yellow corn with good results.

melissa newman
DANVILLE, PENNSYLVANIA

My husband makes the best chili. His recipe is filled to the brim with healthy vegetables and just enough heat to warm you to your toes!

santa fe chili

2 pounds lean ground beef (90% lean)
1 medium onion, chopped
2 cans (16 ounces each) kidney beans, rinsed and drained
2 cans (15 ounces each) black beans, rinsed and drained
2 cans (15 ounces each) pinto beans, rinsed and drained
3 cans (7 ounces each) white or shoepeg corn, drained
1 can (14-1/2 ounces) diced tomatoes, undrained
1 can (10 ounces) diced tomatoes and green chilies
1 can (11-1/2 ounces) V8 juice
2 envelopes ranch salad dressing mix
2 envelopes taco seasoning
Sour cream, shredded cheddar cheese and corn chips, optional

In a large skillet, cook beef and onion over medium heat until meat is no longer pink; drain. Transfer to a 5- or 6-qt. slow cooker. Stir in the beans, corn, tomatoes, juice, salad dressing mix and taco seasoning.

Cover and cook on high for 4-6 hours or until heated through. Serve with sour cream, cheese and corn chips if desired.

YIELD: 16 servings.

spicy hearty chili

1 pound lean ground beef (90% lean)
1 cup chopped onion
10 garlic cloves, minced
2 cups chopped green peppers
1-1/2 cups chopped sweet red peppers
1-1/2 cups chopped celery

3 jalapeno peppers, seeded and chopped
3 cans (14-1/2 ounces each) petite diced tomatoes, undrained
2 cans (16 ounces each) kidney beans, rinsed and drained
1 can (28 ounces) tomato sauce
1 can (12 ounces) tomato paste
1 cup water
1/2 cup light beer or nonalcoholic beer
3 tablespoons chili powder
1 teaspoon crushed red pepper flakes

In a large saucepan or Dutch oven coated with cooking spray, cook the beef, onion and garlic over medium heat until meat is no longer pink; drain. Stir in the peppers, celery and jalapenos. Cook and stir for 8 minutes or until vegetables are crisp-tender.

Stir in the remaining ingredients. Bring to a boil. Reduce heat; simmer, uncovered, for 1 hour, stirring occasionally.

YIELD: 10 servings.

EDITOR'S NOTE: We recommend wearing disposable gloves when cutting hot peppers. Avoid touching your face.

anytime turkey chili

2/3 cup chopped sweet onion
1/2 cup chopped green pepper
1-1/2 teaspoons dried oregano
1 teaspoon ground cumin
1 teaspoon olive oil
2 garlic cloves, minced
1 can (16 ounces) kidney beans, rinsed and drained
1 can (15-1/2 ounces) great northern beans, rinsed and drained
1 can (15 ounces) solid-pack pumpkin
1 can (15 ounces) crushed tomatoes
1 can (14-1/2 ounces) reduced-sodium chicken broth
1/2 cup water

2 tablespoons brown sugar
2 tablespoons chili powder
1/2 teaspoon pepper
3 cups cubed cooked turkey breast

In a large saucepan, saute the onion, green pepper, oregano and cumin in oil until vegetables are tender. Add garlic; cook 1 minute longer.

Stir in the beans, pumpkin, tomatoes, broth, water, brown sugar, chili powder and pepper; bring to a boil. Reduce heat; cover and simmer for 1 hour. Add turkey; heat through.

YIELD: 8 servings.

brad bailey
CARY, NORTH CAROLINA

I created this dish for a chili contest we held in our backyard. With pumpkin, brown sugar and turkey, it tastes like Thanksgiving dinner in a bowl!

lime chicken chili

diane randazzo

SINKING SPRING, PENNSYLVANIA

Lime juice gives this chili a zesty twist, while canned tomatoes and beans make preparation a snap. Serve bowls with toasted tortilla strips.

lemon or lime?

Lemon and lime juice or zest can be used interchangeably in equal amounts in most recipes. Add a little of both for a refreshing lemon-lime flavor.

1 medium onion, chopped
1 *each* medium sweet yellow, red and green pepper, chopped
2 tablespoons olive oil
3 garlic cloves, minced
1 pound ground chicken
1 tablespoon all-purpose flour
1 tablespoon baking cocoa
1 tablespoon ground cumin
1 tablespoon chili powder
2 teaspoons ground coriander
1/2 teaspoon salt
1/2 teaspoon garlic pepper blend
1/4 teaspoon pepper
2 cans (14-1/2 ounces each) diced tomatoes, undrained
1/4 cup lime juice
1 teaspoon grated lime peel
1 can (15 ounces) white kidney *or* cannellini beans, rinsed and drained
2 flour tortillas (8 inches), cut into 1/4-inch strips
6 tablespoons reduced-fat sour cream

In a large saucepan, saute the onion and peppers in oil for 7-8 minutes or until crisp-tender. Add garlic; cook 1 minute longer. Add the chicken; cook and stir over medium heat for 8-9 minutes or until the meat is no longer pink.

Stir in the flour, cocoa and seasonings. Add the tomatoes, lime juice and lime peel. Bring to a boil. Reduce heat; simmer, uncovered, for 20-25 minutes or until thickened, stirring frequently. Stir in beans; heat through.

Meanwhile, place tortilla strips on a baking sheet coated with cooking spray. Bake at 400° for 8-10 minutes or until crisp. Serve chili with sour cream and tortilla strips.

YIELD: 6 servings.

barbecued turkey chili

- 1 can (16 ounces) kidney beans, rinsed and drained
- 1 can (16 ounces) hot chili beans, undrained
- 1 can (15 ounces) turkey chili with beans
- 1 can (14-1/2 ounces) diced tomatoes, undrained
- 1/3 cup barbecue sauce

In a 3-qt. slow cooker, combine all of the ingredients. Cover and cook on high for 4 hours or until heated through and flavors are blended.

YIELD: 4-6 servings.

melissa webb
ELLSWORTH, SOUTH DAKOTA

The first time I tried my hand at this recipe was for a chili cook-off—and I won first prize! Just toss together all the ingredients and let your slow cooker do the work.

chipotle turkey chili

- 1 can (7 ounces) chipotle peppers in adobo sauce
- 1-1/4 pounds lean ground turkey
- 3 medium carrots, chopped
- 1 medium green pepper, chopped
- 1/2 cup chopped onion
- 4 garlic cloves, minced
- 1 can (28 ounces) crushed tomatoes
- 1 can (14-1/2 ounces) reduced-sodium chicken broth
- 1 can (8 ounces) tomato sauce
- 1-1/2 teaspoons dried oregano
- 1-1/2 teaspoons dried basil
- 1 teaspoon chili powder
- 1/2 teaspoon ground cumin
- 1 can (16 ounces) kidney beans, rinsed and drained
- 1 can (15 ounces) garbanzo beans *or* chickpeas, rinsed and drained

Drain chipotle peppers; set aside 2 tablespoons adobo sauce. Seed and chop three peppers; set aside. (Save remaining peppers and sauce for another use.)

In a large Dutch oven or soup kettle coated with cooking spray, cook the turkey, carrots, green pepper, onion, garlic and reserved peppers over medium heat until meat is no longer pink; drain if necessary. Stir in the tomatoes, broth, tomato sauce, oregano, basil, chili powder, cumin and reserved adobo sauce. Bring to a boil. Reduce heat; cover and simmer for 1 hour.

Stir in the beans. Cover and simmer for 15-20 minutes or until heated through.

YIELD: 8 servings.

EDITOR'S NOTE: We recommend wearing disposable gloves when cutting hot peppers. Avoid touching your face.

christie ladd
MECHANICSBURG, PENNSYLVANIA

I combined a few chili recipes to come up with this low-fat rendition. It's great served with baked tortilla chips.

four-star chili

- 1-1/2 pounds lean ground beef (90% lean)
- 2 large green peppers, diced
- 1 medium onion, diced
- 4 garlic cloves, minced
- 1 can (28 ounces) crushed tomatoes
- 1 can (15-1/2 ounces) great northern beans, rinsed and drained
- 1 can (14-1/2 ounces) chicken broth
- 1 medium carrot, chopped
- 1 celery rib, chopped
- 2 jalapeno peppers, finely chopped
- 2-1/2 teaspoons pepper blend
- 1 teaspoon paprika
- 1/2 teaspoon crushed red pepper flakes
- Hot cooked rice
- Sour cream
- Shredded Colby cheese

In a stockpot, cook the beef, green peppers and onion over medium heat until meat is no longer pink. Add garlic; cook 1 minute longer. Drain. Add the tomatoes, beans, broth, carrot, celery, jalapenos and seasonings; bring to a boil. Reduce heat; cover and simmer for 1-1/2 hours or until thick and bubbly.

Serve with rice, sour cream and cheese.

YIELD: 18 servings.

EDITOR'S NOTES: We recommend wearing disposable gloves when cutting hot peppers. Avoid touching your face. This recipe was tested with McCormick's Hot Shot Black & Red Pepper.

frank fenti
HORNELL, NEW YORK

My spicy chili features all the traditional ingredients, but carrots and white beans make it deliciously different. Serve it over rice for a hearty meal.

audra duvall
CANOGA PARK, CALIFORNIA

This combines all the flavors of a chili dog in one bowl! I make it when I need a hot, hearty meal in a hurry. It's also great for football games.

karen golden
PHOENIX, ARIZONA

The cooks in our school cafeteria in Rocky Ford, Colorado, introduced my brother and sister to their famous chili. My siblings described it to our mother so she could duplicate it. We all enjoy preparing it for our own families now.

cynthia baca
CRANBERRY TOWNSHIP, PENNSYLVANIA

With lean ground beef, four types of beans, lots of seasonings and tons of toppings, this chili truly lives up to its name. Each serving provides a hefty 26 grams of protein and 11 grams of fiber.

kielbasa chili

- 1 pound smoked kielbasa *or* Polish sausage, halved and sliced
- 2 cans (14-1/2 ounces each) diced tomatoes, undrained
- 1 can (15 ounces) chili with beans
- 1 can (8-3/4 ounces) whole kernel corn, drained
- 1 can (2-1/4 ounces) sliced ripe olives, drained

In a Dutch oven coated with cooking spray, saute kielbasa until browned. Stir in remaining ingredients. Bring to a boil. Reduce heat; simmer, uncovered, for 4-5 minutes or until heated through.

YIELD: 7 servings.

rocky ford chili

- 2 cans (14.3 ounces each) chili with beans
- 1 package (10 ounces) frozen corn
- 4 cups corn chips
- 1 cup shredded lettuce
- 1 cup (4 ounces) shredded Mexican cheese blend
- 1 can (2-1/4 ounces) sliced ripe olives, drained
- 1/4 cup sour cream
- 1/4 cup salsa

In a large microwave-safe bowl, cook the chili and corn on high for 2-4 minutes or until heated through. Place corn chips in four large soup bowls; top with chili mixture, lettuce, cheese, olives, sour cream and salsa.

YIELD: 4 servings.

EDITOR'S NOTE: This recipe was tested in a 1,100-watt microwave.

fully loaded chili

- 1 pound lean ground beef (90% lean)
- 1 medium onion, chopped
- 1 medium green pepper, chopped
- 1-3/4 cups water
- 2 cans (8 ounces *each*) tomato sauce
- 1 can (16 ounces) kidney beans, rinsed and drained
- 1 can (15-1/2 ounces) great northern beans, rinsed and drained
- 1 can (15 ounces) garbanzo beans *or* chickpeas, rinsed and drained
- 1 can (15 ounces) black beans, rinsed and drained
- 1 tablespoon baking cocoa
- 2 teaspoons Louisiana-style hot sauce
- 1/2 teaspoon pepper
- 1/2 teaspoon chili powder
- 1/4 teaspoon garlic powder
- 1/8 teaspoon cayenne pepper

GARNISHES:
- 1/2 cup reduced-fat sour cream
- 1/2 cup crushed baked tortilla chip scoops
- 1/2 cup shredded reduced-fat cheddar cheese

In a Dutch oven over medium heat, cook the beef, onion and pepper until meat is no longer pink; drain.

Stir in the water, tomato sauce, beans, cocoa, hot sauce and seasonings. Bring to a boil. Reduce heat; cover and simmer for 30 minutes.

Garnish each serving with 1 tablespoon each of sour cream, crushed chips and cheese.

YIELD: 8 servings.

two-bean chili

1/2 pound sliced fresh mushrooms

1 large green pepper, chopped

1 large sweet red pepper, chopped

2 celery ribs, chopped

1 medium onion, chopped

1 jalapeno pepper, seeded and chopped

1 tablespoon olive oil

4 garlic cloves, minced

2 teaspoons ground cumin

1 teaspoon dried oregano

1 can (28 ounces) diced tomatoes, undrained

1 can (16 ounces) red beans, rinsed and drained

1 can (15 ounces) black beans, rinsed and drained

1 large carrot, chopped

1/2 cup water

1/2 cup barbecue sauce

1/4 cup chili powder

1 teaspoon Liquid Smoke, optional

OPTIONAL TOPPINGS:

Reduced-fat sour cream, hot pepper sauce, shredded cheddar cheese, chopped onion *and/or* crushed baked tortilla chip scoops

In a large skillet over medium heat, cook and stir the mushrooms, peppers, celery, onion and jalapeno in oil until onion is lightly browned. Add the garlic, cumin and oregano; cook and stir 1 minute longer.

Transfer to a 5-qt. slow cooker. Stir in the tomatoes, beans, carrot, water, barbecue sauce, chili powder and Liquid Smoke if desired. Cover and cook on low for 8 hours or until vegetables are tender. Serve with sour cream, pepper sauce, cheese, onion and/or chips if desired.

YIELD: 6 servings.

EDITOR'S NOTE: We recommend wearing disposable gloves when cutting hot peppers. Avoid touching your face.

ronald johnson
ELMHURST, ILLINOIS

The first time I had this chili at game-day party, I was on my second bowl before I realized it was meatless! It's so chock-full of ingredients and flavor that it's hard to believe it's a low-fat recipe.

judy niemeyer
BRENHAM, TEXAS

My mother-in-law introduced our family to her turkey chili a few years ago, and we can't get enough! This recipe makes a lot, so freeze extra portions for a delicious dinner even on hectic nights.

hearty turkey chili

2 pounds lean ground turkey
1 large onion, chopped
2 celery ribs, chopped
4 garlic cloves, minced
2 cans (16 ounces *each*) kidney beans, rinsed and drained
6 cans (5-1/2 ounces *each*) reduced-sodium V8 juice
1 cup reduced-sodium beef broth
1 can (6 ounces) tomato paste
3 teaspoons ground cumin
1 teaspoon salt
1/2 teaspoon crushed red pepper flakes
2 bay leaves

In a Dutch oven, cook the turkey, onion and celery over medium heat or until the meat is no longer pink. Add garlic; cook 1 minute longer. Drain. Stir in the remaining ingredients. Bring to a boil.

Reduce heat; simmer, uncovered, for 15 minutes to allow flavors to blend. Discard bay leaves.

YIELD: 8 servings.

spicy chicken chili

- 1 small onion, chopped
- 1 small green pepper, chopped
- 1 small sweet red pepper, chopped
- 2 jalapeno peppers, seeded and chopped
- 1 serrano pepper, seeded and chopped
- 1 tablespoon olive oil
- 3 garlic cloves, minced
- 1 can (28 ounces) crushed tomatoes
- 1 can (14-1/2 ounces) stewed tomatoes, cut up
- 1 can (14-1/2 ounces) diced tomatoes with mild green chilies
- 1 can (16 ounces) kidney beans, rinsed and drained
- 1 can (15 ounces) black beans, rinsed and drained
- 1 carton (32 ounces) reduced-sodium chicken broth
- 3 tablespoons chili powder
- 1 tablespoon ground cumin
- 1 to 2 teaspoons crushed red pepper flakes
- 2 to 4 tablespoons Louisiana-style hot sauce
- 2-1/2 cups cubed cooked chicken breast
- 2 cups frozen corn
- 3/4 cup reduced-fat sour cream
- 3/4 cup shredded reduced-fat cheddar cheese

In a Dutch oven, saute the first five ingredients in oil until tender. Add garlic, cook 1 minute longer. Add the tomatoes, beans, broth, seasonings and hot sauce. Bring to a boil. Reduce heat; simmer, uncovered, for 15 minutes. Stir in chicken and corn; heat through. Garnish each serving with 1 tablespoon each of sour cream and cheese.

YIELD: 12 servings.

EDITOR'S NOTE: We recommend wearing disposable gloves when cutting hot peppers. Avoid touching your face.

natalie hughes
JOPLIN, MISSOURI

I was inspired to create this recipe when I was on a low-calorie, low-fat, high-fiber diet. I entered it in a chili cook-off and got lots of compliments.

super spicy chili

This recipe for spicy chicken chili really packs some heat! But if you want to take it up even a notch further, try leaving the seeds in the hot peppers.

speedy weeknight chili

- 1-1/2 pounds lean ground beef (90% lean)
- 2 small onions, chopped
- 1/2 cup chopped green pepper
- 1 teaspoon minced garlic
- 2 cans (16 ounces each) kidney beans, rinsed and drained
- 2 cans (14-1/2 ounces each) stewed tomatoes
- 1 can (28 ounces) crushed tomatoes
- 1 bottle (12 ounces) beer or nonalcoholic beer
- 1 can (6 ounces) tomato paste
- 1/4 cup chili powder
- 3/4 teaspoon dried oregano
- 1/2 teaspoon hot pepper sauce
- 1/4 teaspoon sugar
- 1/4 teaspoon salt
- 1/4 teaspoon pepper

In a large saucepan or Dutch oven, cook the beef, onions and green pepper over medium heat until meat is no longer pink. Add garlic; cook 1 minute longer. Drain. Add the remaining ingredients; bring to a boil. Reduce the heat; simmer, uncovered, for 10 minutes.

YIELD: 15 servings.

cynthia hudson
GREENVILLE, SOUTH CAROLINA

This hearty chili makes a big batch, so it's great when you need a quick dish for a party or potluck. Toss the veggies in a food processor to cut down on prep time.

jolene britten
GIG HARBOR, WASHINGTON

My family, especially my dad, loves chili. After experimenting with several recipes, I came up with my own version that uses ground turkey and is conveniently prepared in a slow cooker.

chunky chili

- 1 pound ground turkey *or* beef
- 1 medium onion, chopped
- 2 medium tomatoes, cut up
- 1 can (16 ounces) kidney beans, rinsed and drained
- 1 can (16 ounces) chili beans, undrained
- 1 can (15 ounces) tomato sauce
- 1 cup water
- 1 can (4 ounces) chopped green chilies
- 1 tablespoon chili powder
- 2 teaspoons salt
- 1 teaspoon ground cumin
- 3/4 teaspoon pepper

Sour cream and sliced jalapenos, optional

In a large skillet, cook turkey and onion over medium heat until meat is no longer pink; drain.

Transfer to a 3-1/2-qt. slow cooker. Stir in the tomatoes, beans, tomato sauce, water, chilies, chili powder, salt, cumin and pepper. Cover and cook on low for 5-6 hours or until heated through. Garnish with sour cream and jalapenos if desired.

YIELD: 6-8 servings.

**taste of home
test kitchen**
GREENDALE, WISCONSIN

This specialty is filled to the brim with flavor and fulfillment. It's a great make-ahead recipe, too.

white chili with hominy

- 1 pound boneless skinless chicken breasts, cut into 1/2-inch cubes
- 1 medium onion, chopped
- 1 tablespoon canola oil
- 1 can (15-1/2 ounces) white hominy, drained
- 1 can (15 ounces) white kidney *or* cannellini beans, rinsed and drained
- 1 can (14-1/2 ounces) chicken broth
- 2 cans (4 ounces *each*) chopped green chilies
- 1 teaspoon garlic salt
- 1 teaspoon dried basil
- 1 teaspoon ground cumin
- 1/4 teaspoon white pepper
- 1/8 to 1/4 teaspoon cayenne pepper
- 1 cup (8 ounces) sour cream
- 1/3 cup half-and-half cream
- 2 tablespoons minced fresh cilantro, *divided*

In a large saucepan, saute the chicken and onion in oil until chicken is no longer pink. Add the hominy, beans, broth, chilies and seasonings. Bring to a boil. Reduce heat; simmer, uncovered, for 30 minutes.

Remove from the heat; stir in the sour cream, half-and-half and 1 tablespoon cilantro. Sprinkle with remaining cilantro.

YIELD: 6 servings.

heartwarming chili

1 pound lean ground beef (90% lean)

1 large onion, chopped

2 cans (16 ounces *each*) kidney beans, rinsed and drained

2 cans (14-1/2 ounces *each*) diced tomatoes

1 can (8 ounces) tomato sauce

1 medium green pepper

3 tablespoons chili powder

1 tablespoon ground cumin

2 garlic cloves, minced

1 teaspoon baking cocoa

1 teaspoon dried oregano

1 teaspoon Worcestershire sauce, optional

Salt and pepper to taste

In a large saucepan, cook the beef and onion over medium heat until the meat is no longer pink; drain. Add the remaining ingredients; bring to a boil. Reduce heat; cover and simmer for 3 hours, stirring occasionally.

YIELD: 4 servings.

audrey byrne

LILLIAN, TEXAS

A touch of baking cocoa gives this chili a rich flavor without adding sweetness. When I was growing up in the North, we scooped chili over hot rice. But after I married a Texan, I learned to love it served in a bowl with a side of corn bread.

soup
for two

Looking to make a hearty, home-cooked meal without any leftovers? Try one of these no-fail, two- or three-serving soups designed just for a cozy couple's table. And since all of the soups in this chapter serve just a few, you won't waste food either. So make a soup for two and enjoy a great lunch or light dinner that you won't have to eat all week!

275   282   284

autumn chowder

sheena hoffman

NORTH VANCOUVER,
BRITISH COLUMBIA

We enjoy this hearty soup when the weather turns chilly. The aroma will make mouths water with sweet anticipation.

2 bacon strips, diced

1/4 cup chopped onion

1 medium red potato, cubed

1 small carrot, halved lengthwise and thinly sliced

1/2 cup water

3/4 teaspoon chicken bouillon granules

1 cup milk

2/3 cup frozen corn

1/8 teaspoon pepper

2-1/2 teaspoons all-purpose flour

2 tablespoons cold water

3/4 cup shredded cheddar cheese

In a large saucepan, cook bacon over medium heat until crisp; remove to paper towels. Drain, reserving 1 teaspoon drippings. In the drippings, saute onion until tender. Add the potato, carrot, water and bouillon. Bring to a boil. Reduce heat; cover and simmer for 15-20 minutes or until the vegetables are almost tender.

Stir in the milk, corn and pepper. Cook 5 minutes longer. Combine the flour and cold water until smooth; gradually whisk into soup. Bring to a boil; cook and stir for 1-2 minutes or until thickened. Remove from the heat; stir in cheese until melted. Sprinkle with bacon.

YIELD: 2 servings.

anniversary chowder

2 small red potatoes, cubed
1/2 medium carrot, finely chopped
1/4 cup finely chopped onion

2 tablespoons butter
2 cups half-and-half cream
1 pouch (6 ounces) boneless skinless pink salmon
1/2 cup fresh *or* frozen corn
1/4 teaspoon dried rosemary, crushed
1/4 teaspoon dried parsley flakes
1/4 teaspoon salt
1/8 teaspoon pepper
1/8 teaspoon rubbed sage
1/8 teaspoon dried thyme

In a large saucepan, saute the potatoes, carrot and onion in butter until tender. Reduce heat; stir in remaining ingredients. Cook and stir for 10 minutes or until heated through.

YIELD: 2 servings.

barbara harrison
RINGOES, NEW JERSEY

My husband treated me to a night on the town on our 35th anniversary. At the restaurant, I ordered a thick salmon chowder that was so delicious I ended up creating a similar version at home. I named my recipe in honor of our special day.

spicy turkey chili

1/4 pound lean ground turkey
1 small onion, chopped
1 cup canned Italian diced tomatoes with juice
1 can (8 ounces) tomato sauce
1/2 cup canned kidney beans, rinsed and drained
1-1/2 teaspoons chili powder
3/4 teaspoon white wine vinegar
1/2 teaspoon Worcestershire sauce
1 bay leaf
1/8 teaspoon salt, optional
1/8 teaspoon garlic powder
1/8 teaspoon crushed red pepper flakes
Dash ground cinnamon
Dash ground allspice
2 tablespoons shredded cheddar cheese, optional

Crumble turkey into a saucepan; add onion. Cook over medium heat until the meat is no longer pink; drain. Add the tomatoes, tomato sauce, beans, chili powder, vinegar, Worcestershire sauce and seasonings. Bring to a boil. Reduce heat; simmer, uncovered, for 15 minutes or until thickened. Discard bay leaf. Garnish with cheese if desired.

YIELD: 2 servings.

marlene gravat
ST LOUIS, MISSOURI

This chili is a scrumptious change of pace thanks to ground turkey, cinnamon and allspice. My hubby ususally favors traditional beef chili, but he said this one was a keeper!

kaylyn vanderveen
GRAND RAPIDS, MICHIGAN

My husband and I both fell in a love with stuffed green pepper soup after we tried it at restaurant. I created a healthier rendition that calls for turkey sausage links rather than pork sausage.

🥄 broth substitute

You can use chicken or beef bouillon in place of broth if you don't have any broth on hand. One bouillon cube or 1 teaspoon of granules dissolved in 1 cup of boiling water may be substituted for 1 cup of broth in any recipe.

ginger ellsworth
CALDWELL, IDAHO

Here's a tasty way to use leftover roast beef and get a delicious supper on the table in about a half hour.

🥄 mushrooms

Fresh mushrooms should be used within a few days of purchase. If that's not possible, you can blanch then freeze them for up to 1 month. Slice larger mushrooms or use small whole mushroom caps. Bring 1 quart of water to a boil; add mushrooms and 1 tablespoon lemon juice to prevent darkening. Cook in boiling water 3 minutes for slices or 4 minutes for mushroom caps. Immediately remove with a slotted spoon and cool in ice water for 3 to 4 minutes. Drain well and pack into freezer containers.

stuffed green pepper soup

6 uncooked breakfast turkey sausage links
1/2 cup diced green pepper
1/4 cup finely chopped onion
1/4 cup water
3/4 cup chicken broth
1 can (10-3/4 ounces) condensed tomato soup, undiluted
1/8 teaspoon garlic powder
Dash pepper
3/4 cup cooked rice

Crumble the sausage into a saucepan; cook over medium heat until no longer pink. Drain. Add the green pepper, onion and water. Cover and cook for 5 minutes.

Stir in broth; bring to a boil. Reduce heat; cover and simmer until vegetables are tender. Stir in the tomato soup, garlic powder and pepper; cover and simmer for 30 minutes. Add rice; heat through.

YIELD: 3 servings.

beefy mushroom soup

1 medium onion, chopped
1/2 cup sliced fresh mushrooms
2 tablespoons butter

2 tablespoons all-purpose flour
2 cups reduced-sodium beef broth
2/3 cup cubed cooked roast beef
1/2 teaspoon garlic powder
1/4 teaspoon paprika
1/4 teaspoon pepper
1/8 teaspoon salt
Dash hot pepper sauce
1/4 cup shredded part-skim mozzarella cheese, optional

In a large saucepan, saute onion and mushrooms in butter until onion is tender; remove with a slotted spoon and set aside. In a small bowl, whisk flour and broth until smooth; gradually add to the pan. Bring to a boil; cook and stir for 1-2 minutes or until thickened.

Add the roast beef, garlic powder, paprika, pepper, salt, pepper sauce and onion mixture; cook and stir until heated through. Garnish with cheese if desired.

YIELD: 3 servings.

golden asparagus soup

3/4 pound fresh asparagus, trimmed
1/2 cup chopped onion
  2 tablespoons butter
  2 garlic cloves, minced
  1 cup thinly sliced carrots
  1 can (14-1/2 ounces) chicken broth
1/4 cup minced fresh parsley
  1 tablespoon minced fresh basil
1/4 teaspoon salt
1/4 teaspoon pepper

Cut tips off asparagus and set aside; cut stalks into 1-1/2-in. pieces. In a large saucepan, saute onion in butter until tender. Add the garlic; cook 1 minute longer. Add the carrots and asparagus pieces; cook for 2 minutes.

Stir in the broth, parsley, basil, salt and pepper. Bring to a boil. Reduce the heat; cover and simmer for 20-25 minutes or until the vegetables are tender. Cool slightly.

In a blender, cover and process the soup until blended. Return to pan. Stir in asparagus tips; cook for 8-10 minutes or until tender.

YIELD: 2 servings.

heather ahrens
AVON, OHIO

It doesn't matter how many times I serve my thick, buttery soup, it's always a hit! It's a tasty way to get your daily dose of veggies.

flavorful italian soup

shirley taylor
RUSSIAVILLE, INDIANA

I tasted a similar Italian soup at a restaurant. The staff wouldn't reveal the recipe, so I went home and created my own version. It's delicious with a few garlic breadsticks.

1 Italian sausage link, casing removed
1 can (14-1/2 ounces) chicken broth
1/2 cup water
1/2 cup cubed peeled potatoes
1/4 cup chopped carrot
1/4 cup chopped onion
1/4 cup canned sliced mushrooms
1/4 teaspoon dried basil
1/8 teaspoon Italian seasoning
1/8 to 1/4 teaspoon hot pepper sauce
Dash celery seed
Dash garlic salt
1/3 cup broken uncooked spaghetti (2-inch pieces)

Crumble sausage into a large saucepan; cook over medium heat until no longer pink. Drain. Add the broth, water, vegetables and seasonings; bring to a boil. Reduce the heat; cover and simmer for 30 minutes.

Add spaghetti. Cover and simmer 8-10 minutes longer or until the spaghetti and vegetables are tender.

YIELD: 2 servings.

soup for two

- 1/2 cup chopped onion
- 1/2 cup chopped carrot
- 1 tablespoon butter
- 1 can (14-1/2 ounces) chicken broth
- 2/3 cup cubed cooked chicken
- 1/2 cup cauliflowerets
- 1/2 cup canned kidney beans, rinsed and drained
- 1/4 cup uncooked elbow macaroni
- 1 cup torn fresh spinach
- 1/8 teaspoon pepper
- Seasoned salad croutons, optional

In a saucepan, saute onion and carrot in butter for 4 minutes. Stir in the broth, chicken, cauliflower, beans and macaroni. Bring to a boil. Reduce heat; cover and simmer for 15-20 minutes or until macaroni and vegetables are tender. Add spinach and pepper; cook and stir until spinach is wilted. Garnish with croutons if desired.

YIELD: 2 servings.

margery bryan
ROYAL CITY, WASHINGTON

My comforting and colorful soup is loaded with the old-fashioned goodness of veggies, chicken and macaroni. Mix up the vegetables to get a different outcome every time you make it.

asian shrimp soup

- 1 ounce uncooked thin spaghetti, broken into 1-inch pieces
- 3 cups plus 1 tablespoon water, *divided*
- 3 teaspoons reduced-sodium chicken bouillon granules
- 1/2 teaspoon salt
- 1/2 cup sliced fresh mushrooms
- 1/2 cup fresh *or* frozen corn
- 1 teaspoon cornstarch
- 1-1/2 teaspoons reduced-sodium teriyaki sauce
- 1 cup thinly sliced romaine lettuce
- 1 can (6 ounces) small shrimp, rinsed and drained
- 2 tablespoons sliced green onion

Cook pasta according to package directions.

In a large saucepan, combine 3 cups water, bouillon and salt; bring to a boil. Stir in mushrooms and corn. Reduce heat; cook, uncovered, until vegetables are tender.

Combine the cornstarch, teriyaki sauce and remaining water until smooth; stir into soup. Bring to a boil; cook and stir for 1-2 minutes or until slightly thickened. Reduce heat. Drain pasta; add the pasta, lettuce, shrimp and green onion to the soup; heat through.

YIELD: 3-4 servings.

michelle smith
SYKESVILLE, MARYLAND

I make this soup so much, I nicknamed it "The House Specialty!" It will appeal to anyone with a taste for Asian fare. Use chicken or pork if you don't have any shrimp on hand.

hominy sausage soup

- 1/4 pound bulk pork sausage
- 1 teaspoon cumin seeds
- 1/8 teaspoon ground coriander
- 1/8 teaspoon cayenne pepper
- 2 cups reduced-sodium chicken broth
- 3/4 cup canned hominy, rinsed and drained
- 1 to 2 tablespoons chopped jalapeno pepper
- 1/4 teaspoon pepper
- 1 tablespoon minced fresh cilantro

Crumble sausage into a small skillet. Cook over medium heat for 3-4 minutes or until no longer pink; drain. In a small saucepan, toast cumin seeds

over medium heat for 2-3 minutes or until browned. Stir in coriander and cayenne; cook and stir for 30 seconds.

Add the broth, hominy, jalapeno, pepper and sausage. Bring to a boil. Reduce heat; simmer, uncovered, for 12-15 minutes or until heated through. Stir in cilantro.

YIELD: 2 servings.

jessie gunn stephens
SHERMAN, TEXAS

This subtle soup filled with sausage and hominy makes a great starter for Southwestern-style meals.

cilantro

To easily mince cilantro, hold the bunch, then angle the blade of a chef's knife almost parallel with the stems. Using short, downward strokes, shave off the leaves where they meet the stems.

jan hancock
EVANSVILLE, WISCONSIN

Full of colorful veggies, this comforting soup is perfect for a twosome.

🥄 **salad bar servings**

When you're preparing a recipe that serves two, you may only need half an onion or pepper, or just one rib of celery. The rest goes to waste. An easy solution is to visit the salad bar at your local grocery store. There, you can stock up on only as much as you need. It's a time-saver, too, because you don't have to chop or clean the veggies.

potato vegetable soup

- 1 bacon strip, diced
- 1 medium potato, peeled and cubed
- 1/2 medium carrot, sliced
- 1/2 cup water
- 2 tablespoons chopped celery
- 2 tablespoons chopped onion
- 1/4 teaspoon salt
- 1/8 teaspoon pepper
- 1 tablespoon all-purpose flour
- 1 cup 2% milk
- 1/4 cup shredded cheddar cheese
- 2 teaspoons butter

In a small saucepan, cook bacon over medium heat until crisp. Using a slotted spoon, remove to paper towels; drain. In the same pan, combine the potato, carrot, water, celery, onion, salt and pepper. Bring

to a boil. Reduce the heat; cover and simmer for 15 minutes or until vegetables are tender.

In a small bowl, combine the flour and milk until smooth; stir into the vegetable mixture. Bring to a boil; cook and stir for 2 minutes or until thickened. Reduce heat. Add the cheese and butter; stir until cheese is melted. Garnish with bacon.

YIELD: 2 servings.

diane ventimiglia
ATLANTA, MICHIGAN

My smooth soup is a tasty way to add nutritious broccoli to your diet. It's so thick and filling you won't miss the meat.

creamy broccoli soup

- 3/4 cup cubed peeled potatoes
- 1 medium carrot, sliced
- 2 cups frozen chopped broccoli
- 2 tablespoons butter
- 2 tablespoons all-purpose flour
- 1-1/2 cups 2% milk, *divided*
- 1/4 to 1/2 teaspoon salt
- 1/4 teaspoon dried thyme
- Dash ground nutmeg
- Dash pepper

Place potatoes and carrot in a small saucepan; cover with water. Bring to a boil. Reduce heat; cover and simmer for 15-20 minutes or until tender. Meanwhile, cook broccoli according to package directions; drain and set aside.

In a saucepan, melt butter. Stir in flour until smooth; gradually add 1/2 cup milk. Bring to a boil; cook and stir for 1 minute or until thickened. Add the salt, thyme, nutmeg and pepper.

Drain potato mixture; cool slightly. In a blender, combine the potato mixture, broccoli and remaining milk; cover and process until smooth. Add to the thickened milk mixture. Return to a boil. Reduce heat; simmer, uncovered, for 10 minutes or until heated through, stirring occasionally.

YIELD: 2 servings.

golden carrot soup

1/2 cup chopped onion
1/4 teaspoon minced garlic
  2 tablespoons reduced-fat butter
  2 cups water
  1 cup sliced carrots
  2 tablespoons uncooked long grain rice
  2 teaspoons chicken bouillon granules
  2 tablespoons minced fresh parsley

In a small saucepan, saute onion and garlic in butter until tender. Add the water, carrots, rice and bouillon; bring to a boil. Reduce heat; cover and simmer for 20-25 minutes or until carrots and rice are very tender.

Remove from the heat; cool slightly. Transfer to a blender or food processor; cover and process until pureed. Return to the saucepan; heat through. Sprinkle with parsley.

YIELD: 2 servings.

aline winje
SLOCAN, BRITISH COLUMBIA

You'll love my creamy, easy-to-fix soup on a cold day. It features a mild chicken flavor with just a hint of garlic.

parsley

To prevent fresh parsley from spoiling before you get the chance to use it all, place washed sprigs in an ice cube tray, then fill the tray with water. After the cubes are frozen, store them in a freezer bag. This makes it easy to pull out as many as needed when you want to add them to soups and stews.

creamy spring soup

dora handy

ALLIANCE, OHIO

At the end of a long day, there's nothing better than indulging in a bowl of this warm, creamy soup. It comes together in a flash, and with so many fresh, delicious veggies, you'll know you're filling up on nutrition, too!

1 can (14-1/2 ounces) reduced-sodium chicken broth

4 fresh asparagus spears, trimmed and cut into 2-inch pieces

4 baby carrots, julienned

1/2 celery rib, chopped

1 green onion, chopped

Dash garlic powder

Dash pepper

3/4 cup cooked elbow macaroni

1 can (5-1/2 ounces) evaporated milk

3/4 cup fresh baby spinach

In a large saucepan, combine the first seven ingredients. Bring to a boil. Reduce heat; cover and simmer for 5 minutes or until vegetables are tender. Stir in the macaroni, milk and spinach; heat through.

YIELD: 2 servings.

lemony mushroom-orzo soup

2-1/2 cups sliced fresh mushrooms
2 green onions, chopped
1 tablespoon olive oil
1 garlic clove, minced
1-1/2 cups chicken broth
1-1/2 teaspoons minced fresh parsley
1/4 teaspoon dried thyme
1/8 teaspoon pepper
1/4 cup uncooked orzo pasta
1-1/2 teaspoons lemon juice
1/8 teaspoon grated lemon peel

In a small saucepan, saute mushrooms and onions in oil until tender. Add garlic; cook 1 minute longer. Stir in the broth, parsley, thyme and pepper.

Bring to a boil. Stir in the orzo, lemon juice and peel. Cook for 5-6 minutes or until pasta is tender.

YIELD: 2 servings.

edrie o'brien,
DENVER, COLORADO

Here's a versatile soup that works as an appetizer or a side dish. It's loaded with mushrooms and orzo pasta, and a burst of lemon perks up its mild flavor.

caramelized french onion soup

1 medium onion, sliced
1 tablespoon butter
1 to 2 teaspoons sugar
1 teaspoon Worcestershire sauce
1-1/3 cups beef broth
1 tablespoon white wine *or* water
Coarsely ground pepper to taste
2 slices French bread (1 inch thick)
1/3 cup shredded Swiss cheese
3 tablespoons grated Parmesan cheese

In a saucepan, saute onion in butter until tender. Sprinkle with sugar and Worcestershire sauce; cook and stir for 13-15 minutes or until the onion is caramelized.

Add the broth, wine or water and pepper. Bring to a boil. Reduce the heat; cover and simmer for 15 minutes.

Place bread on an ungreased baking sheet. Broil 4 in. from the heat until toasted. Turn; sprinkle with cheeses. Broil until cheese is melted and bubbly. Ladle soup into bowls; top with toast.

YIELD: 2 servings.

pat stevens
GRANBURY, TEXAS

Carmelized onions give a touch of sweetness to my French onion soup that's topped with toasted cheese bread. It's an easy version of a classic.

potato corn chowder

2/3 cup fresh *or* frozen corn, thawed
1/3 cup chopped onion
1/4 cup chopped sweet red pepper
1/4 cup chopped green pepper
1 teaspoon canola oil
1 medium red potato, diced
2/3 cup reduced-sodium chicken broth
1/2 cup silken firm tofu
1/2 cup soy milk
1/4 teaspoon salt
1/8 teaspoon pepper

In a small saucepan, saute the corn, onion and peppers in oil until onion is tender. Add potato and broth. Bring to a boil. Reduce heat; cover and simmer for 8-10 minutes or until potato is tender.

Process tofu in a blender until smooth. Gradually stir tofu and soy milk into soup. Bring to a boil. Reduce heat; simmer, uncovered, for 10-15 minutes or until thickened, stirring occasionally. Season with salt and pepper.

YIELD: 2 servings.

taste of home test kitchen
GREENDALE, WISCONSIN

No one will guess that this chunky soup is made with tofu and soy milk. Even folks who don't have a problem with lactose will eat it up!

marilyn ausland
COLUMBUS, GEORGIA

My sweetheart and I count this soup among our favorites. We never grow tired of it—no matter how many times we eat it!

storing celery

To keep celery crisp, remove it from the plastic bag and wrap in paper towel. Then wrap again in aluminum foil. Store in the refrigerator. When you need some, break off what your recipe calls for, then re-wrap the rest and return it the fridge.

creamy wild rice soup

1/4 cup chopped onion
1/4 cup thinly sliced celery
1/4 cup sliced fresh mushrooms
 1 green onion, thinly sliced
1/4 cup reduced-fat butter
1/4 cup all-purpose flour
1/8 teaspoon pepper
 1 can (14-1/2 ounces) reduced-sodium chicken broth
 1 cup cooked wild rice
1/4 cup diced fully cooked lean ham
1-1/2 teaspoons diced pimientos
1/2 cup fat-free half-and-half
 1 tablespoon sliced almonds, toasted, optional

In a large saucepan, saute the onion, celery, mushrooms and green onion in butter until tender. Stir in the flour and pepper until blended. Gradually stir in the broth. Bring to a boil; cook and stir for 1-2 minutes or until thickened. Reduce heat. Stir in the rice, ham and pimientos; heat through. Stir in half-and-half; heat through (do not boil). Sprinkle with almonds if desired.

YIELD: 3 servings.

betty lineaweaver
PARADISE, CALIFORNIA

Chopped clams add big flavor to this full-bodied chowder. I serve it with garlic bread and a salad.

clams

Clams are great in chowders and pasta sauces. The key to plump and tender clams is to add them at the end of the cooking time and heat for just a few minutes. If clams cook too long, they become tough.

bacon clam chowder

 1 can (6-1/2 ounces) minced clams
 1 cup reduced-sodium chicken broth
 1 medium potato, peeled and cubed

1/2 cup chopped celery
1/4 cup chopped onion
1/2 teaspoon chicken bouillon granules
1/4 teaspoon dried thyme
 1 tablespoon cornstarch
1/2 cup half-and-half cream
1-1/2 teaspoons butter
Dash cayenne pepper
 2 bacon strips, cooked and crumbled

Drain clams, reserving juice; set aside. Place the clams in a food processor; cover and process until finely chopped. Set aside.

In a large saucepan, combine the broth, potato, celery, onion, bouillon and thyme. Bring to a boil. Reduce heat; simmer, uncovered, for 10-12 minutes or until vegetables are tender. Stir in the reserved clam juice.

Combine cornstarch and cream until smooth; gradually stir into soup. Bring to a boil; cook and stir for 2 minutes or until thickened. Stir in the butter, cayenne and clams. Cook and stir over medium heat for 3-4 minutes or until heated through. Garnish with bacon.

YIELD: 3 servings.

broccoli-cauliflower cheese soup

3/4 cup small cauliflowerets
3/4 cup small broccoli florets
1/4 cup chopped onion
1/4 cup halved thinly sliced carrot
1 to 2 tablespoons butter
1-1/2 cups 2% milk, *divided*
1/2 teaspoon chicken bouillon granules
1/4 teaspoon salt
Dash pepper
2 tablespoons all-purpose flour
1/3 cup cubed process cheese (Velveeta)

In a large saucepan, cook the cauliflower, broccoli, onion and carrot in butter for 5 minutes or until vegetables are crisp-tender. Stir in 1-1/4 cups milk, bouillon, salt and pepper. Bring to a boil. Reduce heat; simmer, uncovered, for about 5 minutes or until vegetables are tender, stirring occasionally.

Combine the flour and remaining milk until smooth; add to saucepan. Bring to a boil; cook and stir for 1-2 minutes or until thickened. Reduce the heat; add the cheese and stir until melted. Serve immediately.

YIELD: 2 servings.

betty corliss
STRATTON, COLORADO

Even my husband, who's never been a fan of broccoli, likes this creamy soup. It's a great way to use up the vegetables from our garden.

tomato-basil orzo soup

mary lu wasniewski
ORLAND PARK, ILLINOIS

Filled with tender pasta, sauteed vegetables and lots of flavor, this soup tastes just like the tomato rosa marina soup they serve in the best Greek restaurants in Chicago. I serve it with a small Greek salad and pita chips. Enjoy!

1/2 cup *each* chopped carrot, celery and onion

1/8 teaspoon *each* dried basil, oregano and thyme

2 tablespoons olive oil

1 can (19 ounces) ready-to-serve tomato basil *or* hearty tomato soup

1 cup chicken broth

1/3 cup uncooked orzo pasta

In a small saucepan, saute the carrot, celery, onion, basil, oregano and thyme in oil for 8-10 minutes or until vegetables are crisp-tender.

Add soup and broth. Bring to a boil. Stir in orzo. Reduce heat; simmer, uncovered, for 10-12 minutes or until orzo and vegetables are tender.

YIELD: 2 servings.

EDITOR'S NOTE: This recipe was tested with ready-to-serve Progresso Tomato Basil soup.

green chili tomato soup

- 1 can (10-3/4 ounces) condensed tomato soup, undiluted
- 3/4 cup whole milk
- 1 can (4 ounces) chopped green chilies
- 1/2 cup shredded cheddar cheese

In a small saucepan, combine the soup, milk and chilies until blended. Cook and stir over medium heat until heated through. Sprinkle with cheese.

YIELD: 2 servings.

mrs. chris christopher
ALBUQUERQUE, NEW MEXICO

I created this recipe after trying a tangy tomato soup at a restaurant. The chef wouldn't divulge the ingredients, but after some experimentation, I came up with my very own tasty version.

broccoli cheese soup for two

- 2 tablespoons chopped onion
- 1 tablespoon butter
- 1 cup chicken broth
- 1 package (10 ounces) frozen broccoli and cheese sauce, thawed
- 1/2 cup cooked long grain rice
- 1/4 cup heavy whipping cream

In a small saucepan, cook the onion in butter until tender. Stir in the broth and broccoli with the sauce. Bring to a boil. Reduce heat; simmer, uncovered, for 4 minutes.

Add rice and cream. Cook 3-4 minutes longer or until heated through and broccoli is tender (do not boil).

YIELD: 2 servings.

laura mihalenko-devoe
CHARLOTTE, NORTH CAROLINA

Frozen broccoli-cheese sauce makes my hearty soup a speedy addition to a lunchtime or evening meal. It's a great way to use up leftover rice.

mixed veggie soup

- 1/2 small carrot, grated
- 1/2 celery rib, chopped
- 2 tablespoons chopped green pepper
- 1 tablespoon chopped onion
- 1 tablespoon butter
- 1 cup reduced-sodium chicken broth
- 1 can (14-1/2 ounces) diced tomatoes, undrained
- 3/4 teaspoon sugar
- Dash pepper
- 1-1/2 teaspoons cornstarch

In a small saucepan, saute the carrot, celery, green pepper and onion in butter until tender. Set aside 2 tablespoons broth. Add the tomatoes, sugar, pepper and remaining broth to the vegetable mixture; bring to a boil. Reduce the heat; cover and simmer for 10 minutes.

Combine the cornstarch and reserved broth and stir until smooth; gradually add to the soup. Bring to a boil; cook and stir for 2 minutes or until slightly thickened.

YIELD: 2 servings.

lucille franck
INDEPENDENCE, IOWA

My sister is a dietitian, and she recommended this soup to anyone counting calories. I will double or triple the ingredients when I want a larger batch to feed my relatives around the holidays.

the value of veggies

Vegetables are great sources of many vitamins, minerals and other natural substances that may help prevent chronic diseases. To get a healthy variety, think color. Eating veggies of different colors gives your body a wide range of valuable nutrients, such as fiber, folate, potassium and vitamins A and C.

soup mixes & breads

Convenience abounds in this chapter filled with homemade soup mixes that you can make ahead in batches and cook up when you're ready. You'll also find a selection of breads that complement the textures and flavors of the soups featured throughout this book. Soup mixes and breads can also make thoughtful gifts for friends, new parents or anyone who likes to eat well but doesn't have a lot of time to cook.

288   293   306

joan anderson
WEST COVINA, CALIFORNIA

My bubbly bread features a pleasant herb flavor that everyone will love.

frozen bread dough

Frozen bread dough is quite a time-saver for busy cooks. If you take it out of the freezer at lunchtime, set it on the counter and cover it with plastic wrap coated with nonstick cooking spray, it will be ready to pop in the oven when you come home before dinner. You can break off small portions, roll them into balls and have fresh-baked rolls in no time.

wendy taylor
MASON CITY, IOWA

I layer this pretty, delicious soup mix in glass jars to give as gifts.

herb bubble bread

1/2 cup grated Parmesan cheese
3/4 teaspoon dried parsley flakes
1/4 teaspoon dill weed
1/8 teaspoon *each* dried thyme, basil and rosemary, crushed
1/4 cup butter, melted
2 teaspoons minced garlic
1 loaf (1 pound) frozen bread dough, thawed

In a small bowl, combine cheese and seasonings. In another bowl, combine butter and garlic; set aside.

Divide dough into 16 pieces. Roll into balls. Coat balls in butter mixture, then dip in cheese mixture. Place in a greased 9-in. x 5-in. loaf pan.

Cover and let rise in a warm place until doubled, about 1 hour. Bake at 350° for 22-26 minutes or until golden brown. (Cover loosely with foil if top browns too quickly.) Cool for 10 minutes before removing from pan to a wire rack. Serve warm.

YIELD: 16 servings.

friendship soup mix

1/2 cup dried green split peas
1/3 cup beef bouillon granules
1/4 cup medium pearl barley

1/2 cup dried lentils, rinsed and well dried
1/4 cup dried minced onion
2 teaspoons Italian seasoning
1/2 cup uncooked long grain rice
1/2 cup uncooked alphabet pasta *or* other small pasta

ADDITIONAL INGREDIENTS:
1 pound ground beef (90% lean)
3 quarts water
1 can (28 ounces) diced tomatoes, undrained

In a 1-1/2-pint jar, layer the first seven ingredients in the order listed. Wrap pasta in a small sheet of plastic wrap; add to jar. Seal tightly. Store in a cool, dry place for up to 3 months.

TO PREPARE SOUP: Remove pasta from jar and set aside. In a Dutch oven over medium heat, cook the beef until no longer pink; drain. Add the water, tomatoes and soup mix; bring to a boil. Reduce heat; cover and simmer for 45 minutes. Stir in the reserved pasta; cover and simmer for 15-20 minutes or until the pasta, peas, barley and lentils are tender.

YIELD: 16 servings.

classic chili mix

1 cup plus 2 tablespoons all-purpose flour

3/4 cup dried minced onion

4 to 6 tablespoons chili powder

1/4 cup paprika

2 tablespoons salt

1 tablespoon ground cumin

1 tablespoon dried minced garlic

1 tablespoon sugar

ADDITIONAL INGREDIENTS (FOR EACH BATCH):

1 pound ground beef

1 can (15 ounces) pinto beans, rinsed and drained

1 can (14-1/2 ounces) diced tomatoes, undrained

1 small green pepper, chopped

1/2 to 3/4 cup water

Sour cream, optional

Combine the first eight ingredients; divide into six batches (a scant 1/2 cup each). Store in airtight containers. **YIELD:** 6 batches (2-3/4 cups total).

TO PREPARE CHILI: In a large saucepan, cook beef over medium heat until no longer pink; drain. Stir in one batch of chili mix, beans, tomatoes, green pepper and water; bring to a boil. Reduce heat; simmer, uncovered, for 30 minutes. Garnish with sour cream if desired.

YIELD: 4 servings per batch.

bernice morris

MARSHFIELD, MISSOURI

This full-flavored chili seasoning will warm up your holiday gift-giving. The mix is on the mild side, which is nice for those who aren't partial to extra-spicy food.

cheese straws

ann nace

PERKASIE, PENNSYLVANIA

You'll have a hard time eating just one of these cheesy, buttery treats. They make a fun appetizer or side for soups or salads. Try twisting the sticks for an extra-fancy look.

1 cup all-purpose flour

1-1/2 teaspoons baking powder

1/2 teaspoon salt

1/2 cup shredded reduced-fat cheddar cheese

2 tablespoons plus 1-1/2 teaspoons cold butter

1/3 cup fat-free milk

2 teaspoons paprika

In a small bowl, combine the flour, baking powder and salt; stir in cheese. Cut in butter until mixture resembles coarse crumbs. Gradually add milk, tossing with a fork until dough forms a ball.

On a lightly floured surface, roll dough into a 12-in. square. Cut in half lengthwise; cut each half widthwise into 1/2-in. strips. Sprinkle with paprika.

Place 1 in. apart on baking sheets coated with cooking spray. Bake at 425° for 6-8 minutes or until golden brown. Serve warm.

YIELD: 4 dozen.

confetti bean soup mix

1 pound *each* dried navy beans, great northern beans, red kidney beans, pinto beans and green split peas

SEASONING MIX:

12 beef bouillon cubes

3/4 cup dried minced chives

4 teaspoons dried savory

2 teaspoons ground cumin

2 teaspoons coarsely ground pepper

4 bay leaves

ADDITIONAL INGREDIENTS FOR SOUP:

12 cups water, *divided*

1 can (14-1/2 ounces) stewed tomatoes, undrained

1-1/2 teaspoons salt

1/4 teaspoon hot pepper sauce, optional

In a large bowl, combine beans and peas; place 3 cups each in four large resealable plastic bags. Set aside.

In four snack-size resealable plastic bags place 3 bouillon cubes, 3 tablespoons chives, 1 teaspoon savory, 1/2 teaspoon cumin, 1/2 teaspoon pepper and 1 bay leaf. Seal bags or tie plastic wrap with ribbon if desired. **YIELD:** 4 batches.

TO PREPARE SOUP: Place the contents of one bag of beans in a Dutch oven; add 7 cups water. Bring to a boil; boil for 2 minutes. Remove from the heat; cover and let stand for 1 hour.

Drain beans and discard liquid. Add remaining water and contents of one seasoning bag. Bring to a boil. Reduce heat; cover and simmer for 1 hour or until beans are tender, stirring occasionally.

Add tomatoes, salt and pepper sauce if desired. Simmer, uncovered, for 20 minutes. Discard bay leaf.

YIELD: 9 servings per batch.

rebecca lambert
STAUNTON, VIRGINIA

With its colorful variety of beans and delicious flavor, this soup is so satisfying! I like to give jars of the mix, along with the recipe, to friends each Christmas.

---

paradise buns

1 loaf (1 pound) frozen bread dough, thawed

1 cup (4 ounces) shredded cheddar cheese

1/4 cup *each* diced mushrooms, broccoli and sweet red and yellow pepper

1 tablespoon chopped green onion

1 garlic clove, minced

1/2 teaspoon garlic powder

Divide bread dough into eight pieces. In a shallow bowl, combine the cheese, vegetables, garlic and garlic powder. Roll each piece of dough into an 8-in. rope. Roll in cheese mixture, pressing mixture into dough. Tie into a knot and press vegetables into dough; tuck ends under.

Place 2 in. apart on greased baking sheets. Cover and let rise until doubled, about 30 minutes.

Bake at 375° for 15-20 minutes or until tops are golden brown.

YIELD: 8 servings.

liz lazenby
VICTORIA, BRITISH COLUMBIA

I think frozen bread dough should be called magic dough because there is so much you can do with it. These flavorful knots are delicious with soup or salad.

---

homemade cream-style soup mix

2 cups nonfat dry milk powder

1/2 cup plus 2 tablespoons cornstarch

1/2 cup mashed potato flakes

1/4 cup chicken bouillon granules

2 teaspoons dried parsley flakes

2 teaspoons dried minced onion

1 teaspoon dried celery flakes

1 teaspoon dried minced garlic

1 teaspoon onion powder

1/2 teaspoon dried marjoram

1/4 teaspoon garlic powder

1/8 teaspoon white pepper

In a small bowl, combine all ingredients. Store in an airtight container in a cool dry place for up to 1 year.

Use as a substitute for half of a 10-3/4-oz. can of condensed cream of chicken, mushroom or celery soup.

In a microwave-safe bowl, whisk 2/3 cup water and 3 tablespoons soup mix. Microwave, uncovered, on high for 2 to 2-1/2 minutes or until thickened and bubbly, whisking occasionally.

For mushroom soup, add 1/4 to 1/2 cup sauteed sliced mushrooms. For celery soup, add 1/8 teaspoon celery salt and one sauteed, sliced or chopped celery rib.

YIELD: 16 batches (3 cups).

deann alleva
WORTHINGTON, OHIO

This easy soup mix is a wonderful substitute for canned cream soup in a recipe. It's great to have on hand for those nights when you need to whip up supper in a hurry.

taste of home test kitchen
GREENDALE, WISCONSIN

A seasoned Parmesan cheese coating gives refrigerated breadsticks a terrific taste twist. The wonderful aroma of these breadsticks baking is so irresistible you just may need to make another batch!

italian garlic breadsticks

1/2 cup grated Parmesan cheese
2 teaspoons Italian seasoning
1 teaspoon garlic powder
1/4 cup butter, melted
1 tube (11 ounces) refrigerated breadsticks

In a shallow bowl, combine the cheese, Italian seasoning and garlic powder. Place butter in another shallow bowl. Separate dough into individual breadsticks. Dip in the butter, then in the cheese mixture. Twist 2-3 times and place on an ungreased baking sheet.

Bake at 375° for 12-14 minutes or until golden brown. Serve immediately.

YIELD: 1 dozen.

jennifer bermingham
SHILLINGTON, PENNSYLVANIA

I'm a sixth grade special education teacher with little time on my hands. These easy-to-make breadsticks go well with my hearty vegetable beef soup.

caramelized onion breadsticks

1 large sweet onion, halved and thinly sliced
6 tablespoons butter, *divided*
1 teaspoon sugar
1 loaf (1 pound) frozen bread dough, thawed

In a large skillet over medium-low heat, cook onion in 4 tablespoons butter for 5 minutes or until tender. Add sugar; cook over low heat for 30-40 minutes longer or until onion is golden brown, stirring frequently.

On a lightly floured surface, roll bread dough into an 18-in. x 12-in. rectangle. Spoon onion mixture lengthwise over half of the dough; fold plain half of dough over onion mixture. Cut into eighteen 1-in. strips. Twist each strip twice; pinch ends to seal.

Place 2 in. apart on greased baking sheets. Melt the remaining butter; brush over breadsticks. Cover and let rise in a warm place until doubled, about 40 minutes.

Bake at 350° for 12-15 minutes or until lightly browned. Serve warm.

YIELD: 1-1/2 dozen.

bazaar soup mix

1/4 cup dried lentils, sorted

1/4 cup dried green split peas, sorted

1/4 cup uncooked long grain rice

2 tablespoons medium pearl barley

4 teaspoons beef *or* chicken bouillon granules

2 tablespoons dried minced onion

1 teaspoon celery salt

1/2 teaspoon Italian seasoning

3 tablespoons dried parsley flakes

1/2 cup uncooked small pasta shells

ADDITIONAL INGREDIENTS:

1/2 pound lean ground beef (90% lean)

8 cups water

1 can (14-1/2 ounces) diced tomatoes, undrained

In a 1-pint jar or container with a tight-fitting lid, layer the first nine ingredients in the order listed. Wrap pasta in a small piece of plastic wrap; add to jar. Seal tightly. Store in a cool dry place for up to 3 months. **YIELD:** 1 batch (1-1/2 cups).

TO PREPARE SOUP: Remove pasta from top of jar and set aside. In a Dutch oven, cook beef over medium heat until no longer pink; drain. Add the water, tomatoes and soup mix; bring to a boil. Reduce heat; cover and simmer for 45 minutes.

Stir in reserved pasta; cover and simmer 15-20 minutes longer or until pasta, lentils, peas and barley are tender.

YIELD: 8 servings.

pearl brock
COUDERSPORT, PENNSYLVANIA

Our church women's group assembles this soup mix to give to visitors and to sell at our annual bazaar. Each container is labeled with the directions to make it and additional ingredients needed.

swiss beer bread

debi wallace
CHESTERTOWN, NEW YORK

This recipe is a favorite because it isn't greasy like other cheese breads I have tried. A loaf will not last long in your kitchen!

- 4 ounces Jarlsberg *or* Swiss cheese
- 3 cups all-purpose flour
- 3 tablespoons sugar
- 3 teaspoons baking powder
- 1-1/2 teaspoons salt
- 1/2 teaspoon pepper
- 1 bottle (12 ounces) beer *or* nonalcoholic beer
- 2 tablespoons butter, melted

Divide cheese in half. Cut half of cheese into 1/4-inch cubes; shred remaining cheese. In a large bowl, combine the flour, sugar, baking powder, salt and pepper. Stir beer into dry ingredients just until moistened. Fold in cheese.

Transfer to a greased 8-in. x 4-in. loaf pan. Drizzle with butter. Bake at 375° for 50-60 minutes or until a toothpick inserted near the center comes out clean. Cool for 10 minutes before removing from pan to a wire rack.

YIELD: 1 loaf.

chicken rice soup mix

2 cups uncooked long grain brown rice
1/2 cup chicken bouillon granules
4 teaspoons dried tarragon
4 teaspoons dried parsley flakes
1 teaspoon white pepper

ADDITIONAL INGREDIENTS:

3 cups water
1 tablespoon butter

In a large bowl, combine the first five ingredients. Cover and store in a cool dry place for up to 6 months. **YIELD:** 4 batches (about 2-2/3 cups).

TO PREPARE SOUP: Shake rice mix before measuring. In a large saucepan, bring the water, butter and 2/3 cup soup mix to a boil. Reduce heat; cover and simmer for 30-35 minutes or until the rice is tender.

YIELD: 2-3 servings per batch.

iola egle
BELLA VISTA, ARKANSAS

This quick combination makes a great gift any time of the year!

cooking with rice

Instant rice (which is precooked before packaging) and long grain rice require different amounts of liquid during cooking, so they cannot be substituted measure for measure. Once prepared, you can use either kind of rice interchangeably in a recipe that calls for cooked rice.

five-bean soup mix

5 packages (16 ounces *each*) dried beans: lima, great northern, kidney, pinto and split peas (enough for four batches of soup)
3 tablespoons minced chives
1 teaspoon dried savory
1 teaspoon salt, optional
1/2 teaspoon ground cumin
1/2 teaspoon pepper
1 bay leaf
3 beef bouillon cubes
2-1/2 quarts water
1 can (14-1/2 ounces) stewed tomatoes

Combine the beans; divide into four even batches, about 3-3/4 cups each.

TO PREPARE SOUP: Wash one batch of beans. Place in a large kettle; add enough water to cover. Bring to a boil; cook for 3-4 minutes. Remove from heat; cover and let stand 1 hour.

Tie spices in a cheesecloth bag. Drain and rinse beans. Return to kettle; add bouillon, spices and water. Bring to a boil. Reduce heat; cover and simmer 1-1/2 hours or until beans are tender, stirring occasionally. Remove spices. Add tomatoes and heat through.

YIELD: 4 servings per batch.

lynne dodd
MENTOR, OHIO

I discovered this recipe a few years ago and now it's one of my family's favorites. Served with a salad and bread or rolls, it makes a savory supper.

cooking dried beans

When cooking dried lima or navy beans in a recipe with tomatoes, the acidity of the tomatoes slows down the cooking of dry beans. So tomato or tomato products should be added after the beans are nearly tender. Salt can also inhibit the cooking and should be added at the same time as the tomatoes.

rhonda letendre
EPSOM, NEW HAMPSHIRE

Loaded with beans of all shapes and sizes, this colorful combination cooks up into a satisfying soup that'll stand by itself or serve as a side dish. Not only do I give the mix away as a gift, I keep it on hand to make for my family, too. They love it!

🥄 dried herbs

Dried herbs don't spoil, but they do lose flavor and potency over time. For maximum flavor in your cooking, replace herbs that are over a year old. Store them in airtight containers and keep away from heat and light.

traci collins
CHEYENNE, WYOMING

I stumbled across this recipe while looking for something different to take to a brunch. Everyone asked for the recipe and could not believe it only called for a handful of ingredients.

🥄 storing bread

Store bread at room temperature in a cool, dry place for up to 2-3 days. Heat and humidity cause homemade bread to mold. Storing it in the refrigerator turns it stale quickly. To keep bread soft and fresh, store in an airtight plastic bag. Most breads will stay fresh in the freezer for up to 3 months. Slice it before freezing, then just take out one or two slices at a time as needed.

calico soup mix

BEAN MIX:

1-1/2 cups *each* dried lentils, baby lima beans, yellow split peas, red kidney beans, great northern beans, pinto beans, green split peas and navy beans

ADDITIONAL INGREDIENTS (FOR EACH BATCH):

2-1/4 quarts water
2 cups cubed fully cooked ham
1 can (14-1/2 ounces) stewed tomatoes
1 medium onion, sliced
1 medium green pepper, chopped
1 garlic clove, minced
2 teaspoons salt
1 teaspoon *each* dried marjoram, oregano, parsley flakes and Italian seasoning

In a large bowl, combine beans; divide into six batches (2 cups each). Store in airtight containers. **YIELD:** 6 batches.

    TO PREPARE SOUP: Place one batch of bean mix in a Dutch oven or soup kettle; add water to cover by

2 in. Bring to a boil; boil for 2 minutes. Remove from the heat; cover and let stand for 1 hour.

    Drain. Add 2-1/4 qts. water; bring to a boil. Reduce heat; cover and simmer for 1-1/2 to 2 hours or until beans are tender. Add ham, tomatoes, onion, green pepper, garlic and seasonings; return to boil. Reduce heat; simmer for 45-50 minutes.

YIELD: 6 servings per batch.

pull-apart bacon bread

12 bacon strips, diced
1 loaf (1 pound) frozen bread dough, thawed

2 tablespoons olive oil, *divided*
1 cup (4 ounces) shredded part-skim mozzarella cheese
1 envelope (1 ounce) ranch salad dressing mix

In a large skillet, cook bacon over medium heat for 5 minutes or until partially cooked; drain on paper towels. Roll out dough to 1/2-in. thickness; brush with 1 tablespoon of oil. Cut into 1-in. pieces; place in a large bowl. Add the bacon, cheese, dressing mix and remaining oil; toss to coat.

    Arrange pieces in a 9-in. x 5-in. oval on a greased baking sheet, layering as needed. Cover and let rise in a warm place for 30 minutes or until doubled.

    Bake at 350° for 15 minutes. Cover with foil; bake 5-10 minutes longer or until golden brown.

YIELD: 1 loaf.

pasta fagioli soup mix

- 1 cup small pasta shells
- 3/4 cup dried great northern beans
- 3/4 cup dried pinto beans
- 3/4 cup dried kidney beans
- 1/4 cup dried minced onion
- 3 tablespoons dried parsley flakes
- 1 teaspoon dried basil
- 1 teaspoon dried oregano
- 1/2 teaspoon dried rosemary, crushed
- 1/4 teaspoon dried minced garlic
- 1 bay leaf
- Dash crushed red pepper flakes

ADDITIONAL INGREDIENTS:

- 14 cups water, *divided*
- 1 can (28 ounces) diced tomatoes, undrained
- 3 medium carrots, chopped
- 1 celery rib, chopped
- 1 teaspoon salt
- Grated Parmesan cheese, optional

Place pasta in a small resealable plastic bag; place in a 1-qt. glass jar. Layer with beans. Place seasonings in another plastic bag; place in jar. Cover and store in a cool dry place for up to 3 months. **YIELD:** 1 batch.

TO PREPARE SOUP: Remove seasoning packet from jar. Remove beans; sort and rinse. Set pasta aside.

Place beans in a Dutch oven; add 6 cups water. Bring to a boil; boil for 2 minutes. Remove from the heat; cover and let stand for 1 to 4 hours or until beans are softened. Drain and discard liquid.

Return beans to the pan. Add contents of seasoning packet and remaining water. Bring to a boil. Reduce heat; cover and simmer for 1 hour or until beans are tender. Add the tomatoes, carrots, celery and salt; cover and simmer 30 minutes longer, stirring occasionally.

Stir in pasta. Cover and simmer for 5-10 minutes or until pasta and carrots are tender, stirring occasionally. Remove bay leaf before serving. Garnish with cheese if desired.

YIELD: 14 servings.

tamra duncan
LINCOLN, ARKANSAS

This mix will create a meatless soup that is both economical and flavorful.

decorative jar covers

Here's an easy way to put pretty cloth toppers and a bow on jars of homemade soup mix. Cut a circular piece of cloth to fit over the lid of the jar with a little extra to fold over the top. Put the cloth over the jar and use a rubber band to hold it in place. Tie a ribbon around the jar, then carefully snip off the rubber band.

tortellini bean soup mix

doris simmons
BROWNING, ILLINOIS

*I like to use mixes for
Christmas gifts. One year,
I gave this soup mix in a
jar and included a kettle,
a mug and a pint of my
home-canned tomatoes.*

1 cup dried great northern beans
1/4 cup dried lentils
1/4 cup dried green split peas
3/4 cup uncooked dried tricolor tortellini
1 tablespoon dried parsley flakes
1 tablespoon chicken bouillon granules
2 teaspoons dried minced garlic
1 teaspoon dried thyme
1/2 teaspoon salt

ADDITIONAL INGREDIENTS:

8 cups water
1 can (49-1/2 ounces) chicken broth
1 can (14-1/2 ounces) diced tomatoes, drained
2 medium carrots, chopped
2 celery ribs, chopped
Grated Parmesan cheese, optional

In a 3-cup jar or container with a tight-fitting lid, layer the beans, lentils and peas. In a small resealable plastic bag, combine the tortellini, parsley, bouillon, garlic, thyme and salt. Place bag in jar. Replace lid and store in a cool dry place. **YIELD:** 1 batch (about 2-1/4 cups).

TO PREPARE SOUP: Remove bag of tortellini and seasonings; set aside. Rinse the beans, lentils and peas; drain. Place in a Dutch oven. Add 8 cups water. Bring to a boil. Reduce heat; cover and simmer for 45-60 minutes or until beans are tender.

Stir in the tortellini and seasonings, broth, tomatoes, carrots and celery. Bring to a boil. Reduce heat; simmer, uncovered, for 8-10 minutes or until pasta and vegetables are tender. Serve with cheese if desired.

YIELD: 15 servings.

savory pull-apart bread

1/4 cup grated Parmesan cheese
3 tablespoons sesame seeds
1/2 teaspoon dried basil
1 package (30 ounces) frozen roll dough (24 rolls)
1/4 cup butter, melted
2 tablespoons bacon bits, optional

In a small bowl, combine the Parmesan cheese, sesame seeds and basil; sprinkle one-third in the bottom and up the sides of a greased 12-cup fluted tube pan.

Place half of the thawed rolls in pan; drizzle with half of the butter. Sprinkle with half of the remaining cheese mixture and bacon bits if desired. Arrange remaining rolls on top; drizzle with remaining butter. Sprinkle with remaining cheese mixture. Cover and refrigerate overnight.

Remove from the refrigerator 30 minutes before baking. Bake at 350° for 20 minutes. Cover loosely with foil; bake 10-15 minutes longer.

YIELD: 10-12 servings.

janne rowe
WICHITA, KANSAS

This yummy pull-apart bread is perfect for any gathering, big or small.

mushroom barley soup mix

1-1/2 cups dried lentils
3 cups medium pearl barley
1 package (1 ounce) dried shiitake *or* porcini mushrooms (about 2 cups)
6 bay leaves
18 beef bouillon cubes
6 tablespoons dried celery flakes
6 tablespoons dried parsley flakes
6 tablespoons dried minced onion
3 teaspoons coarsely ground pepper
3 teaspoons garlic salt
3 teaspoons dried thyme

ADDITIONAL INGREDIENTS (FOR EACH BATCH):
2 quarts water
2 medium carrots, chopped

In six pint-size jars or cellophane gift bags, layer 1/4 cup lentils, 1/2 cup barley and 1/3 cup mushrooms. Top with a bay leaf, or attach to jar or bag for decoration.

In six snack-size resealable plastic bags, place three bouillon cubes, 1 tablespoon celery flakes, 1 tablespoon parsley, 1 tablespoon onion, 1/2 teaspoon pepper, 1/2 teaspoon garlic salt and 1/2 teaspoon thyme; seal bags. Place one in each jar or bag and seal. **YIELD: 6 batches.**

TO PREPARE SOUP: Place mix and seasonings in a large saucepan; add water and carrots. Bring to a boil; stir well. Reduce heat; cover and simmer for 45-60 minutes or until barley and lentils are tender. Remove bay leaf before serving.

YIELD: about 5 servings per batch.

**taste of home
test kitchen**
GREENDALE, WISCONSIN

Steaming bowls of homemade soup are less than an hour away when you have this lovely layered soup mix on hand. Filled with lentils and barley, we promise you won't miss the meat!

cracked pepper bread

1-1/2 cups water (70° to 80°)
3 tablespoons olive oil
3 tablespoons sugar
2 teaspoons salt
3 tablespoons minced chives
2 garlic cloves, minced
1 teaspoon garlic powder
1 teaspoon dried basil
1 teaspoon cracked black pepper
1/4 cup grated Parmesan cheese
4 cups bread flour
2-1/2 teaspoons active dry yeast

In bread machine pan, place all ingredients in order suggested by manufacturer. Select basic bread setting. Choose crust color and loaf size if available. Bake according to bread machine directions (check the dough after 5 minutes of mixing; add 1 to 2 tablespoons of water or flour if needed).

YIELD: 1 loaf.

joy mcmillan
THE WOODLANDS, TEXAS

Parmesan cheese and a blend of herbs give big flavor to this bread. The use of a bread machine makes preparation a snap.

elizabeth moore
FRANKFORT, KENTUCKY

This flavorful soup tastes so fresh you'll never know it's been frozen. You can easily double the recipe when tomatoes are plentiful or toss in extra vegetables from your garden. For heartier fare, beef it up with ground beef, sausage or meatballs.

freezer vegetable soup

SOUP BASE:

4 cups chopped tomatoes
1 cup chopped celery
1 cup chopped carrot
1 cup chopped onion
2 teaspoons sugar
1 teaspoon salt, optional
1/2 teaspoon pepper
1/2 teaspoon dill weed

ADDITIONAL INGREDIENTS (FOR EACH BATCH):

2 cups diced potatoes
2 cups water

In a kettle or Dutch oven, combine the soup base ingredients; bring to a boil over medium heat. Reduce the heat; cover and simmer for 45 minutes. Cool.

Place 2 cups each into freezer containers. Soup may be frozen for up to 3 months. **YIELD:** 2 batches (4 cups total).

TO PREPARE SOUP: Thaw soup base in the refrigerator. Transfer to a kettle or Dutch oven. Add potatoes and water; simmer for 30-40 minutes.

YIELD: 4 servings per batch.

gaylene anderson
SANDY, UTAH

These tender breadsticks fill the kitchen with a tempting aroma when they're in the oven, and they're wonderful served warm. My family tells me I can't make them enough.

parmesan breadsticks

2 packages (1/4 ounce *each*) active dry yeast
1-1/2 cups warm water (110° to 115°)
1/2 cup warm milk (110° to 115°)
3 tablespoons sugar
3 tablespoons plus 1/4 cup butter, softened, *divided*

1 teaspoon salt
4-1/2 to 5-1/2 cups all-purpose flour
1/4 cup grated Parmesan cheese
1/2 teaspoon garlic salt

In a large bowl, dissolve yeast in warm water. Add the milk, sugar, 3 tablespoons butter, salt and 2 cups flour. Beat until smooth. Stir in enough remaining flour to form a soft dough.

Turn onto a floured surface; knead until smooth and elastic, about 6-8 minutes. Place in a greased bowl, turning once to grease top. Cover and let rise in a warm place until doubled, about 45 minutes.

Punch the dough down. Turn onto a floured surface; divide into 36 pieces. Shape each piece into a 6-in. rope. Place 2 in. apart on greased baking sheets. Cover and let rise until doubled, about 25 minutes.

Melt remaining butter; brush over dough. Sprinkle with Parmesan cheese and garlic salt. Bake at 400° for 8-10 minutes or until golden brown. Remove from pans to wire racks.

YIELD: 3 dozen.

buttery herb loaves

4 to 5 cups all-purpose flour
1 package (1/4 ounce) active dry yeast
1/4 cup sugar
1 teaspoon salt
1-1/4 cups 2% milk
1/3 cup butter, cubed
2 eggs

FILLING:

1/2 cup butter, softened
1 garlic clove, minced
1/2 teaspoon dried minced onion
1/2 teaspoon dried basil
1/2 teaspoon caraway seeds
1/4 teaspoon dried oregano
1/8 teaspoon cayenne pepper

In a large bowl, combine 2 cups flour, yeast, sugar and salt. In a small saucepan, heat milk and butter to 120°-130°. Add to dry ingredients; beat just until moistened. Add eggs; beat until smooth. Stir in enough remaining flour to form a soft dough.

Turn onto a floured surface; knead until smooth and elastic, about 6-8 minutes. Place in a greased bowl, turning once to grease top. Cover and let rise in a warm place until doubled, about 1 hour.

In a small bowl, combine filling ingredients; set aside. Punch down dough; divide in half. Turn onto a lightly floured surface. Roll each portion into a 15-in. x 9-in. rectangle. Spread filling over each to within 1/2 in. of edges. Roll up jelly-roll style, starting with a short side; pinch seams to seal and tuck ends under.

Place seam side down in two greased 9-in. x 5-in. loaf pans. Cover and let rise in a warm place until doubled, about 30 minutes.

Bake at 350° for 20-25 minutes or until golden brown. Cool for 10 minutes before removing from pans to wire racks to cool completely.

YIELD: 2 loaves.

lillian hatcher
PLAINFIELD, ILLINOIS

This is one of my family's favorite bread recipes. We love it with a warm bowl of soup during autumn.

wrapped bread

Here's a stunning way to present a gift of fresh-baked bread: Purchase, wash and dry an inexpensive kitchen towel. Use it to wrap a cooled loaf of bread. Tie with a strip of ribbon or raffia.

**taste of home
test kitchen**

GREENDALE, WISCONSIN

Warm up loved ones on frosty winter nights with a gift of this hearty, stick-to-your-ribs soup mix. Layered in pretty bow-tied jars, it looks just as good as it tastes! Be sure to include preparation instructions and a list of any additional ingredients necessary with your gift.

hearty pasta soup mix

1/2 cup dried split peas

2 tablespoons chicken bouillon granules

1/2 cup dried lentils

2 tablespoons dried minced onion

1 teaspoon dried basil

1 teaspoon dried parsley flakes

1 envelope savory herb with garlic soup mix *or* vegetable soup mix

2 cups uncooked tricolor spiral pasta

ADDITIONAL INGREDIENTS:

10 cups water

3 cups cubed cooked chicken

1 can (28 ounces) diced tomatoes, undrained

In a 1-qt. glass container, layer the first seven ingredients in the order listed. Place the pasta in a 1-qt. resealable plastic bag; add to the jar. Seal tightly. **YIELD:** 1 batch (4 cups).

TO PREPARE SOUP: Remove pasta from top of jar and set aside. Place water in a Dutch oven; stir in soup mix. Bring to a boil. Reduce heat; cover and simmer for 45 minutes. Add the chicken, tomatoes and pasta. Cover and simmer for 15-20 minutes longer or until pasta, peas and lentils are tender.

YIELD: 14 servings.

wendy chilton

BROOKELAND, TEXAS

These light, golden puffs are super simple to make, but their flavor is sinfully delicious. Their small size makes them easy to munch on for a tiny treat, small appetizer or complement to your favorite soup.

savory biscuit bites

1/4 cup butter, melted

2 tablespoons grated Parmesan cheese

1 tablespoon dried minced onion

1-1/2 teaspoons dried parsley flakes

1 tube (12 ounces) refrigerated biscuits

In a small bowl, combine the butter, cheese, onion and parsley. Cut biscuits into quarters; roll in butter mixture. Place in a greased 15-in. x 10-in. x 1-in. baking pan; let stand for 25 minutes.

Bake at 400° for 8 minutes or until lightly browned.

YIELD: 13-15 servings.

june poepping

QUINCY, ILLINOIS

My daughter has given me many great recipes, but this is one of my all-time favorites. I usually serve them with chili or a fresh green salad.

three-cheese twists

1/2 cup butter, melted

1/4 teaspoon garlic salt

1-1/2 cups (6 ounces) finely shredded cheddar cheese

1-1/2 cups (6 ounces) finely shredded part-skim mozzarella cheese

3/4 cup grated Parmesan cheese

1 tablespoon dried parsley flakes

24 frozen bread dough dinner rolls, thawed

In a shallow bowl, combine butter and garlic salt. In another shallow bowl, combine cheeses and parsley. On a lightly floured surface, roll each dinner roll into a 10-in. rope. Dip in butter mixture, then in cheese mixture.

Fold each rope in half and twist twice; pinch ends together to seal. Place 2 in. apart on greased baking sheets. Cover and let rise in a warm place until almost doubled, about 30 minutes.

Bake at 350° for 15 minutes or until golden brown.

YIELD: 24 servings.

tomato focaccia

2-1/2 to 3 cups all-purpose flour
1 teaspoon salt
1 teaspoon sugar
3 teaspoons active dry yeast
1 cup warm water (110° to 115°)
1 tablespoon olive oil

TOPPING:
1 tablespoon olive oil
2 tablespoons grated Parmesan cheese
1 tablespoon minced fresh rosemary
2 garlic cloves, minced
1/4 teaspoon salt
1 small red onion, thinly sliced and
    separated into rings
3 to 4 medium plum tomatoes, thinly
    sliced

In a large bowl, combine 2-1/2 cups flour, salt and sugar. Dissolve yeast in water; stir in oil. Add to dry ingredients; beat until smooth. Stir in enough remaining flour to form a soft dough.

Turn onto a floured surface; knead until smooth and elastic, about 6-8 minutes. Place in a greased bowl, turning once to grease top. Cover; let rise in a warm place until doubled, about 30 minutes.

Punch the dough down. On a lightly floured surface, roll dough into a 12-in. circle. Place on a greased 12-in. pizza pan. Brush with oil. Combine the Parmesan cheese, rosemary, garlic and salt; sprinkle over dough. Arrange onion rings and tomatoes over top, pressing down lightly.

Bake at 400° for 15-20 minutes or until crust is golden brown. Cut into wedges.

YIELD: 10 servings.

mary lou wayman
SALT LAKE CITY, UTAH

I top these savory appetizers with onion, tomatoes and Parmesan cheese. They make tasty nibblers alongside a steaming bowl of soup.

slicing tomatoes

The best way to cut through the skin of a tomato is with a serrated, not straight-edged, knife. Cut a tomato vertically, from stem end to blossom end, for slices that will be less juicy and hold their shape better.

the best bean soup mix

elizabeth clayton paul
NEPEAN, ONTARIO

An attractive bag of this savory mix makes a lovely gift for the holidays or any special occasion.

rinsing beans

For a quick and easy way to rinse dried beans, place them in a plastic pitcher equipped with a plunger/mixer. Submerge the beans in water and mix to get them thoroughly clean. Pour the water out using the strainer opening on the lid.

BEAN MIX:

- 1 cup *each* dried yellow split peas, green split peas, lentils, medium pearl barley, black-eyed peas, small lima beans, navy beans, great northern beans and pinto beans

SOUP:

- 6 cups water
- 1 large onion, chopped
- 1 large carrot, chopped
- 2 teaspoons chili powder
- 1-1/4 teaspoons salt
- 1/4 teaspoon pepper
- 1/8 teaspoon ground cloves
- 1/2 pound smoked sausage
- 1 can (28 ounces) diced tomatoes, undrained
- 1 tablespoon lemon juice

In a large bowl, combine bean mix ingredients. Divide into six batches, 1-1/2 cups each. Store in airtight containers in a cool dry place for up to 1 year. **YIELD:** 6 batches (2-1/2 quarts per batch).

TO MAKE ONE BATCH OF SOUP: Place 1-1/2 cups bean mix in a Dutch oven; cover with water by 2 in. Bring to a boil; boil for 2 minutes. Remove from the heat; let stand for 1 hour. Drain, discarding liquid. Return beans to kettle; add water. Bring to a boil. Reduce heat; cover and simmer for 1-1/2 to 2 hours or until beans are tender.

Add the onion, carrot, chili powder, salt, pepper and cloves. Return to a boil. Reduce heat and simmer, uncovered, for 30 minutes. Add sausage, tomatoes and lemon juice; simmer 15-20 minutes longer.

YIELD: 8-10 servings.

breadsticks with parmesan butter

2 packages (1/4 ounce *each*) active dry yeast
1/2 cup sugar, *divided*
2 cups warm water (110° to 115°), *divided*
3 tablespoons canola oil
1 egg
1 teaspoon salt
4-1/2 to 5 cups all-purpose flour

PARMESAN BUTTER:

1/2 cup butter, softened
2 tablespoons grated Parmesan cheese
1/4 to 1/2 teaspoon garlic powder

In a large bowl, dissolve yeast and 1 tablespoon sugar in 1 cup warm water. Add the oil, egg, salt, 2 cups flour, and remaining sugar and water. Beat until smooth. Stir in enough remaining flour to form a soft dough.

Turn onto a floured surface; knead until smooth and elastic, about 6-8 minutes. Place in a greased bowl, turning once to grease top. Cover and let rise in a warm place until doubled, about 40 minutes.

Punch the dough down. Turn onto a floured surface; divide into 36 pieces. Shape each piece into a 6-in. rope. Place 2 in. apart on greased baking sheets. Cover and let rise until doubled, about 25 minutes.

Bake at 400° for 10-12 minutes or until golden brown. Meanwhile, in a small bowl, cream the butter, Parmesan cheese and garlic powder. Serve butter with breadsticks.

YIELD: 3 dozen breadsticks and about 2/3 cup butter.

elaine anderson
NEW GALILEE, PENNSYLVANIA

My kids love these tender breadsticks and devour them in a hurry. Any leftovers are great with butter and honey for breakfast the next day.

wild rice and barley soup mix

1 tablespoon brown sugar
2 teaspoons Italian seasoning
1/2 teaspoon dried minced garlic
1/2 teaspoon ground celery seed
1/2 teaspoon pepper
1/2 cup medium pearl barley
1/3 cup dried vegetable flakes
3 tablespoons chicken bouillon granules
1/2 cup uncooked wild rice
1/2 cup dried minced onion

ADDITIONAL INGREDIENTS:

8 cups water
Real bacon bits, optional

In a small bowl, combine the first five ingredients. In a pint-size jar with a tight-fitting lid, layer the barley, vegetable flakes, brown sugar mixture, bouillon granules, rice and onion, packing each layer tightly (do not mix). Cover and store in a cool dry place for up to 4 months. **YIELD: 1 batch.**

TO PREPARE SOUP: Pour mix into a large saucepan. Add water and bring to a boil. Reduce heat; cover and simmer for 1 hour or until rice is tender. Sprinkle with bacon bits if desired.

YIELD: 6 servings.

taste of home test kitchen
GREENDALE, WISCONSIN

Soothe both body and soul by serving up ladles of home-cooked comfort with this classic soup.

basil garlic bread

2/3 cup warm milk (70° to 80°)
1/4 cup warm water (70° to 80°)
1/4 cup warm sour cream (70° to 80°)
1-1/2 teaspoons sugar
1 tablespoon butter, softened
1 tablespoon grated Parmesan cheese
1 teaspoon salt
1/2 teaspoon minced garlic
1/2 teaspoon dried basil
1/2 teaspoon garlic powder
3 cups bread flour
2-1/4 teaspoons active dry yeast

In bread machine pan, place all of the ingredients in the order suggested by the manufacturer. Select basic bread setting. Choose crust color and loaf size if available.

Bake according to bread machine directions (check dough after 5 minutes of mixing; add 1 to 2 tablespoons of water or flour if needed).

YIELD: 1 loaf.

christine burger
GRAFTON, WISCONSIN

I created this simple loaf one night, and now my family asks for it time and again. We toast leftover slices for breakfast in the morning.

cari miller
PHILADELPHIA, PENNSYLVANIA

These pastry pockets are cripsy on the outside and tender on the inside. They can be eaten by hand, so they're great for when you're on the go.

bacon onion turnovers

3 packages (1/4 ounce *each*) active dry yeast
1/2 cup warm water (110° to 115°)
1 cup warm milk (110° to 115°)
1/2 cup butter, melted
2 teaspoons salt
3-1/2 to 4 cups all-purpose flour
1/2 pound sliced bacon, cooked and crumbled
1 large onion, diced
1 egg, lightly beaten

In a large bowl, dissolve yeast in warm water. Add the milk, butter and salt; beat until smooth. Stir in enough flour to form a soft dough.

Turn onto a floured surface; knead until smooth and elastic, about 6-8 minutes. Place in a greased bowl, turning once to grease top. Cover and let rise in a warm place until doubled, about 30 minutes.

Punch dough down. Turn onto a lightly floured surface; divided into 30 pieces. Roll each into a 4-in. circle. Combine bacon and onion; place about 2 teaspoons on one side of each circle. Fold dough over filling; press edges with a fork to seal. Place 3 in. apart on greased baking sheets. Cover and let rise in a warm place until doubled, about 20 minutes.

Brush with egg. Bake at 425° for 10-15 minutes or until golden brown. Remove to wire racks. Serve warm.

YIELD: 2-1/2 dozen.

vivian huizinga
SHALLOW LAKE, ONTARIO

This spice mix comes from my mother's fantastic chili recipe. It will make a great gift for anyone with a hearty appetite.

spice mix for chili

3-1/2 teaspoons garlic salt
3-1/2 teaspoons chili powder
2 teaspoons *each* salt, onion powder, pepper, ground cumin, paprika and dried parsley flakes
1/2 teaspoon cayenne pepper

ADDITIONAL INGREDIENTS (FOR EACH BATCH):
1 pound ground beef
1 medium onion, chopped

1 cup sliced fresh mushrooms, optional
1 can (28 ounces) diced tomatoes, undrained
1 can (16 ounces) kidney beans, rinsed and drained
1 can (16 ounces) hot chili beans, undrained
1 can (10-3/4 ounces) condensed tomato soup, undiluted
1 teaspoon Worcestershire sauce
2 garlic cloves, minced
Shredded cheddar cheese

In a small bowl, combine all of the seasonings. Store in an airtight container in a cool dry place for up to 6 months. **YIELD:** 3 batches.

TO PREPARE CHILI: In a large saucepan or Dutch oven, cook the beef, onion and mushrooms if desired over medium heat until meat is no longer pink; drain.

Stir in the tomatoes, beans, soup, 2 tablespoons spice mix, Worcestershire sauce and garlic. Bring to a boil. Reduce heat; cover and simmer for 20 minutes, stirring occasionally. Garnish with cheese.

YIELD: 8-10 servings per batch.

perk up chili

To a add robust flavor to chili, soak the dried beans in leftover coffee instead of water.

parmesan knots

- 1 tube (12 ounces) refrigerated buttermilk biscuits
- 1/4 cup canola oil
- 3 tablespoons grated Parmesan cheese
- 1 teaspoon garlic powder
- 1 teaspoon dried oregano
- 1 teaspoon dried parsley flakes

Cut each biscuit into thirds. Roll each piece into a 3-in. rope and tie into a knot; tuck ends under. Place 2 in. apart on a greased baking sheet. Bake at 400° for 8-10 minutes or until golden brown.

In a bowl, combine the remaining ingredients; add the warm knots and gently toss to coat.

YIELD: 2-1/2 dozen.

jane paschke
DULUTH, MINNESOTA

These knots are handy, because they can be made in advance and re-heated when needed.

sharon delaney-chronis
SOUTH MILWAUKEE,
WISCONSIN

The convenience of frozen bread dough and dried herbs makes this treat about as easy as it gets. To boost fiber, you can also use frozen whole wheat bread dough.

cheese flatbread

1 loaf (1 pound) frozen bread dough, thawed

2 tablespoons butter, softened

2 teaspoons paprika

1/2 teaspoon garlic powder

1/2 teaspoon dried oregano

1/2 teaspoon dried basil

1 cup (4 ounces) shredded part-skim mozzarella cheese

On a lightly floured surface, roll dough into a 16-in. x 11-in. rectangle. Transfer to a 15-in. x 10-in. x 1-in. baking pan coated with cooking spray; build up edges slightly. Spread with butter. Sprinkle with paprika, garlic powder, oregano and basil. Prick the dough several times with a fork; sprinkle with cheese. Cover and let rise for 30 minutes.

Bake at 375° for 20-25 minutes or until crust is golden brown and cheese is melted. Serve warm.

YIELD: 16 servings.

braided onion loaf

1 package (1/4 ounce) active dry yeast
3/4 cup warm water (110° to 115°)
1/2 cup warm milk (110° to 115°)
1/4 cup butter, softened
1 egg
1/4 cup sugar
1-1/2 teaspoons salt
4 to 4-1/2 cups all-purpose flour

FILLING:

1/4 cup butter, softened
3/4 cup dried minced onion
1 tablespoon grated Parmesan cheese
1 teaspoon paprika
1 teaspoon garlic salt, optional
Melted butter

In a large bowl, dissolve yeast in warm water. Add the milk, butter, egg, sugar, salt and 2 cups flour; beat until smooth. Add enough of the remaining flour to form a soft dough.

Turn onto a floured surface; knead until smooth and elastic, about 6-8 minutes. Place in a greased

bowl, turning once to grease top. Cover and let rise in a warm place until doubled, about 1 hour.

For filling, in a bowl, combine the butter, onion, Parmesan cheese, paprika and garlic salt if desired; set aside. Punch dough down; turn onto a lightly floured surface. Divide into thirds. Roll each portion into a 20-in. x 4-in. rectangle. Spread filling over rectangles. Roll up jelly-roll style, starting from a long side.

Place ropes on an ungreased baking sheet; braid. Pinch ends to seal and tuck under. Cover and let rise until doubled, about 45 minutes.

Bake at 350° for 30-35 minutes or until golden brown. Brush with melted butter. Remove from pan to a wire rack.

YIELD: 1 loaf.

linda knoll
JACKSON, MICHIGAN

This recipe won a blue ribbon at our county fair a few years ago. Take one bite, and you'll see why the tender savory slices appealed to the judges.

storing yeast bread

Don't store homemade yeast breads in the refrigerator as they'll quickly go stale. Instead, store in an airtight container at room temperature.

split pea soup mix

1 package (16 ounces) dried green split peas
1 package (16 ounces) dried yellow split peas
1 package (16 ounces) dried lentils, rinsed
1 package (16 ounces) medium pearl barley
1 package (12 ounces) alphabet pasta
1 jar (1/2 ounce) dried celery flakes
1/2 cup dried parsley flakes

ADDITIONAL INGREDIENTS:

4 cups chicken broth
1/4 teaspoon pepper
1 cup cubed cooked chicken, optional

In a large bowl, combine the first seven ingredients and place in airtight containers, or divide the first seven ingredients equally among 13 plastic bags. Store in a cool dry place for up to 1 year. **YIELD:** 13 batches (13 cups total).

TO PREPARE SOUP: In a large saucepan, combine 1 cup soup mix, broth, pepper and chicken if desired. Bring to a boil. Reduce heat; cover and simmer for 60-70 minutes or until peas and lentils are tender.

YIELD: about 4 servings per batch.

susan ruckert
TANGENT, OREGON

My mother sent this dry blend to me one year. The soup simmers up thick and hearty with lentils, barley, pasta and peas.

pretty gifts

For a lovely gift, put the assembled soup mix into a large basket or decorative bowl along with a few other items, such as a loaf of bread, a large soup mug or additional non-perishable ingredients needed to prepare the soup.

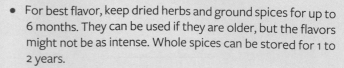

a guide to herbs and spices

- Store dried herbs and spices in tightly closed glass or heavy-duty plastic containers. It's best to keep them in a cool, dry place; avoid storing them in direct sunlight, over the stove or near other heat sources.

- For best flavor, keep dried herbs and ground spices for up to 6 months. They can be used if they are older, but the flavors might not be as intense. Whole spices can be stored for 1 to 2 years.

- Select fresh herbs that are fragrant with bright, fresh-looking leaves. Avoid those with wilted, yellowing or browning leaves. Wrap fresh herbs in a slightly damp paper towel and place in a resealable plastic bag. Press as much air as possible out of the bag and seal. Store in the refrigerator for 5 to 7 days.

- To substitute dried herbs in place of fresh herbs, use one-third of the original amount. For example, if a recipe calls for 1 tablespoon of fresh herbs, use 1 teaspoon dried.

ALLSPICE
Available as whole dried berries or ground. Blend of cinnamon, clove and nutmeg flavors. Use for baked goods, jerked meats, sauces, sausage, preserves, roasts and root vegetables.

ANISEED
Available as oval, greenish-brown seeds. Licorice-like flavor similar to fennel. Use for cookies, cakes, breads, pickles, stews, seafood, beets, cauliflower, pasta sauces.

BASIL
Available as fresh green or purple leaves, or dried and crushed. Sweet flavor with hints of mint, pepper and cloves. Use for tomato sauce, pestos, chicken, meat, zucchini, summer squashes.

BAY LEAF
Available fresh or dried as whole, dull-green leaves. Savory, spicy and aromatic. Use for soups, stews, casseroles, pickles, meat.

BLACK/WHITE PEPPER
Available whole, cracked, coarse or ground (black); whole or ground (white). Black has a sharp, hot, piney flavor; white has mild pepper flavor without flecks. Use for all types of cooking.

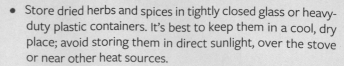

CARAWAY SEEDS
Available as light- to dark-brown seeds. Sweet blend of dill and anise flavors. Use for breads, cakes, biscuits, pork, cheese, potatoes, sauerkraut.

CARDAMOM
Available as green pods, brownish-black seeds or in ground form. Sweet, spicy flavor and slightly pungent. Use for baked goods, chicken, curries, meat.

CAYENNE PEPPER
Available ground, also known as ground red pepper. Pungent, hot flavor. Use for chili, soups, sauces, beans, poultry, meat, seafood.

CELERY SEED
Available as light-brown or tan seeds. Strong and bitter flavor. Use for fish, eggs, cheese and salad dressings.

CUMIN
Available as seeds and in ground form. Pungent, earthy, slightly bitter flavor. Use for beans, chili, pork, chicken, stews.

CHERVIL
Available as fresh leaves, or dried and crushed. Fresh has a hint of anise; dry has a hint of parsley flavor. Use for fish, eggs, poultry, salads.

DILL
Available as fresh leaves, dried and crushed, or seeds. Fresh, sweet, grassy flavor. Use for pickles, fish, cucumbers, breads, tomatoes.

CHIVES
Available as fresh or freeze-dried hollow stems. Delicate and peppery, mild onion flavor. Use for potatoes, eggs, sauces, seafood, salads.

FENNEL
Available as seeds. Sweet and mildly licorice-like flavor. Use for baked goods, seafood, sausage, pork.

CILANTRO
Available as fresh leaves. Pungent, strong flavor. Use for ethnic dishes (Mexican or Asian), salsa, tomatoes, chicken, pork, seafood.

GINGER
Available as fresh root, crystallized or ground. Pungent, sweet, spicy, hot flavor. Use for baked goods, pumpkin, pork, chicken.

CINNAMON
Available ground or as sticks. Sweet and pungent flavor. Use for baked goods, fruit desserts, warm beverages.

MACE
Available ground. Nutmeg-like flavor. Use for baked goods, poultry, fish.

CLOVES
Available whole or ground. Pungent, medicinal, sweet flavor. Use for baked goods, fruit desserts, ham, lamb and even warm beverages.

MARJORAM
Available as fresh leaves or dried and crushed. Oregano-like flavor. Use for tomato dishes, meat, poultry, seafood, vegetables.

CORIANDER
Available as seeds or ground. Mildly sweet, spicy flavor. Use for ethnic dishes (North African, Mediterranean, Asian), stews, curries, pork, lentils.

MINT
Available as fresh leaves or dried and crushed. Fresh, strong, cool flavor. Use for lamb, salsas, vegetables, meats.

MUSTARD

Available ground or as seeds. Pungent, sharp, hot flavor. Use for meats, vinaigrettes, seafood, sauces.

NUTMEG

Available whole or ground. Sweet, spicy flavor. Use for baked goods, custards, vegetables, poultry, meats.

OREGANO

Available as fresh leaves, or dried and crushed or ground. Pungent, slightly bitter flavor. Use for tomato dishes, chicken, pork, lamb, vegetables.

PAPRIKA

Available ground. Mild to hot, sweet flavor. Use for poultry, shellfish, meat, vegetables.

PARSLEY

Available as fresh leaves, curly or Italian (flat-leaf), or dried and flaked. Fresh, slightly peppery flavor. Use for poultry, seafood, tomatoes, pasta, vegetables.

POPPY SEEDS

Available as seeds. Nut-like flavor. Use for baked goods, fruits, pasta.

ROSEMARY

Available as fresh leaves on stems or dried. Pungent flavor with a hint of pine. Use for lamb, poultry, pork, vegetables.

SAFFRON

Available as threads (whole stigmas) or powder. Pungent, bitter flavor. Use for bouillabaisse, curries, fish, poultry, rice.

SAGE

Available as fresh leaves or dried leaves that are crushed or rubbed. Pungent, slightly bitter, musty, mint flavor. Use for pork, poultry, soups, stuffing.

SAVORY

Available as fresh leaves or as dried leaves that are crushed or ground. Piquant blend of mint and thyme flavors. Use for beans, lentils, lamb, poultry.

SESAME SEEDS

Available as seeds. Nut-like flavor. Use for breads, chicken, seafood, noodles, chickpeas.

TARRAGON

Available as fresh leaves or dried leaves that are crushed. Strong, spicy, anise-like flavors. Use for poultry, seafood, meats, soups, stews, vegetables.

THYME

Available as fresh leaves or dried and crushed. Pungent, earthy, spicy flavor. Use for meat, poultry, lentils, soups, stews.

TURMERIC

Available ground. Pungent, bitter, earthy flavor. Use for curries, lamb, chicken, meat, beans, lentils.

MINCING AND CHOPPING

Holding the handle of a chef's knife with one hand, rest the fingers of your other hand on the top of the blade near the tip. Using the handle to guide and apply pressure, move knife in an arc across the food with a rocking motion until pieces of food are the desired size. Mincing results in pieces no larger than 1/8 in., and chopping can produce 1/4-in. to 1/2-in. pieces.

CHOPPING AN ONION

1 To quickly chop an onion, peel and cut in half from the root to the top. Leaving the root attached, place the flat side down on a work surface. Cut vertically through the onion, leaving the root end uncut.

2 Cut across the onion, discarding the root end. The closer the cuts, the finer the onion will be chopped. This method can also be used for shallots.

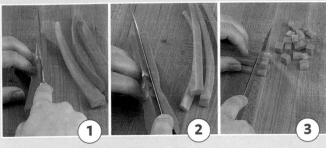

DICING AND CUBING VEGETABLES

1 Using a utility knife, trim each side of the vegetable, squaring it off. Cut lengthwise into evenly spaced strips. The narrower the strips, the smaller the pieces will be. Dicing results in 1/8-in. to 1/4-in. uniform pieces, and cubing yields 1/2-in. to 1-in. uniform pieces.

2 Stack the strips and cut lengthwise into uniform-sized strips.

3 Arrange the square-shaped strips into a pile and cut widthwise into cubes.

PEELING AND MINCING FRESH GARLIC

Using the blade of a chef's knife, crush garlic clove. Peel away skin. Mince as directed at top left.

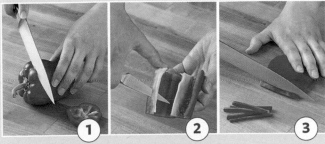

SLICING OR CHOPPING A SWEET PEPPER

1 To slice or chop, cut each side from pepper by cutting close to the stem and down. Discard top and scrape out seeds.

2 Cut away any ribs.

3 Place cut side down on work surface and flatten slightly with your hand. Cut lengthwise into strips, then widthwise into pieces if desired.

SNIPPING FRESH HERBS

Hold herbs over a small bowl and make 1/8-in. to 1/4-in. cuts with a kitchen shears.

alphabetical index